Humanistic Buddhism

Holding True to the Original Intents of Buddha

©2016 Fo Guang Cultural Enterprise Co., Ltd.

By Venerable Master Hsing Yun
Translated by Miao Guang
Edited by Arthur Van Sevendonck

Fo Guang Cultural Enterprise Co., Ltd.
Fo Guang Shan Monastery
153 Hsin-tien Rd, Dashu, Kaohsiung City
Taiwan, R.O.C.

Distributed by Buddha's Light Missionary Association, Chunghua
Originally published as *renjianfojiao fotuo benhuai* (人間佛教佛陀本懷)

©Fo Guang Cultural Enterprise Co., Ltd.
For Free Distribution Only.
NOT FOR SALE.

Printed in Taiwan (Republic of China).
May 2017. Third English Edition.

Publisher's Catalogue-in-Publication Data

Hsing Yun, 1927-.
       [Renjianfojiao fotuo benhuai. English]
       Humanistic Buddhism: Holding True to the Original Intents of Buddha /
       Written by Venerable Master Hsing Yun;
       Translated by Miao Guang – 3rd English Edition
       Translated from Chinese.
       ISBN 978-957-457-398-1
       1. Humanistic Buddhism. I. Title.

人間佛教 佛陀本懷

Humanistic Buddhism

Holding True to the Original Intents of Buddha

Venerable Master Hsing Yun

Translated by Venerable Miao Guang

Acknowledgments

We would like to thank Arthur Van Sevendonck from IBPS Paris for assisting in the editing of the translation and clarifying issues concerning cross-cultural understandings that has helped greatly in avoiding any misuse of word choice or expressions. Thank you to Venerable Zhi Yue for doing the layout design and managing the production process. Thank you to Chunyun Cheng for compiling the list of text titles, people's names, and dates, as well as for doing anything and everything. Thank you to Hsin-Yu Huang for compiling the list of Buddhist terms and expressions in English, and also for the translation of the Chronology of Buddha's Life. Last but not least, we would like to express our gratitude to all those who have supported this project from its conception to its completion.

Table of Contents

Biography of Venerable Master Hsing Yun

Venerable Master Hsing Yun was born in Jiangsu Province, China in 1927. He studied at various renowned Buddhist institutions such as Qixia Vinaya College and Jiaoshan Buddhist College.

Soon after his arrival in Taiwan in 1949, he became the chief editor of Human Life, a Buddhist Magazine. In 1952, his efforts in establishing Buddhist Chanting Groups strengthened the foundation for his subsequent endeavors in the promotion of the Dharma. The Master founded Fo Guang Shan Monastery in 1967, with the primary goal of promoting Humanistic Buddhism through Buddhist education, culture, charity, and propagation of the Dharma. Since then, over two hundred branch temples have been established in major cities around the world. He has also set up art galleries, libraries, publishing houses, bookstores, mobile clinics, Buddhist colleges, and universities including University of the West, Fo Guang University, Nan Hua University, Nan Tien Institute, and Guang Ming College. In 1977, the Fo Guang Tripitaka Editorial Board was formed to compile the *Fo Guang Buddhist Canon* and the *Fo Guang Dictionary of Buddhism*. Many other works on Buddhism have also been published.

Master Hsing Yun has dedicated his life to propagating Humanistic Buddhism. As a global citizen, he continues to foster "joy and harmony," "oneness and coexistence," "respect and tolerance," and "equality and peace" throughout the world. When he founded the Buddha's Light International Association in 1991, and was elected president of its world headquarters, he was closer to realizing the ideal of having "the Buddha's light shining throughout the three thousand realms, and the Dharma water flowing across the five continents."

Foreword

"What is your faith?" A asks B.

"Humanistic Buddhism," answers B.

"If your faith is Buddhism, then it is just Buddhism. Why add 'Humanistic' in front?" asks A again.

"Because the founder of Buddhism, Sakyamuni Buddha, was not a god but simply a human being. The uniqueness of Buddhism lies in that it was founded by a human being, that is why it is called Humanistic Buddhism."

"What is good about Humanistic Buddhism?"

"Just to name a few. Humanistic Buddhism purifies the body and mind, enhances our moral ethics, makes us compassionate, helps us understand ourselves, gives us strength to rely on ourselves, inspires us to help and accept others, teaches us the Truth of Dependent Origination, helps us uncover our wisdom to transcend the mundane world and attain a state of ultimate true existence, and shows a life of liberation and perfect ease."

"Would any of these benefits disappear if we turn to just 'Buddhism'?"

"Certainly not, just as traditional Buddhism has branched into the Eight Schools of Chinese Buddhism, no matter which you follow, their essence is always the same."

"Then why bother specifying the belief of Humanistic Buddhism?"

"For over two thousand years, traditional Buddhism has been tainted by beliefs that, under the guise of Buddhism, have preached superstitions such as divination by time, fengshui, geography, picking sticks, and fortune telling. Buddhism was almost turned into a superstitious belief that worshipped deities and spirits.

As the saying goes, "Out of prevailing rules arise faults." These misunderstandings arose due to the fact that long periods of Buddhist dissemination enabled the infiltration of teachings and practices into Buddhism that have gone against the Buddha's original intents. As a result, the Buddha's humanistic character became lost, and the overall image of Buddhism distorted, which is a true pity. Without Humanistic Buddhism, how else could the true identities of heretics who feed off the advantages of Buddhism have been exposed?

Today, we abide by the humanistic teachings of Buddhist masters such as "Dharma can only be found in the world, and enlightenment cannot be attained away from it" by Huineng the Sixth Patriarch, or "Who we shall look up to is none other than the Buddha, and what we shall regard as our goal is none other than the perfection of our character" by Master Taixu, for these are all teachings urging Buddhists to unite as one and reinstate Buddha's original intents.

As we look at Zhao Puchu and Venerable Xuecheng, one former and the other current President of the Buddhist Association of China, are their endeavors not also the propagation of Humanistic Buddhism? A clear evidence is that Venerable Xuecheng included "the establishment of Buddhist undertakings with the mission of propagating the Humanistic Buddhist philosophy" in the Association's Constitution.

One of the most arduous tasks required of traditional Buddhism is to clarify false understandings and reinstate the true goal of Buddhism by tracing it back to the Buddha's humanistic character. Is this not at all feasible?

If it is, a common realization of what the Buddha had originally intended to teach will arise among all Buddhists, and consequently, all shall realize the importance of advocating Humanistic Buddhism."

"There already exist various traditions such as Northern, Southern, Tibetan, Japanese, Sectarian, and Early Buddhism. Why add another called 'Humanistic Buddhism'?"

"In light of the complex system of Buddhist sects and terminology, which has caused deviation from the earliest form of Buddhism, we now hold true to Buddha's original intents by tracing back to the historical facts of Buddha's birth, enlightenment, teaching, and death, all of which took place in this world to call upon a faith in Humanistic Buddhism.

I have also come across many Buddhists, scholars, and professors who have mentioned the need to separate Buddhism and traditional Chinese folk religions, as well as religions in deities and spirits. This is indeed a way of Humanistic Buddhism.

In effectively eliminating fallacious views, correcting biases, and rediscovering right view and right thought, Humanistic Buddhism is a ray of hope to society that shall bring happiness and provide a means of liberation to all."

"What happens if people refuse to recognize Humanistic Buddhism?"

"This failure to recognize Humanistic Buddhism comes from their ignorance, lack of understanding in the Dharma, and ego. Not only do they not see Buddha's original intents, they also do not recognize Buddhist history. For over two thousand years, Buddhism underwent heretic attacks, political persecutions, and subjected to public bias and misunderstandings. As a result, Buddhists were driven from cities into mountain forests. Monastics were confined to temple grounds and away from people, faith as a family legacy neglected, and awareness of the need to be of service and contribution to the purification of society disappeared. Instead, the focus shifted to mere metaphysical discussions and inappropriate means of teaching Buddhism that held a passive attitude in encouraging seclusion from the world rather than actively helping people."

"Buddhism speaks of transcending the cycle of birth and death. Where would we go after that?"

"Where would you like to go? You would still be in this world. Even if you become a sage, a saint or even a buddha, you still cannot be away from this world. All of the Ten Dharma Realms exist within our mind, for the mind embodies the great void and the entire universe. If not, where would you like to go?"

"I thought we would be headed to the Western Pure Land of Ultimate Bliss?"

"The Western Pure Land is indeed one of our future abodes, but ultimately, a Pure Land is only a creation of the mind, while Amitabha Buddha is found in our intrinsic nature. Thus Pure Land is also found within this world.

Imagine a faith that only encourages individual cultivation away from society without having any regard for the people, how would this faith be of any help to the world?

It must be known that Buddha carried the original intention of helping humans when he spoke of the Five Vehicles. Only with compassion, prajna, and bodhi can liberation be sought. To participate in this-worldly endeavors with an other-worldly attitude would be a realization of the Bodhi Mind.

"What then, is the essence of Humanistic Buddhism?"

"That would be Buddhism. Humanistic Buddhism is 'what the Buddha taught, what is essential to human beings, what purifies, and what is virtuous and beautiful.' The essence of Humanistic Buddhism is found within the Threefold Training—discipline, concentration, and wisdom. Its core concepts are found within Dependent Origination, the Middle Path, and its mission found within guiding modern day people in finding peace and stability."

"Is there an alternative to the name 'Humanistic Buddhism'?"

"No, there cannot be, because Sakyamuni Buddha, the founder of Buddhism, was born in the human world to teach human beings how to discover guidance and happiness. He never taught his Dharma to animals, thus we cannot attribute Buddhism to animals. He never taught it to deities or ghosts, therefore we cannot call it Buddhism for Deities and Ghosts. He never taught it to people with fallacious or superstitious views, thus we cannot call it Superstitious Buddhism. Having been established in the human world and taught to humans, it shall therefore be named 'Humanistic Buddhism.'"

"Wouldn't the 'Humanistic' prefix take away the sacredness of Buddhism?"

"Buddha claimed that all living beings have the buddha-nature. By admitting that we are buddhas, we are elevating ourselves to the same status as that of the Buddha, holding the same True-Thusness. Is this not sacred?

Is not your reliance on the Buddha's teachings on the Three Dharma Seals, Four Noble Truths, Twelve Links of Dependent Origination, Six Paramitas, the Bodhi Mind, and the Bodhisattva Path also sacred?

When each of us keeps faith that Humanistic Buddhism will bring harmony, family happiness, a positive mind, and liberation, is this also not sacred?

Since Humanistic Buddhism is centered on human beings, the true Buddhist teachings shall carry the aim of finding ultimate happiness by relying on oneself, and the Dharma. Is this not sacred?

By reaching out to society and serving the people, are not the great ideals and aspirations of 'propagating the Dharma to benefit living beings' and 'to reach for Buddhahood and at the same time deliver living beings' sacred?"

"Just as you have said, Buddha had a humanistic character. Then where is he in this world right now?"

"'The sounds of the creeks are voices spoken by the Buddha's broad and long tongue; the mountains are none but manifestations of Buddha's pure body.' The Buddha's Dharma-body has become one with the universe. So where is he not found? The Buddha is found within faith. When you have faith and practice his teachings accordingly, then he will be found in your heart, and in everything that you do."

"What are the benefits of having faith in Humanistic Buddhism?"

"Faith in Humanistic Buddhism shall lead to the purification of body and mind. With an open mind, you shall transcend all differences between the self and others, as well as free yourself from attachment, delusion, and affliction. Additionally, you shall feel the joy of Chan and Dharma. These are all benefits that can be attained through the practice of Humanistic Buddhism."

"Who are the advocates of Humanistic Buddhism as Buddha's original intent?"

"Zhang Taiyan, one of the prominent Chinese thinkers once said, 'Those claiming to be intellectuals cannot do so without Buddhist philosophy, because the Buddha's teachings such as causes and conditions, and karmic retribution are universal rules applicable to all, and therefore important to all.'

Liang Qichao, one of the greatest Chinese scholars also claimed, 'The Buddhist faith is one of wisdom, not of superstition. It emphasizes the greater good over the lesser, and advocates a this-worldly mindset over an other-worldly one.'

In addition, Sun Yat-sen also said, 'Buddhism is a world-saving grace, the mother of philosophy; the study of Buddhism amends the biases of science. The Dharma complements the Law; the latter stops crime, while the former prevents it.'

Mao Zedong, whose mother was a devout Buddhist, mentioned the need to promote the outstanding Buddhist traditions and regard religion as culture, not superstition.

Albert Einstein once said, 'Buddhism has the characteristics expected in a cosmic religion of the future: it transcends a personal God, avoids dogmas and theology; it covers both the natural and spiritual, and is based on a religious sense aspiring from the experience of all things in meaningful unity. Buddhism fits this description. If there is any religion that would cope with modern scientific needs, it would be Buddhism.'

Therefore, what is needed today is a consensus on Humanistic

Buddhism, that it shall benefit humanity and resolve human concerns. Once these problems are resolved, what further problems could possibly arise?"

"What references and resources on Humanistic Buddhism are available?"

"After reading this book, you shall gain an overall understanding of Buddhism. Furthermore, by practicing accordingly we shall progress smoothly from being an improving human to becoming a buddha. Our faith in Humanistic Buddhism shall lead us towards the perfection of life."

"How difficult is it to read this book?"

It is not.

The book consists of six chapters:

Chapter One provides an overview of the spread of Buddhism across the world over the past two thousand years and its subsequent influences on different countries.

Chapter Two elaborates on Buddha's lifetime conducts such as his daily life and teachings to disciples, devotees, and society.

Chapter Three is a discussion on the core concepts of the Buddha Dharma.

Chapter Four expounds on the spread of Buddhism in China. Furthermore, Buddhism has already become an essential part of the Chinese culture. Without the elements of Buddhism, we would have trouble speaking the Chinese language. Without the spread of Buddhism, the idea of vegetarianism probably would not exist today. Even the elements of our daily routine, language, culture, and arts are deeply related to the Buddhist culture. Thus Buddhism is no longer just Buddhism; Buddhism itself is already a type of culture.

Chapter Five continues with the progress of Humanistic Buddhism.

Chapter Six concludes with an elaboration of the rise and fall of Buddhism.

星雲

Hsing Yun
April 2016
Founder's Quarter

Translator's Introduction

This translation has been completed with the hopes of guiding English speaking readers along Venerable Master Hsing Yun's latest work on the elaboration of Humanistic Buddhism and its close connection to Sakyamuni Buddha, the founder of Buddhism, as well as everyday life. For the first time, Fo Guang Shan's English speaking audience can appreciate Venerable Master's work together with the Chinese readers without the usual six to ten month wait.

Chinese and Sanskrit titles cited have been translated into English and a list of pinyin and Chinese original of the titles have been included in the back. A Chronology of Buddha's Life has also been attached to provide a brief introduction of Sakyamuni Buddha.

The names of people have been romanized in Hanyu Pinyin. Exceptions are those from Taiwan, which are romanized in Wade-Giles, and instances where the name is a transliteration from Sanskrit or another language. Provided after the names are their names in Chinese and years.

In this third edition, sutra quotes in Chapter One previously omitted have been added, whilst misspelled words and other minor mistakes in the translation are also corrected.

Meticulous readers will observe that we refer to Sakyamuni Buddha as "the Buddha" and "Buddha" throughout this book. We have done so for cultural reasons and out of profound respect. In American English, it is often "the Buddha," while in British English, it is often simply "Buddha." With great reverence for our teacher, both are one and the same as they are the titles given to the founder of Buddhism, Sakyamuni Buddha.

May this gift of Dharma bring us closer to the origin of our spiritual path through the wisdom and compassion of our dear Venerable Master Hsing Yun.

I would also like to express my deepest gratitude to Venerable Master and the entire Fo Guang Shan Order for your guidance and endless support.

Miao Guang
May 16, 2017

My Understanding about Humanistic Buddhism

Fo Guang Shan
Buddha Museum
TAIWAN, Kaohsiung

As far as Humanistic Buddhism has developed, many queries about this teaching exist and await clarification. I hereby list a few of them:

---

1. Humanistic Buddhism is a secular and prosaic tradition taught only for the Human Vehicle, and does not lead to supreme Buddhahood.

2. Humanistic Buddhism only focuses on mundane activities that do not bear much relevance to the practice of Dharma.

3. Humanistic Buddhism does not involve spiritual cultivation, and only focuses on ways of personal relationships and dealing with matters irrelevant to the Buddhist practices of transcendence, spiritual growth, and attainment of Buddhahood.

4. Humanistic Buddhism is aimed at lay Buddhists, and does not bear sacredness pertained to the monastic ways of living, austerity or enlightenment.

5. What is the heritage of Humanistic Buddhism? Who of this tradition has achieved spiritual attainment? Since there are no clear answers, the propagation of Humanistic Buddhism has thus become a challenge.

6. Insufficient promotion and the absence of a clear theoretical system of Humanistic Buddhism have added to the challenge for people to thoroughly understand it, especially when only understood or encountered through small segments, one-sided views, and

bereft a system.

7. Humanistic Buddhism is not yet generally recognized as a core concept of Buddhism. Without general support, it is not easy for the public to accept it solely based on the effort of any single tradition or organization.

8. Humanistic Buddhism does not involve a path to liberation, nor leads one to the state of attainment, therefore not easily accepted by traditional Buddhists.

Besides the above issues of concern regarding Humanistic Buddhism, others include: the relation between modern and traditional Buddhism, monastic and lay Buddhists, social seclusion and participation, primitive and contemporary forms of Buddhism, spiritual cultivation and activities. It can be said that general acceptance of Humanistic Buddhism still needs to be enhanced.

There was a time when Buddhists retreated to an other-worldly lifestyle, focusing solely on cultivation of the self. This caused Buddhism's this-worldly spirit to disappear. They retreated in isolation into mountain forests, no longer concerned with helping the people. Their focus shifted to empty metaphysical talks and abandonned the development of Buddhist undertakings. They simply spoke of the Dharma, and assumed a passive mindset. This was a complete regression from proactive Buddhism, namely the search for the Truth and to benefit all beings. In my journey to restore the original and genuine meaning of Humanistic Buddhism, I present the following elaborations on its meanings and contents:

1. Humanistic Buddhism inspires us to elevate and have faith in ourselves; because this self embodies the wisdom and virtue of the Buddha. Thus we must realize that we are all buddhas and be proud to say that "I am a buddha." Such is the spirit of Humanistic Buddhism. Instead of placing our fate in the hands of divine entities, we should take responsibility for our own lives. The saying in the *Agamas*, "Rely on the self, rely on the Dharma, rely on nothing else," is a rendition of the faith of Humanistic Buddhism.

2. The spirit of Humanistic Buddhism encourages us to blend in with others instead of seeing the self and others as separate beings on opposite stances. All beings are connected as one, and everything in this world is related to us. We believe that the Truths of Dependent Origination and Middle Path, as realized by the Buddha, are in fact the Truths taught in Humanistic Buddhism. The inheritance of belief in these Truths symbolizes the faith of Humanistic Buddhism.

3. Faith can be complex and diverse, yet everything becomes simple in Humanistic Buddhism based on the belief that our buddha-nature can make anything possible. While the levels and categories of faith may vary, the teachings of all faiths can be harmonized by the concept of Humanistic Buddhism, which embraces all, and serves as a faith for humanity as a whole.

4. Humanistic Buddhism is a faith in an eternal life. While it is said in the Bible: "He who believes has eternal life," the truth is, he who does not believe also has eternal life. Life is like the arms of a clock that move in a cyclical direction. If it were linear, then it would mean that life moves from the point of birth to the point

of death, and then ends. On the other hand, in a cyclical manner, once the arms of a clock pass twelve, it will begin anew again and again without end. Life can also be compared to the four seasons of spring, summer, autumn, and winter; the cycle of formation, existence, disintegration, emptiness; the mental process of arising, abiding, change, and cessation; and cycle of old age, sickness, death, and rebirth. Since birth follows death, there will be a future, and there will be hope.

Therefore, I believe that the Humanistic Buddhist view on rebirth offers an infinite future. From now on, the Six Realms of Rebirth are less likely to be mentioned in Humanistic Buddhism. The belief that every being is a buddha deems it unnecessary to draw a clear line between sacred and ordinary beings if rebirth occurs within all ten realms. This is what Humanistic Buddhism advocates.

5. It is true to say that everyone has the buddha-nature. Like a seed which, when presented with the right conditions, will sprout and grow. Unfortunately, without the necessary nutrients, these barren seeds are then known as *icchantika*—one without the potential of attaining Buddhahood. As the theories of natural selection and survival of the fittest both hold, the removal of an unfit minority is also part of the process. Generally speaking, life is eternal only with a few exceptions; that is to say, in terms of time, life never dies. In terms of evolution, it is natural for certain beings to eclipse others. This is entirely natural.

6. While it is said that everyone has the buddha-nature, faith nevertheless differs amongst individuals. For example, differences in depth, level of transcendence, elevation, and breadth of one's faith.

In fact, though faith is sacred, the levels of devotion, transcendence, and potential still differ. Just as the functions of different brands of microphones vary, it is also natural for some to fall behind in energy and devotion to faith. This is likewise altogether normal.

7. We believe that humanity can be better, bigger, and more transcending. Even the so-called arhat, bodhisattva, and buddha are only conventional names. Human nature is extremely diverse, and life can be limitless, whilst faith has differing levels. In Humanistic Buddhism, it is believed that faith is what determines our future destinations; faith is also what leads us to the state of eternity, one that frees us from birth and death.

8. Human society can be quite complex. While each human is an individual, they also depend on the conditions of the communities to exist, just as everything in this universe depends on one another to survive. However, while there is no difference between the sacred and ordinary, ordinary beings nevertheless still possess a sense of discrimination.

As much as world peace is a common ideal, the possibility of realizing it in the human world is minimal, because the worlds of Buddha and Mara will always be regarded as separate. Therefore, rather than expecting others to achieve peace, we should depend on ourselves to do so. While it is said that external peace may never be achieved, we can still achieve inner peace. Just as Ksitigarbha Bodhisattva has vowed to never attain Buddhahood until hells are emptied, though hells may never be empty, the power of Ksitigarbha's vow has already emptied the hells, and he will eventually attain Buddhahood.

9. While lives are regarded as individual beings, they are never-theless interconnected as one. In the faith of Humanistic Buddhism, there are no dualities of time and space or concerns of birth and death. From a passive perspective, what we seek is freedom from fear, delusion, depravity, and distress. From a proactive perspective, life can be happier, more tranquil, more peaceful, more harmonious, and more liberated. In the end, the faith of Humanistic Buddhism helps pursue a life lived in joy, in the boundless space and time, as well as within unlimited connections and achievements.

10. The ultimate goal of Humanistic Buddhism does not inher-ently reside in the attainment of Buddhahood. Since the Buddha declared that everyone possesses the buddha-nature, what we need to do now is "to awaken." Awaken to the fact that we can harmonize ourselves with the rest of the world. Humanistic Buddhism advo-cates that everything in this world is part of the self. Concurrently, everything in this world is without a self. If the self can be harmo-nized with the dharma realms, it would also mean that the self is equal and coexists with all beings within the Ten Dharma Realms.

11. The faith of Humanistic Buddhism is simple and undivided. It is freedom from birth and death, and a state of existence that neither arises nor ceases. The faith of Humanistic Buddhism in-spires one to pursue a life and spiritual state of perfection, eternity, awakening, liberation and purification. It allows one to transcend all living beings.

12. Humanistic Buddhism aims to achieve a state of mind that is free from worries, fears, and delusions. Through the virtues of

kindness, honesty, and compassion, we shall be able to take life onto an even higher level that is free from doubts, fear of death, distress, and instead follow our faith and the natural process of life. Within this higher state, we are not at the mercy of divine entities; instead, we depend on ourselves to reach our destinations.

Be it present or future lives, or even that disrememberment in-between lives, confusion about birth and death, or disbelief in the possibility of liberation, none of these will ever prevail in an awakened mind. We also believe that the state of enlightenment is the uncovering of our own original face, that is, the true Thusness of buddha-nature. This so happens to be the sacredness of Humanistic Buddhism. In terms of the three great asamkya-kalpas, the Eastern Pure Land, and Western Pure Land, an awakened mind will help us realize that these are nothing but expedient means. Liberation and perfection of the world will eventually come true under the blessings of the Buddha.

13. Humanistic Buddhism believes that we can unify ourselves with others. Just as the saying, "the mind, Buddha, and all living beings are no different from one another," both self and time are infinite, both self and space are boundless; furthermore, both self and countless living beings coexist as one.

14. Liberation can be rightly attained within the cycle of rebirth. Rebirth should not be distinguished by suffering caused within it and joy attained outside of it, because the cycle is also a world within itself in which elevation and freedom can be achieved. Now, where exactly is the cycle of rebirth? It is inside the great void. The concept of a harmonized dharma realm is omnipresent. One is all, and all is one. In other words, it can be explained by the

idea: "With wisdom, one does not abide in birth and death; with compassion, one does not abide in nirvana." This is the world of Humanistic Buddhism.

15. Upon the moment of awakening, one will discover prajna wisdom to guide oneself through life. Like an enlightened traveler, one will be able to travel the world with infinite energy. Once awakened, one will realize that the dualities of good and bad, right and wrong, or virtue and evil no longer matter. Furthermore, one will no longer be influenced by the Five Desires and Six Sense Fields*. Is this not a state of liberation?

16. The value of faith lies in broadening one's horizons, elevating oneself, liberating oneself, and harmonizing self and the world. I believe that these ultimate goals of Humanistic Buddhism can only be accomplished by self-effort. "Be your own mentor." This is what being a buddha is about.

17. No religions in this world, not even Humanistic Buddhism, can solve people's problems for them. This world is comprised of half Buddha and half Mara. One principle the Buddha taught us is that even if he may show you the way by which he attained liberation, he nevertheless cannot liberate you from your own karma. The saying, "We all stand before God's judgment" leaves much to be questioned. Where will this judgment take place? In Buddhism, we stand before our own judgments, no one else's. We are the only ones who will be facing our own karma.

18. Humanistic Buddhism as a faith can never be too vast, too profound, or too considerable, for it embodies all dharmas. It is

about self-purification, self-management, and self-education. The purpose of collective cultivation is to maintain mutual respect of people's conducts, shared values, equal distribution of benefits, harmonious social coexistence, loving and kind speech, as well as mental joy of spiritual attainment. This concept of collective harmony introduced by the Buddha, when he first established the monastic community, is truly what Humanistic Buddhism advocates today.

19. Humanistic Buddhism is a faith that encourages us to have self-recognition. No matter what others may say, my chosen faith is supreme and unsurpassed. The depth of faith may vary like the different stages of schooling: kindergarten, primary, secondary, and tertiary school; yet all of us are still known as students. Just because I am still in kindergarten does not mean that I lack potential, or just because you are pursuing a doctorate degree does not make you any different since we are all in the process of learning. On the journey of faith, we can each be great in our own ways.

20. Life is eternal and never dies; by stating this I am referring to the True Thusness of buddha-nature, which bears sacredness, which is Humanistic Buddhism. When human beings aspire to broaden and expand transcendental lives, purify and sublimate their faith, what they practice so happens to be Humanistic Buddhism.

---

* The Five Desires refer to human desires for: wealth, sensual pleasure, fame, food and sleep; and the Six Sense fields refer to the objects of the six sense faculties: form, sound, smell, taste, touch, and concepts.

Chapter One

Overview

Summary of Chapter One

In the 2,600 years of Buddhism's dissemination, many traditions arose as adaptations to the diverse needs of distinctive countries. Whom they all follow is the Buddha, propagating the teachings of Buddha; all are Buddhism. Specifically, all are Humanistic Buddhism.

Humanistic Buddhism is what the Buddha 'conveyed' to the "human world" with the original intents "to teach, instruct, benefit, and bring joy" and "to attain the Buddha's insight." It is closely related to society and individuals, evident in the Buddha's declaration of equality, "all sentient beings possess the buddha-nature," fitting the modern mentality of freedom, democracy, and equality.

The Buddha established precepts to ensure that the Sangha prevails, with the spirit of "not trespassing upon others." It is the root of social harmony and humanity. In addition, all Buddhist concepts are derived from the Buddha's teachings of Dependent Origination, guiding us to hope and perfection.

The essence of Humanistic Buddhism is negating superstition and blind faith, in its inspiration of wisdom and clarity. It emphasizes self-awareness, self-enlightenment, and self-improvement by offering insights into the Truths, peace and stability, freedom from the fear and sorrow caused by birth and death, and ultimately the perfection of life.

Humanistic Buddhism is Buddhism as needed by humanity, so we put it forth as the original intents of the Buddha so that his teachings can be seen in a new light. Denying biased notions and coming together in Humanistic Buddhism, we allow the Buddha's compassion and wisdom to shine a light of hope on humanity.

Overview

1) Humanistic Buddhism: Holding True to the Original Intents of Buddha

Sakyamuni Buddha, the founder of Buddhism, was born some twenty-six hundred years ago in the Indian kingdom of Kapilavastu as Prince Siddhartha Gautama, son of King Suddhodana.

Before Prince Siddhartha renounced and attained enlightenment, he lived a princely life of luxury in the palace. However, what he also discovered were the hardships suffered by ordinary people. Especially distressing to him was the caste system, its segregation of people into specific and perpetual classifications, the epitome of inequality. Once born as a Brahmin (priest), Ksatriya (nobility), Vaisya (agriculturalist, cattle rearer and trader), or Sudra (slave), a person was fated to consent to how they were treated by society, even if prejudicial or unequal. Predictably, those with 'lesser' rankings experienced greater misery.

Nevertheless, whilst still a prince and dwelling in the palace, Siddhartha demonstrated love and concern for his people. Markedly, due to his outside excursions, he drew nearer to the reality of sufferings caused by life and death in order to overcome the strict caste system and realize equality for all beings. (*Abhiniskramana Sutra*, T03 No.190)

After becoming the Buddha, he taught the world that only by following the Middle Path and living a life free from the dualities of suffering and joy can one truly resolve problems in life. For this reason, he spent forty-nine years teaching at over three hundred assemblies for the purposes of instructing, benefiting, and bringing

Angkor Wat: Life of the Buddha, Birth of Prince Siddhartha
CAMBODIA, Siem Reap, Angkor; 12th century; Stone;
H: 74.6 cm; Bangkok National Museum, Thailand

joy to society (*Lotus Sutra*). Consequently, the Buddha's compassion and teaching bequeathed 'Buddhism' to the human world.

One can say that Buddhism had been taught by the Buddha to the human world for the purpose of helping people resolve their difficulties in life. Everything the Buddha ever taught serves the purpose of discovering happiness and peace in this world. That is why it can be said that Buddhism is in fact Humanistic Buddhism— the original intent of the Buddha's birth into this world and sharing of his teachings. Everything he taught is Humanistic Buddhism, and everything about Humanistic Buddhism is Buddhism itself.

Since Buddhism embodies the spirit of Humanistic Buddhism, and that everything about Humanistic Buddhism is Buddhism itself, then why the necessity to insert 'Humanistic' in front of 'Buddhism?'

The inference behind this is the time span of 2,600 years separating the Buddha's era from the present. Along this considerable amount of time, various sects and reflections of Buddhism arose due to the differences in opinion among Buddhist disciples regarding teachings and precepts. These disparities have added to the challenge of unity among Buddhists. For this reason, cooperation between Buddhists and the development of Buddhism became rather difficult.

Furthermore, after Buddhism spread to China, political oppressions and social changes impelled Buddhism into the mountain forests, causing Buddhism to become a religion that focused on spiritual cultivation in seclusion for the sole benefit of oneself. The situation was exacerbated by monastics who spoke the Dharma solely from their own perspectives, exaggerating the need to be other-worldly, dismissing people's needs in life for wealth, love, and family. For instance, on the topic of wealth, they would speak of money as a poisonous snake; when speaking about marriage, they would describe husband and wife as adversaries; when talking about children, they would call them debtors come to collect their due. The lack of value for human life in "traditional" Buddhism has drawn criticism from society for being unhumanly and its irrelevance to real life.

We now propose "Humanistic Buddhism: Holding True to the Original Intents of Buddha," for the purpose of re-presenting a lifetime of the Buddha's teachings through a comprehensive review of his original intents on teaching the Dharma. It is hoped that through advocating Humanistic Buddhism, we are able to grasp the true meaning of the Buddha's core teachings and his spirit of liberation for this world. Through the unification of different theories and opinions, we hope to reconnect Buddhism with the human world. Only then can we truly realize Buddha's original teachings today. Furthermore, it is to ensure a thorough understanding and practice of the Dharma by people to discover greater happiness and perfection of life. These are the Buddha's original intents in choosing to be born and teaching the Dharma in this world.

2) The Five Precepts and Ten Wholesome Deeds as the Basis of a Human Being

Embodying Buddha's lifetime teachings it is believed that, one day, the light of Humanistic Buddhism will surely shine on humanity. Today, the whole world is pursuing peace through advocating freedom, democracy, and equality. From as early as the moment of Buddha's enlightenment, he had already made a very important declaration: "How amazing! How amazing! All living beings possess the wisdom and virtue of the Buddha." (*Avatamsaka Sutra*, Fascicle 51)

What he meant is that our intrinsic nature is the same as his; we retain the buddha-nature within. When it is revealed, we can find peace and liberation, be our own masters, and never let our future fall into the hands of divine entities. That is why taking refuge in the Three Jewels in Buddhism is to take refuge in ourselves, just as the Buddha encouraged his disciples to "rely on oneself, rely on the Dharma, and rely on nothing else." In other words, to take refuge means to rediscover our buddha-nature. (*Samyuktagama*, T02 No.99)

All beings are equal in terms of buddha-nature. This core Buddhist notion is what makes Buddhism unique from other religions. It is also one of the greatest ideals of democracy and equality. Just as stated in the *Ekottaragama*, "Once waters from all rivers flow into the ocean, they shall no longer bear their individual names; once people from all castes renounce, they will share the Sakya name." In particular, Buddha placed special emphasis on equality between men and women, as well as equality between all four categories of Buddhists. Disappointedly, a number of Buddhists today not only fail to comprehend Buddha's original intentions but also conceitedly place themselves as superior and better than others. This certainly is a great fallacy.

The saying, "All beings are equal in buddha-nature" holds that all beings merit to be treated equally. This is a respectful, sacred, and noble statement! The Buddha also established the Sangha community under the rules of the Six Points of Reverent Harmony, including various precepts to maintain the tranquility and welfare of the Sangha. He even taught lay Buddhists to uphold the Five Precepts and to practice the Ten Wholesome Deeds.

Sarnath: Seated Buddha; INDIA, Uttar Pradesh, Varanasi;
circa mid to late 5th century; Sandstone; H: 160 cm;
Archaeological Museum, Sarnath, Uttar Pradesh, India

The Five Precepts and Ten Wholesome Deeds are the foundations of a happy family; more so, they are the foundations of personal liberty. Once, people lacked proper understanding of the precepts and hence believed that they were merely constraints and shackles on life. The truth is, real freedom can only be gained through observing precepts. Those who have violated the precepts are sanctioned by law and imprisoned for the transgressions committed. That is why they have been deprived of their freedom.

The spirit of precepts in Humanistic Buddhism is to not trespass upon but to respect others:

1. **No killing:** not to trespass upon others' lives means to respect their right to life.
2. **No stealing:** not to trespass upon others' assets means to respect their right to possession of wealth.
3. **No sexual misconduct:** not to trespass upon others' reputation and integrity means to respect their right to dignity.
4. **No lying:** not to trespass upon others' honor means to respect their trust and character.
5. **No intoxicants:** not taking drugs, intoxicants, or substances that arouse delusions, violence, and cruelty, means to respect others' right to good health.

Precepts are the basis for all spiritual cultivation. All roots of virtue and merits arise from precepts. That is why the *Avatamsaka Sutra* says, "Precepts are the basis of supreme Bodhi wisdom, for they nurture all roots of virtue." It is further emphasized in the *Mahaparinirvana Sutra* (T12 No.374), "Although it is said that buddha-nature is intrinsic in all living beings, it nevertheless cannot be revealed without the practice of precepts." From this, one can see the importance of upholding precepts.

The Five Precepts are the foundations of being human. One who observes the precepts will refrain from trespassing upon others, and inherently, will not create karmic retributions. By observing the precepts, freedom is ensured for both self and others, and will become an intangible power of stability within society. Continuing from the Five Precepts to the Ten Wholesome Deeds, it means to refrain from: 1) the corporal misdeeds of killing, stealing, and sexual misconduct; 2) the spoken misdeeds of lying, idle talk, duplicity, and profanity; and 3) the spiritual misdeeds of the Three Poisons—greed, anger, and ignorance.

The Five Precepts and Ten Wholesome Deeds are the Buddha's initial instructions for the human world. Not only do they set the standards for social behavior, they also provide a clear direction for life. Thus, these are the basis for the development of Humanistic Buddhism. That is why Humanistic Buddhism can be deemed as the original teachings of Buddha. In fact, Humanistic Buddhism can unquestionably be traced from the Buddha's teachings. Just as Master Taixu (太虛 , 1890-1947) said, "Who we shall look up to is none other than the Buddha, and what we shall regard as our goal is none other than perfection of our character, and buddhahood is attained the instant our characters are perfected. This is true reality." In other words, the perfection of our character as human beings is the attainment of Buddhahood.

As Buddhism continues to evolve, the bodhisattva spirit as advocated in Mahayana Buddhism, comes even closer to the Buddha's original intents, as well as the essence of the human world. Bodhisattvahood is attained through the development of the Bodhi mind, complementing the fundamental values of Humanistic Buddhism.

Nevertheless, differences in the aptitudes of disciples have led to differences in the levels of understanding and realizations of the Buddha's teachings. Their differences in spiritual attainment have thus given rise to varying opinions and beliefs in the Dharma. People's insistence upon their own opinion and ideas has also complicated the situation. Their purported attachments to the self and to the Dharma have caused further discord amongst Buddhists, hindering the overall development of Buddhism.

For instance, soon after the Buddha entered nirvana, his disciples had distinct disparities in opinion and understanding of his teachings and the precepts, causing a major schism and the creation of Sectarian Buddhism. As time passed, further schisms ensued and came Early Buddhism and Mahayana Buddhism. By geography, Buddhism was further split into Southern Buddhism, Northern Buddhism, Chinese Buddhism and Tibetan Buddhism. Eventually, there are also Korean Buddhism, Japanese Buddhism, Thai Buddhism, and Western Buddhism. In particular, Chinese Buddhism alone split into the Eight Schools followed by the spread of Chan Buddhism into the Five Houses and Seven Schools.

However, heedless of the fact that the Dharma was spoken by the voice of the Buddha and interpreted by living beings (*Vimalakirti-Nirdesa Sutra*), it must be known that ultimately, all expedient means lead to a single path (*Lankavatara Sutra*). These differences in opinion were not personal, just as the Eight Schools of Chinese Buddhism each held to their own standards of classification. Instead of further schism, the outcome has allowed Buddhism more diversity and a greater range of expedient means to cater to the aptitudes of living beings. On balance, all these individuals believe in the same Buddha and propagate the same Dharma based on the Truths of the Three Dharma Seals,

Humanistic Buddhism Magazine

which the Buddha has dedicated his entire life to teaching.

Nonetheless, in recent years, as Western knowledge prevails over waning Eastern philosophy, many scholars study Buddhism not for the purpose of faith, but for bias, comparison, and criticism. This has created further misunderstanding and division among Buddhists. In light of this, a group of Buddhists have come together to search for common understanding in the future development of Buddhism. For this reason, Humanistic Buddhism has come to exist.

In Mainland China, Master Taixu spoke about *Rensheng Fojiao* (人生佛教, lit. Life Buddhism) in various places. In 1932, he published an article, "How to Develop Humanistic Buddhism." During the same period, in Singapore and Malaysia, Venerable Tzu Hang (慈航, 1893-1954) founded the *Humanistic Buddhism* Magazine to propagate the teachings of Humanistic Buddhism. Open-minded contemporaries such as Yang Renshan (楊仁山, 1837-1911) and Ouyang Jingwu (歐陽竟無, 1871-1943) co-founded Jinling Sutra Publishing House (金凌刻經處) in Nanjing to promote Chinese culture. Zhao Puchu (趙樸初, 1907-2000), then President of the Buddhist Association of China, was also an advocate of Humanistic Buddhism. All these forerunners believed that Humanistic Buddhism was the original intents of the Buddha. It includes the Buddhist teachings of "teaching, instructing, benefiting, and bringing joy" to both oneself and others, to become enlightened through concepts such as Dependent Origination, the Middle Path, the unity of all within the dharma realms, as well as oneness and coexistence. It also includes equality among all living beings to achieve world peace and happiness. Humanistic Buddhism has since been regarded as mainstream Buddhism for the modern age.

3) The Three Acts of Goodness and Four Givings as Fundamental Concepts of Humanistic Buddhism

As aforementioned, Humanistic Buddhism holds true to the Buddha's original intents. The Buddha was born in the human world, cultivated and attained enlightenment in the human world, and taught everything to human beings. If not Humanistic Buddhism, would it be better to call his teachings Rebirth Buddhism? Animal Buddhism? Hell Buddhism, Asura Buddhism, or even Hungry Ghost Buddhism?

The Buddha taught 'Buddhism' to human beings. That is why the discussion of Humanistic Buddhism should begin with his 'humanistic' qualities. The historical records of Buddhism clearly state that the Buddha was a human, not a god. In the *Mahaparinirvana Sutra*, the Buddha said, "I too, am constantly among the community of bhiksus." He was a historical figure whose existence in this world can be proven. Instead of an imaginary deity such as Xuan Wu (玄武), the Eternal Mother (無生老母), or the Jade Emperor (玉皇大帝), the Buddha was an awakened sage.

He was not a divine being who came and went without a trace. Even if the deification of the Buddha were true, it is not consequent from people's pronounced admiration of him. Rather, it is the result of his arduous journey of spiritual cultivation. His thorough enlightenment of the human mind; the ways of human nature and characters led to the attainment of his virtue, character, compassion, and wisdom. The teachings expounded by him such as Dependent Origination, Middle Path, Twelve Links of Dependent Origination, Three Dharma Seals, Four Noble Truths, Cause and Effect, karmic retribution, Five Precepts, Ten Wholesome Deeds, Six Paramitas, and the Four Means of Embracing are all supreme Truths that reveal the path to mental and physical well-being. They show the means by which we liberate ourselves from life's predicaments, and present solutions to life's problems such as birth and death, as well as everyday living.

Let us illustrate this in the instance of karmic retribution.

Lumbini, NEPAL, Bhairahawa

Karma denotes deeds or actions. The fortunes and misfortunes that we experience all arise from our respective actions. Namely, it is our karma. Accordingly, when Buddhists pray to the Buddha, the wish to eradicate karma carries greater importance than the wish for good fortune. Provided that we practice the Three Acts of Goodness—do good deeds (virtue), speak good words (truthfulness), and think good thoughts (beauty), our minds will be filled with the power of integrity, and we shall inherently be relieved from adversity and calamity. We thereby accumulate merits whilst removing unwholesome karma. That is why practicing the Three Acts of Goodness and the Four Givings are fundamental.

The Four Givings symbolize the Four Immeasurable States of Mind. These are further detailed as: "Give others faith, give others joy, give others hope, and give others convenience." Being willing to give others faith, one will naturally speak comforting words. In the willingness to give others joy, one will innately see the good in others and praise them. Essentially, this is speaking good words, thus purifying one's verbal karma. Owing to the willingness to give others hope, one will instinctively show care, concern, and encouragement. In essence, it is to think good thoughts—the purification of one's mental karma. Befitting the willingness to give others convenience, one will naturally offer a helping hand altruistically. This is to do good deeds, subsequently the purification of one's corporal karma. Thus, the Three Acts of Goodness and the Four Givings both embody the Four Immeasurable States of Mind cultivated by bodhisattvas. Collectively, these are the core concepts of Humanistic Buddhism.

Nonetheless, it is human nature to prefer gaining over giving due to our fear of loss and the disadvantages resulting from the acts of charity and virtuous deeds. For this reason, people regard virtuous deeds as difficult and fruitless practices. The truth is, the act of giving is like sowing seeds. How can one harvest without sowing? How can there be crops if seedlings were never cultivated? How can flowers and fruit grow if seeds were never planted? Within these notions of Cause and Effect, as well as karmic retribution, Buddhists stand resolute. As early as two thousand years ago, the Buddha was already propagating this universal truth of life to the world. This is Humanistic Buddhism.

Therefore, what Humanistic Buddhism advocates is neither blind faith nor unquestioning belief. Rather, Humanistic Buddhism aims to inspire wisdom and rationality. Those willing to accept and practice Humanistic Buddhism will be mindful to the wisdom of the Dharma, and its insights to the truths of life. By doing so, mental and physical well-being will not only be possible in our present life, but we will also free ourselves from the fear and sorrow caused by life and death. Ultimately, a consummate life will be attained.

Moreover, we will not be the sole beneficiaries of our faith. Our descendants and future generations shall inherit our faith in the Dharma. Fittingly, we shall convey to our descendants bountiful knowledge. They shall bathe in everlasting light. Their minds shall awaken to their intrinsic buddha-nature. They will grasp the Truth through the Three Dharma Seals. They shall strengthen their faith in the Four Noble Truths. With the Five Vehicles, all dharma realms shall be open to them. They shall contemplate the world of buddhas through the gate of the Six Paramitas. The Seven Factors of Enlightenment shall nurture their wisdom. By adhering to the Noble Eightfold Path, they shall further cultivate their practices.

In other words, Humanistic Buddhism will open our eyes to a faith that is real, virtuous, and has true potential. This faith will empower us to find peace and stability, relieve us from the constraints of daily worries, and allow us to clearly perceive all phenomenon through Dependent Origination and its emptiness. Understanding the true meaning of emptiness can awaken our buddha-nature, the true Thusness. Therefore, this world needs Humanistic Buddhism as it can help all living beings realize a happy and peaceful life. To encourage people to achieving these goals was the original intent of the Buddha.

Humanistic Buddhism is not exclusive to any individual. Humanistic Buddhism is Buddhism that is essential to humanity. It carries the mission of guiding sentient beings to awaken to the Buddha's insight, through expedient teachings (*Lotus Sutra*). Accordingly, Humanistic Buddhism should focus on expounding the teachings that Buddha awakened to. For example, teachings such as Dependent Origination, Cause and Effect, karmic retribution, impermanence, suffering, and emptiness are all essential teachings for this world.

Particularly, Humanistic Buddhism holds true to the Buddha's spirit and unique characteristics. It is humanistic, relevant, altruistic, joyful, universal, and timely. To elaborate on this, I often cite the essence of Humanistic Buddhism as "what the Buddha taught, what is essential to humans, what purifies, what is virtuous and beautiful." A clear comprehension of these principles is decidedly more vital than mere arguments over trivial matters such as regulations and rituals, which only prompt criticism, accusation, rejection, and even slander amongst Buddhists.

In 1963, when we traveled to Japan as the Chinese Buddhist delegation, Ishibashi Tanzan, President of Taisho University, said in his address to the delegation:

"Today, you represent Chinese Buddhists on this visit to Japan, yet inwardly you may not think much of Japanese Buddhism conceivably because contemporary Japanese monastics are married with children, which shapes a perception of negligence in regards to precepts in Japanese Buddhism. Perhaps you also dismiss Thai Buddhism, because they depend solely on the devotion and offerings of their followers, and seldom engage in doctrinal propagation or academic activities. Perchance, Thai Buddhists doubtless have reciprocal feelings about Chinese Buddhism. They feel that you have deviated far from the precepts established in the Buddha's time. You speak in the name of Mahayana Buddhism, yet you also lack thorough understanding of the Dharma. Even Japanese Buddhists may belittle Chinese Buddhism, because while Japanese Buddhism is divided by sects, they are undivided in thought. On the other hand, Chinese Buddhism is filled with divisions both of sects and thoughts, which is its weakness."

In this situation, the conference clearly exuded a sense of prejudice and repudiation. Deprived of trust, fellowship, and willingness to confer, how can Buddhists find common ground? For this reason, the study of Humanistic Buddhism emphasizes the recognition of humanistic characteristics, unity, cooperation, and consensus. Undoubtedly, this is a rather difficult endeavor.

Consequently, it is pointless to insist on rules and formalities. In its place, if teachings such as the Three Dharma Seals, Four Noble Truths, Six Paramitas, Noble Eightfold Path, Twelve Links of Dependent Origination, Cause and Effect, and karmic retribution are easy to understand, subsequent universal acceptance of Buddhism is feasible. Conversely, an excessive emphasis on metaphysics and overly profound concepts not only results in antipathy towards Buddhism, but also its potential extinction.

Furthermore, differing cultural, linguistic, custom, environmental, and geographical backgrounds have given rise to varied lifestyles around the world. For instance, consider the Sangha community from the Buddha's era. Then, monastics exposed their right shoulder, fed on offerings of alms, and slept under trees. This is only feasible in the warm tropical weather of India. For monastics living in the snowy climate of Siberia or Harbin in Northeast China, a lifestyle analogous with alms begging and exposing one's shoulder would be unfeasible. Markedly, the Chinese see alms begging as the behavior of homeless beggars. Assuming this, is it still practical for today's bhiksus and bhiksunis to observe the Buddha's precept of alms begging?

It is said in the *Avatamsaka Sutra*'s Chapter on the Arising Nature of Tathagata the Jeweled King, "Moreover, sons of the Buddha, take the taste of water for example, though of one taste, when placed in different vessels, the taste therefore varies. Yet is is never the water's intention to change. 'I take on the flavors of all.'

The same goes for Tathagata's wondrous voice. It is of one taste, but taken by sentient beings differently with different aptitudes." Therefore, a reconsideration of Buddhist formalities is necessary. The core principles of faith should be prioritized to meet the mental, doctrinal, spiritual, and practical needs of the practitioner. For this very reason, it is evident that Humanistic Buddhism is ideal for the present-day mentality.

4) Lifestyle and Ways of Cultivation in Humanistic Buddhism

From as early as the ancient times, it is easy to discern the traits of Humanistic Buddhism within the teachings and practices of Chinese Buddhist masters. For example, Huineng (惠能 , 638-713) the Sixth Patriarch stated, "Dharma can only be found in the world, and enlightenment cannot be attained away from it." Baizhang's (百丈, 749-814) insistence on "A day without work means a day without food" integrates the Chan practices with agricultural life. Similar Chan monastery lifestyles were also established according to the Buddha's expectations for Sangha communities.

The different ways of life in China and India have made it impossible for Chinese monastics to follow the traditions of primitive Sangha communities. Mazu Daoyi (馬祖道一, 709-788) thus established "monasteries," whilst Baizhang Huaihai introduced the Pure Regulations as adaptations to the Buddha's precepts. Monastery rules and pure regulations thus became a unique feature of Chinese Buddhism, and furthered the development of the Eight Schools of Chinese Buddhism throughout the Sui and Tang dynasties.

Further on the subject of the Eight Schools of Chinese Buddhism, we have sects such as the Tiantai, Huayan, Three Treatises,

Mogao Cave 17: Frontispiece of the Diamond Sutra; CHINA, Gansu, Dunhuang; Tang dynasty (618–907), dated 868; Commissioned by Wang Jie; Print on paper; 23.7 x 28.5 cm; British Library, London, United Kingdom

or Yogacara Sects that emphasize doctrinal interpretations. On the other hand we also have sects such as the Pure Land, Chan, Vinaya, and Esoteric that stress actual practice. However, what they all have in common is the Dharma's relevance to daily life and ceaseless social participation. Many inspired faith in people by benefiting society through charitable activities, while others taught and transformed people's minds by expounding the Dharma, attracting the interest of scholars and even royalty. This is similar to how the Buddha taught the Dharma to kings, royalty, and ministers. Thus one can clearly see their humanistic characteristics.

Humanistic Buddhism can be defined as "what the Buddha taught," but also "what is essential to humans beings." Both represent the essence of Humanistic Buddhism. In this world, people cannot survive without the protection of their country and the supporting conditions of society. From the moment one is born, they become dependent on a material life provided for by scholars, farmers, artisans and merchants. A human being also has the need for family, love, friendship, and kindness. In order to elevate one's character, a spiritual and aesthetic life is also necessary. Moreover, since the issues of life and death are inevitable, people seek faith. In light of this, I have proposed the following principles:

1. Glory goes to the Buddha
2. Success goes to the multitude
3. Benefit goes to society
4. Merit goes to devotees

Additionally, I have also proposed the following principal creeds of Humanistic Buddhism:

1. To honor one's family and country
2. To lead a moderate lifestyle
3. To value worldly interconnectedness
4. To maintain a peaceful and joyful mind

In my view, only Buddhism that is widely accepted can be called Humanistic Buddhism.

There is a Chinese proverb that says, "the same moon is now different in the presence of plum blossoms." Our lives as human beings, when guided by the Dharma, will become more diverse and meaningful.

The most renowned Buddhist text in China, the *Diamond Sutra*, begins with:

> *At one time, when came the time to eat, the World-Honored One donned his robe, carried his alms bowl, and entered Sravasti to beg for alms in an orderly manner. After returning to his place, having partaken of the food, he straightened his robe, put away his alms bowl, washed his feet, and sat down on his mat....*

Describing the seemingly ordinary occasion of eating breakfast, it embodies a considerably more profound meaning. This opening text reveals the ways of practice, compassion, and wisdom. All of

Mogao Cave 254: King Sibi Jataka
CHINA, Gansu, Dunhuang; Northern Wei dynasty (386–534)

these retained by an awakened one, abiding in the daily routines of life while resolving to enlighten and deliver both oneself and others.

"When came the time to eat, the World-Honored One donned his robe, carried his alms bowl," demonstrating his upholding of the precepts. In this part, the Buddha displayed the discipline of dressing properly, maintaining his demeanor, and begging in a peaceful and orderly manner. To "beg for alms in an orderly manner" symbolizes the spirit of patience, equality, and abiding in present conditions. It also shows equality in the treatment of nobility and the poor, as well as being satisfied with both delicate and coarse food. Moreover, whilst begging for alms, devotees offered food to

Mogao Cave 257: Ruru Jataka
CHINA, Gansu, Dunhuang; Northern Wei dynasty (386–534)

monastics who in turn reciprocated by teaching the Dharma. This symbolizes the spirit of generosity as it recognizes the equality between the giving of Dharma and the giving of wealth. Lastly, to straighten his robe, wash his feet, put away his bowl, arrange his sitting mat, and sit down in meditation to pacify his body and mind serve to demonstrate the Paramita of Diligence.

In conditions where the quality of food and the social acceptance of Buddhism vary, the Paramita of Patience is essential. In order to perfect the practices of generosity, discipline, patience, diligence, and meditative concentration, prajna wisdom plays a guiding role. Together, the Six Paramitas represent the daily life of a humanistic Buddhist.

The Buddha illuminated the world with the great light of prajna wisdom through the simple procedure of alms-begging. Light radiated from the Buddha's hands when he donned his robe and carried his bowl. Light exuded from the Buddha's feet when he walked into the city to beg for alms. Light emanated from the Buddha's eyes when he begged for alms in an orderly fashion. Light issued from the Buddha's mouth when he put away his robe and alms bowl after partaking of the alms. Having washed his feet and sat down, the Buddha's entire body shone with light.

In the simple matters of everyday life, the Buddha was able to thoroughly express the relevance of Buddhism and its humanistic spirit. He not only demonstrated the Six Paramitas, but also the profound meaning of Humanistic Buddhism. Therefore, instead of a cursory look at the Dharma, we need to gain deeper insight into the compassionate intentions and aspirations hidden behind the Buddha's every action. Only then can we truly comprehend the meaning of the Dharma.

5) Aspiring for the Bodhi Mind and Bodhisattva Path

In the past, the spread of Buddhism mainly depended on devotees who, lacking self-confidence and faith, used Buddhism to grant their wishes, hopeful that the buddhas would make the sick healthy, resolve family quarrels, and make the poor rich.

While it is reasonable to rely on the Buddha's virtue to enhance our confidence and personal growth, if we expect Buddha to fulfill our selfish desires, then we lose the true meaning of faith. Like children expecting their parents to fulfill their every need, the only thing that grows would be greed. On the contrary, faith should be balanced around sacrifice, service, and giving for the greater good.

Thus, Humanistic Buddhism holds true to the Buddha's spirit by advocating an altruistic faith. In one of the Buddha's previous lives, he fed his flesh to an eagle to protect a rabbit, and in another, fed himself to a tiger as a rabbit. Such acts of sacrifice and giving are truly the rarest, noblest, and most precious in the world. Therefore, in order to enhance the relevance of Buddhism, the concepts of Humanistic Buddhism must be established first. As said in the *Shorter Chinese Samyuktagama* (T02 No.100), "The Buddha, having aspired for great loving-kindness, benefits all worlds." With the teachings of Humanistic Buddhism, it is easier to actualize practices that praise virtue, beauty, harmony, and joy. It also inspires one to reach out and help others.

An exemplar practitioner of Humanistic Buddhism would be the layman in the *Vimalakirti Sutra*. Additionally, the Chapter on "A Parable" in the *Lotus Sutra*, and the concept of the "mutual-unobstructedness of all phenomena" in the *Avatamsaka Sutra* are all core concepts of Humanistic Buddhism.

Specifically, Humanistic Buddhism must embody the characteristics of altruism and universality. It is based on the Bodhi mind and the Bodhisattva path, namely, reaching upwards for Buddhahood while delivering sentient beings below. To aspire for the Bodhi mind is to practice the Buddha's teachings and to emulate his acts of sacrifice and giving.

The Nine-Colored Deer King who sacrificed his life for his kind, and the parrot who attempted to extinguish a forest fire with small mouthfuls of water are both examples of aspiring for the Bodhi mind. What matters is not whether the fire will be extinguished but the parrot's vow and Bodhi mind. The two combined are the bodhisattva path, which is Humanistic Buddhism. Otherwise, one is nothing but a "barren seed." That is why it is said in the *Avatamsaka Sutra*, "Any virtuous deed practiced in the absence of the Bodhi mind is destined to become the acts of Mara."

The Bodhi mind symbolizes "this-worldly" spirit along with an "other-worldly" transcendental mind. Specifically, it means to remain in this world without becoming attached to it. Yue Fei (岳飛 , 1103-1142) from the Song Dynasty once said, "A prosperous nation is only possible with honorable ministers and courageous generals." The same is true for Buddhism. A good future for Buddhism is only possible with the harmonization of "this-worldly" and "other-worldly" thoughts. In Humanistic Buddhism, the Bodhi mind serves as the basis of faith and spiritual cultivation.

Humanistic Buddhism prioritizes this-worldly issues over other-worldly transcendence, real life over birth and death, the greater good over the lesser, and universal deliverance over individual liberation. There is no bodhisattva path without the Bodhi mind. Only those with the Bodhi mind are worthy propagators of Humanistic Buddhism.

Most Buddhists today wish to attain buddhahood. However, according to the sutras, it takes three great asamkya kalpas for one to attain buddhahood. The affirmation of faith alone takes one great asamkya kalpa. Would the attainment of buddhahood then not take forever? Therefore, the most significant undertaking for Buddhists is not chanting, praying, or prostrating to the Buddha. To practice the way of the Buddha is to go through a thousand deaths and endless trials before finally attaining enlightenment and uniting with the Buddha's mind. Once enlightened, the fear of failure in said attainment is superfluous.

Humanistic Buddhism emphasizes actual practice of the Buddha's ways, which is to realize the bodhisattva path. Even though the ultimate goal of Buddhists is to attain buddhahood, the only way to reach it is through one's connection with sentient beings. The journey from being human to becoming buddha cannot be accomplished by shirking the bodhisattva path. Only through the Bodhi mind, and the Bodhisattva path, and awakening oneself and others, can buddhahood be possible.

The Bodhi mind is the main driving force behind buddhas and bodhisattvas in liberating sentient beings. For example, the Four Renowned Mountains in China embody the Four Great Bodhisattvas in Chinese Buddhism:

1. *Avalokitesvara* — great compassion in alleviating living beings from suffering

2. *Manjusri* — great prajna wisdom

3. *Samantabhadra* — the exemplary practice of his vows

4. *Ksitigarbha* — great altruism in entering hell to redeem all beings within

Longmen Grotto 140: Buddha Pentad (back wall)
CHINA, Henan, Luoyang

The dispositions of these bodhisattvas are the only means by which Buddhism can gain universal recognition. If we neglect these unique characteristics of compassion, wisdom, vow, and practice, and rely only on prayer and devotion, Humanistic Buddhism can never have any effects.

In order to propagate Humanistic Buddhism through these attributes, I once penned an article, "From the Four Noble Truths to the Four Universal Vows," in an attempt to integrate the early Buddhist and Mahayana teachings. In order to resolve the most paramount problem in life—suffering—one must "vow to deliver the endless sentient beings." In order to liberate all beings from the karmic retributions of greed, anger, and ignorance—all causes of suffering—one must "vow to eradicate the endless vexations." In order to enable sentient beings to practice all Dharmas, one must "vow to learn the inexhaustible Dharma"—the path leading to the end of suffering. Finally, the ultimate goal in our pursuit of the Buddhist faith is to guide all living beings towards ultimate liberation, therefore they must "vow to attain supreme Buddhahood"—the end of suffering.

6) The Future and Development of Humanistic Buddhism

Master Taixu and Venerable Tzu Hang both emphasized the importance of education, culture, and charity in the future of Buddhism. I have likewise established four objectives for the future development of Humanistic Buddhism:

1. To propagate Dharma through culture.
2. To foster talents through education.
3. To benefit society through charity.
4. To purify human minds through spiritual cultivation.

In terms of culture, education, and charity, secular society has already been fostering talents and raising social awareness. However, their equivalents in Buddhism are even more excelled and transcending. The Buddhist philosophy of formlessness, selflessness, detachment, and desirelessness implies a world that is inexhaustible, everlasting, boundless, and infinite. It is also what makes Buddhist endeavors distinctive from secular undertakings.

That is why in Humanistic Buddhism, the Four Noble Truths are expanded into the Four Universal Vows and the Six Paramitas. These not only are ways of individual cultivation; but also paths of liberation. Thus, it is Buddhism that places dual emphasis on understanding and practice, as well as the harmony of past and present.

Another important question: Why did the practitioners of Mahayana Buddhism integrate the Four Universal Vows with Buddha's early teachings on the Four Noble Truths? In my opinion, Buddhism should not merely be theory; it should help to resolve life's problems. That is why the Dharma offers more than just insights into the truth of suffering, cause of suffering, end of suffering, and the path leading to the end of suffering. Vows, spiritual cultivation, and actual practice are also needed. Within the Four Noble Truths, to eradicate suffering and its causes, the practices of spiritual cultivation must be perfected. The Four Noble Truths and achieving them through the path of the Four Universal Vows thus becomes the core concept of Humanistic Buddhism. Sustained by the power of the Four Universal Vows, we must reach out to sentient beings in need. This is how, in the future, Humanistic Buddhism will shine a ray of hope on the world and be recognized.

Notably, many scholars are inclined to compare different schools of Buddhism based on personal prejudices and opinions. Some compare Indian Buddhism with Chinese Buddhism; others early Buddhism with modern Buddhism. Some compare Buddhist texts and even scholars in Buddhist studies, criticizing one another for a lack of insight or clarity in concepts. This only serves to incite division, which unquestionably is not the Buddha's original intent.

For committed Buddhists, this deeply tarnishes Buddhism. Has anyone ever compared and scrutinized the Bible or the Koran in a similar manner? Candidly, to treat the holy teachings with such insolence in the name of scholarly work causes nothing but harm to Buddhism. The singular purpose of Buddhism is to encourage faith and enlightenment; it is not something to be scrutinized or compared. The holy texts by which a religion abides should not be treated in this manner.

A professor from the China Central Academy of Fine Arts, Tian Qing once said, "Scholars who simply regard Buddhism as a study will never become enlightened. The attainment of buddha-hood is only possible to those who abide by and practice the Buddha's teachings." This is indeed true! Any discussion of the Dharma without a sincere appreciation or actual practice is futile. While there is the need to discuss the formality of Buddhist practice as well as the core teachings, mere criticism and denigration should not be tolerated. A lack of respect, tolerance, and understanding; to simply criticize, prejudge, or impulsively render conclusions based upon prejudices are severe deviations from faith. Any provocation made will only hinder the development of Buddhism. It is truly regretful to see this happen.

The Dharma exists not just in writing but also within the mind, the whole universe, and as part of our faith. Anyone who neglects to see the supreme Buddha and the purifying effects of the Dharma within the faith carries no legitimacy in criticizing or judging Buddhism.

Essentially, we propose that Humanistic Buddhism holds true to the Buddha's original intents, for the purpose of harmonizing and uniting all Buddhists across time, geographical, customs, and cultural differences. We nevertheless respect, accept and cooperate with those different from us.

For the same reason, we advocate Humanistic Buddhism bears

utmost respect for human beings, as each individual has their own faith. Even if each faith differs in depth and form, there is no need for conformity. We must recognize that each of the seven or eight billion people on Earth has their own perspective and depth of faith. Technically, there are seven to eight billion singular faiths in the world.

For example, a believer of *Tudigong* (土地公 , lit. Earth God) will espouse the *Tudigong* Faith. A worshipper of *Chenghuang* (城隍爺 , lit. City God) will follow the faith of *Chuenghuang*. Those who follow *Mazu* (媽祖) or Jesus will believe in *Mazu* or Jesus. Moreover, genuine religions are divided into different levels. It is similar to how schools are divided into different grades. The bodhisattva path itself is divided into fifty-one stages, and arhatship into four different types of attainments. The difference in levels is understandable, while derision in the ultimate and supreme goal of a faith should not be tolerated.

Although the Buddha declared that we are all the same in terms of buddha-nature, those people with different aptitudes and influences have categorized Buddhism into the Human Vehicle, Heavenly Vehicle, Sravaka Vehicle, Pratyekabuddha Vehicle, and the Bodhisattva Vehicle. The first two represent this-worldly Buddhism. The third and fourth are other-worldly Buddhism. The final one, which harmonizes this-worldly and other-worldly Buddhism is the Mahayana Bodhisattva Path, which represents Humanistic Buddhism.

Therefore, those who lead secluded lives in austerity are deemed practitioners of Humanistic Buddhism. Those with a passion for Dharma propagation are also considered teachers of Humanistic Buddhism. Those who practice the Five Precepts, Ten Wholesome Deeds, Six Paramitas, and the Four Ways of Embracing are all regarded as followers and practitioners of Humanistic Buddhism, providing that they embrace their faith and contribute to the betterment of society.

Humanistic Buddhism directly inherits all of the Buddha's teachings. The chapters that follow shall provide introductions to the Buddha's original teachings, his humanistic lifestyle, the spread and development of Buddhism, and how modern Buddhism holds true to the Buddha's original intents. It is our wish to offer a Dharma guide for daily living so that people will be able to journey through the stages of life—birth, schooling, adulthood, matrimony, career advancement, old age, sickness, and even death—all under the auspices of the Buddha's wisdom.

We hereby present an overview of the past, present, and future of Humanistic Buddhism through enhancing understanding of its core concepts, essence, historical development, and ways of propagation. All so that we may perceive the Buddha's original intents. Otherwise, would we not be looking at Buddhism that is segregated and deviated towards beings in lower realms, heretics, and theocracy? We assert Humanistic Buddhism to be the Buddha's original intents in the fervent hope that Buddhists can unite in shared faith, mutual growth, and coexistence with the Buddha.

As we abide by Humanistic Buddhism, may we join our hands in propagating the teachings, restoring its ties to the Buddha's Dharma. May the Buddha's compassion and wisdom shine light onto the universe and this world with brightness and hope. For this, we hold true to the meaning and purpose of this book—*Humanistic Buddhism: Holding True to the Original Intents of Buddha.*

Fo Guang Shan Monastery Great Buddha Land:
Great Buddha; TAIWAN, Kaohsiung

Chapter Two

Humanistic Lifestyle of the Buddha

Summary of Chapter Two

We should neither regard the Buddha as some apparition nor ethereal deity. Born in a defined time and place, the Buddha was a human being who persevered through years of hardship to become a perfectly enlightened person of great wisdom.

The Awakened One never regarded himself as the Buddha, or the leader of the Sangha. Be it collective meditative practice or begging for food, he conducted his daily activities with the multitude, never deeming himself special in any way. He lived an ordinary life, advancing himself through meditative concentration and teaching the Dharma to benefit others.

The Buddha was apt at catering to different aptitudes and never forsook anyone. With compassion, he touched the hearts of the fearful. With wisdom, he subdued those who challenged him. He taught to kings, ministers, and royalty. He also helped ordinary people and the distressed. He even wrought his own body to blockade a road to save his homeland.

Known as the Honored One, the Buddha used both his wisdom and merits, and always exerted his compassion and insight. This world was his place of cultivation and propagation, as well as his Pure Land. Just as stated in the *Platform Sutra*, "Dharma can only be found in the world, and enlightenment cannot be attained away from it. To seek Bodhi Wisdom away from the world is as futile as to seek the rabbit's horn." Only by understanding the humanistic characteristics of the Buddha's life can we truly perceive Humanistic Buddhism.

Buddhism was never detached from this world and daily living; this is exactly the disposition upheld by Humanistic Buddhism.

Humanistic Lifestyle of the Buddha

1) Renunciation and Pursuit of the Truth

The Buddha lived an extraordinary life. Growing up as the gifted Prince Siddhartha, he mastered the Five Sciences and Four Vedas at a young age. Life inside the palace meant he could have all he desired, including the power to reign over his kingdom. Despite this, he instead drew his attention to the forces of impermanence experienced in life and society such as the significant issues of suffering caused by birth, old age, sickness, and death; discrimination of the caste system, the oppression of power, wealth disparity, and the weak preyed upon by the strong. All these signs of inequality amongst living beings left him perturbed and perplexed.

Notably, what he realized was that no political power could ever relieve people from their sufferings and the cycle of birth and death, or shine a light on ignorant minds. He thus aspired to become renounced so as to accomplish ultimate liberation for the self, discover the Truth which would liberate living beings, better society, relieve people from fear, affliction, attachment, sorrow, and suffering; and ultimately discover the true abode of life.

Having explained his decision to become renounced to his father, King Suddhodana, the answer he received was certainly contradictory.

Rather than obliging his son, the king insisted that he first follow the natural path of life, assume the throne, and then rule the kingdom. In reply, Siddhartha made the following requests:

"Father, if you could grant me these four wishes, then I would

Sikri: Ascetic Sakyamuni; PAKISTAN, Balochistan, Sikri; Kushan period (circa 1st–3rd century), circa 2nd–3rd century; Schist; H: 84 cm; Lahore Museum, Punjab, Pakistan

happily forgo the idea of renunciation:

Let there be no birth, old age, sickness, and death in this world.

Let there be no distresses of sorrow, sadness, suffering, and unhappiness.

Let there be no pain of separation from loved ones.

Let everything in this world never change." (*Sutra on Past and Present Causes and Effects*, T03 No.189)

"How could you propose such requests? Who in this world could ever resolve such problems for you?" replied the King.

"Father, if you are unable to oblige my requests, then please allow me to search for the answers myself."

Despite the ineffectual conversation, and after deep deliberation, Siddhartha remained firm with his decision to relinquish his throne and life of luxury. One quiet night, when the entire palace was dormant, he left with Channa, his attendant.

In order to avoid the subjugations of royal affairs and the pursuit of the muster dispatched by King Suddhodana, Siddhartha tried to travel as far away as possible. When he finally came upon Magadha, a kingdom in the South, he began his austerities in Uruvilva alongside other practitioners, many of whom were yogis and shamans. Notwithstanding, he nevertheless sought advice from them, and even followed as his spiritual master Alara Kalama, seeking for ways to attain liberation. However, when all efforts came to naught, he began practicing on his own.

According to *Shijia-pu* (*Genealogy of the Sakya clan*, T50 No.2040), his life of austerity involved only intake of wheat as sustenance. He was in such deep levels of sitting meditation that he never even raised an eyebrow when birds began to nest over his head. He simply let them be. Thus, one can perceive the harsh conditions of his practices.

At this time, the royal muster caught up with the prince in an attempt to persuade him to return home. Firm with determination the prince instead changed the ministers' minds, and inspired them to practice austerities with him.

As time went by, the prince realized that years of austerity still offered no passage into the world of the Truth or methods of liberating living beings. What he also came to understand was that while unhappiness had come from the constraints created by the Five Desires and Six Dusts, the path of austerity offered no peace either. Ultimately, spiritual cultivation does not entail torturing one's own body. Thus, he rose from his seat, resolving to search for alternative ways.

Lacking physical strength, along his way to the nearby Niranjana River to bathe himself, the prince fell. Fortunately, a shepherdess offered him some goat milk to help replenish his energy. However, his five followers perceived the sight of him forgoing the practices of austerity as a sign of weakness and regression. In enmity, all five abandoned the prince.

Having regained his energy, Siddhartha reached Bodhgaya, took a seat beneath the Bodhi tree, and made a vow: "I shall never relinquish this seat until enlightenment is attained." (*Abhiniskramana Sutra*, T03 No.190)

Throughout the process of meditative concentration, Siddhartha experienced an endless array of afflictions. From the external temptations of fame and gain to the internal unrest caused by greed, hatred, ignorance, and doubt; he nevertheless confronted them all with fortitude. Finally came the eighth day of the twelfth lunar month when, the stars and moon shining at their brightest, Siddhartha became enlightened.

According to Fascicle Thirty of the *Abhiniskramana Sutra*,

upon that moment, heaven and earth shattered, and the delusional world was undone. What appeared before Siddhartha's eyes was a different world, one that shone with the golden light of Truth. Within such a world, all dualities of arising and ceasing, emptiness and existence, principle and phenomena, good and evil are all eliminated in a moment of thought. What Siddhartha awakened to were the Truths of Dependent Origination and emptiness. That all phenomena arise due to causes and conditions, and all phenomena cease due to causes and conditions. What the prince also awakened to was that despite the fact that our physical bodies go through the cycle of birth, old age, sickness, and death, our buddha-nature, the true Thusness is all-pervading and omnipresent.

Upon that moment, his mind was as calm as a still lake, beneath which all living beings within the Ten Realms suddenly manifested distinctly before him. What were once difficult problems suddenly became simple equations. He finally realized that everything was equal, and matters that differed became unified. He knew his life had totally and thoroughly changed. He also knew that the Truth to which he awakened was something he could teach the world. Thus he exclaimed, "How amazing! How amazing! All living beings possess the wisdom and virtue of the Buddha; it is only through delusions and attachments that they have shielded themselves from it." This was Buddha's declaration on the equality among ordinary beings and buddhas. (*Avatamsaka Sutra*, Fascicle 51)

Nevertheless, the awakened Buddha was in no haste to expound the Truth. Instead, he continued to meditate on ways to remedy the mind, steps to attaining enlightenment, his perspective on the universe, his view on life, and even how he would teach such truths in the future; as well as establish the monastic community and promote equality amongst all four categories of Buddhists. The

Mahabodhi Temple
INDIA, Bihar, Bodhgaya

Buddha was well aware that if the people in this world practiced such teachings, they could all be akin to him: to embark on the journey of spiritual cultivation, attain enlightenment, and realize a complete and liberated life.

2) Establishment of the Sangha Community

Having pondered further on the truths he awakened to, his mind was as clear as a bright full moon, ready to illuminate the world. At that moment, he thought of Ajnata Kaundinya and the four others who had followed him in his practices, wishing he could share his enlightenment with them. On a nearby hill, the Buddha found his five companions and expounded on the Truths of suffering: suffering, cause of suffering, path leading to the cessation of suffering, and the cessation of suffering. According to the *Dharma cakra Pravartana Sutra* (T02 No.110), these explanations occurred on three distinct occasions, known as the Three Turnings of the Dharma Wheel.

During the First Turning of the Dharma Wheel, the Buddha said, "The sufferings in the world are oppressive; the cause of life is impelling; the perfection of life is achievable; and the path to liberation is attainable." This historical moment stands for the First Turning of the Dharma Wheel.

The Buddha continued to teach the five practitioners, "This is the oppressive reality of suffering, which you shall know; this is the affliction caused by ignorance, which you shall eradicate; this is the eternal life, which you can attain; this is the way to liberation, which you shall practice and realize." This elocution is known as the Second Turning of the Dharma Wheel.

"All such sufferings are that which I have already come to realize; all such afflictions and ignorance are that which I have already eradicated; such eternal life is that which I have already attained; these Ways are that which I have already tread and completed." This is known as the Third Turning of the Dharma Wheel.

Having heard the Buddha's teachings, the minds of these five practitioners suddenly unraveled. Although they were prone to dismiss the man who had abandoned the practices of austerity; when this man appeared as Buddha and radiated the light of awe-inspiring virtue and compassion, they were so overwhelmed that all fell to their knees. "Siddhartha, we have wronged you before, but now we are willing to be your disciples. Please let us follow and learn from you."

"I am Siddhartha no longer. Henceforth, please call me 'Buddha.' I hereby accept your request so that we can strive together in delivering sentient beings." According to *Sutra on Past and Present Causes and Effects*, these five men thus became the Five Bhiksus who formed the earliest Sangha community, thereby completing the framework of a faith consisting of the Three Jewels: Buddha, Dharma, and Sangha. Today, when tourists visit Rajagriha in India, they can still see the historical site where Buddha first taught the

Dharma to the Five Bhiksus.

Soon after, the Buddha and the Five Bhiksus began their lives as propagators of the Dharma, attracting people from all walks of life, including shamans and spiritual practitioners, all of whom had come to learn from the Buddha. In particular, Uruvela Kasyapa, along with his two brothers and their one thousand or more disciples were the largest group to take refuge in the Buddha. This certainly intensified Buddha's propagation works immensely.

Moreover, the renowned Sariputra and Maudgalyayana, along with their two hundred followers, also took refuge in the Buddha. Yasa, son of a great elder from Varanasi, India, in aversion for his mundane life, also took refuge and became Buddha's disciple along with his fifty followers. Subsequently, even Yasa's father, mother, and wife took refuge and became the first upasakas and upasikas

Chaukhandi Stupa
INDIA, Uttar Pradesh, Sarnath

within the community. These stories are all recorded in the *Sutra on Past and Present Causes and Effects* as the first founding of the 1,255-member Sangha community in the world.

As the Buddha's reputation spread far and wide, he knew that provided the environment, climate, and social conditions in India at that time, other than the establishment of a set of regulations within the Sangha community, a dwelling place was also sorely needed in order to accommodate such a large number of people who would be practicing, living, and propagating with him. The Buddha promptly received help from King Bimbisara, a sovereign who once offered to donate lands from his kingdom to the Buddha.

Not far from Bodhgaya, where Buddha attained enlightenment, King Bimbisara offered a vast land for the construction of the Venuvana Vihara. This dwelling was said to consist of sixteen courts each containing sixty chambers, five hundred buildings, seventy-two halls as teaching spaces for the Buddha, and living as well as cultivation quarters for his one thousand and more disciples. This was also Buddha's first monastery in his endeavor to propagate the Dharma. (*Sutra on Past and Present Causes and Effects*)

While the Buddha was based in Southern India to conduct his propagation works; merchants from the North also came to hear the Dharma. Sudatta, an elder and merchant from the Northern city of Sravasti, inspired by Buddha's teachings, vowed to support the Buddha by building the Jetavana Vihara so that he could spread the Dharma to Northern India. (S*utra on the Wise and Foolish*, T04 No.202)

In the North, Sudatta the Elder thus purchased a garden from Prince Jeta and offered it as a site for the Vihara. With Sariputra assigned as the construction supervisor, it became the Buddha's base of Dharma propagation in Northern India—Jetavana-anathapindasyarama, the ruins of which still remain today.

According to Chapter Twenty-Five of *Vinaya in Five Divisions* (T22 No.1421), Jetavana Vihara was situated over a flat land area of approximately eighty hectares. Eight small chambers along with other facilities such as walking meditation quarters, a lecture hall, greenhouse, dining hall, kitchen, bathroom, sickbays, and lotus ponds surrounded the Central Shrine.

Thus far, there were now monasteries in both Southern and Northern India. The Buddha regularly led his one thousand, two hundred and fifty-five disciples in propagating the Dharma to various places, each time being well received by the local communities. Even King Prasenajit of Kosala from the North became a follower of the Buddha. Initially, the "bottom-up" approach made the spread of Dharma a difficult challenge. But with the timely addition of royal patrons in both the South and North, Buddha's endeavors in Dharma propagation enabled the Buddhist community to grow daily. By then, the Buddha had established the world's first compre-

Jetavana Monastery: Remnants of Stupas
INDIA, Uttar Pradesh, Saheth

hensive Buddhist community.

The greatness of the Buddha lies within his unique approach in delivering sentient beings. Not only had he never regarded himself as the most illustrious in the world, he even asserted that he was but a part of the multitude. He taught his disciples to "rely on oneself, rely on the Dharma, and rely on nothing else." This shows the true meaning of faith is about having faith in oneself, and discovering one's compassion and wisdom. For this reason, Buddha set Dharma as the core spirit of the Sangha community and taught the Four Reliances: "Rely on the Dharma, not on people; rely on the meaning, not on words; rely on the ultimate meaning, not the conventional meanings; and rely on prajna, not on knowledge." There is no reason for such open-minded teachings not to be accepted by the world. It is also not difficult to understand why Buddhism stood out amongst other religions in India.

Establishing the Sangha community was certainly no easy task. One needs to know how to spread the Truth that liberates the world, in other words, to propagate the Dharma. In addition, one also needs to know how to liberate people from suffering and adversity, namely, to deliver them. A comprehensive plan was also needed for the organization and day-to-day maintenance of the Sangha community.

In particular, to meet the needs of daily life, the Buddha established a set of regulations for the community called the Six Points of Reverent Harmony. For example, Harmony of Being is achieved by keeping courtesies such as lining up in order, and refraining from trespassing on others. Harmony of Speech means to speak softly with kind words to prevent conflicts. Harmony of Thought means keeping shared goals and serene minds. Harmony of Discipline means that everyone is equal in front of the law. Harmony of

Profit means all daily necessities are distributed equally among the community, and any surplus given to the poor and needy. Harmony of View means to share the same viewpoints upon having heard the Buddha's teachings. Under these regulations, the Buddhist community thus becomes a complete and more ideal place for spiritual cultivation.

Nonetheless, virtue may be strong, but Mara can be even stronger. In the nascent days of prosperity for Buddhism, heretics retaliated out of jealousy and enmity. As mentioned in the Eight Stages of Buddha's Life, after Buddha underwent painstaking efforts to cultivate and finally subdued external temptations and internal afflictions, he also became immovable against such oppressions.

For example, a Brahmin once challenged Buddha to a debate. In order to be courteous, he brought two pots of flowers to greet the Buddha. Upon seeing the Brahmin, Buddha immediately said, "Let go!" The Brahmin released the pot in his left hand.

However, Buddha continued, "Let go!"

The Brahmin then released the pot in his right hand.

"Let go!" said the Buddha once more.

"I have already put down both pots, what else do you want me to let go of?" asked the Brahmin.

"What I asked you to let go of were not the flowers. What you should let go of are the greed, anger, ignorance, and afflictions in your mind." replied the Buddha. (*Outline of the Buddhas and Patriarchs*, X85 No.1594)

The Brahmin was overwrought by the Buddha's words. What he had regarded as well cultivated attainments were merely ignorance that was instantly dispelled by the Buddha. As a result, he bowed to the Buddha and took refuge in him.

On another occasion, after teaching at Mrgaramatuh Prasada,

Amaravati: Life of the Buddha - Calming the Drunken Elephant
INDIA, Andhra Pradesh, Amaravati; Satavahana period (circa 200 BCE–
250 CE), circa 2nd century; Limestone; Diameter: 89.5 cm;
Government Museum, Chennai, Tamil Nadu, India

the Buddha went into Sravasti to beg for alms as usual. Suddenly, a Brahmin appeared out of nowhere and started to yell at the Buddha. Ignoring him, Buddha continued to proceed peacefully, arousing even greater anger in the Brahmin, who reached down to grab a handful of dust and threw it towards Buddha. A breeze happened to sweep towards the Brahmin and blew the dust back into his face. Upon seeing this, Buddha uttered the following verse,

He who enforces anger upon one who is peaceful,

Since this peaceful and righteous mind
is freed of all ties of afflictions,
Any unwholesome thoughts enforced onto him
Shall be returned to the unwholesome doer;
It is like throwing dust into the wind,
Eventually it will all come back to you.

In other words, anyone who speaks harshly with undue reason merely to hurt others will suffer from his own actions. It is just like throwing dust at others, when the wind blows back, the one throwing will eventually be the one who gets dirty. (*Samyuktagama*, T02 No.99)

Once, a group of heretics threatened the Buddha: "We shall spread all the wrong dharmas to make people feel that your teachings are unsuitable for those living in India."

"I care not for your heretical views," replied the Buddha.

"We will gather a crowd to attack your community."

"The community does not fear your clubs and sticks."

"Then we will don your robe, eat out of your bowls, but act in disaccord to your Dharma and rules to destroy your reputation." said the heretics.

Upon hearing this, the Buddha replied with sadness, "In that case there is nothing I can do." This was the famous story which gave rise to the saying, "That which feeds off the lion's flesh are the bugs living on it."

There were also incidents about Angulimala's lies and Devadatta's betrayal of the Buddha. Devadatta, in particular, attempted to hurt Buddha by pushing boulders off hills or inciting a drunk elephant towards him.

Other than the above, the Buddha's disciples were also often

Venuvana Monastery; INDIA, Bihar, Rajgir

tempted by heretics with money, force or even lust. For example, Matanga's attempt to seduce Ananda, and Maudgalyayana's trouble with Utpalavarnna. Fortunately, these bhiksus were firm in their faith and remained steadfast against temptations. Instead, these incidents actually strengthened them and further safeguarded the Sangha community.

With great wisdom, courage and fearlessness, the Buddha found his way through the challenges of some ninety-six types of heretics and propagated the Dharma with determination, bequeathing India one of her greatest traditions—Humanistic Buddhism.

3) Daily Routine

We are born in an era very distant from the Buddha's time, yet it is certain that many of us must be very interested in the way Buddha lived his days after attaining enlightenment. In fact, from the four *Agamas*, we can discover the way the Buddha and his disciples lived their days. It can best be described with the saying: "To be at ease under all circumstances, to live by following conditions, to undertake every endeavor with joy, and to truly own everything by heart."

The *Sutra of Bequeathed Teachings* says, "During daytime, learn and practice the teachings diligently without neglect. Do not languish during the early and late hours of the night either. In the midst of the night, chant the sutras to extinguish your afflictions." The Buddha's intention is to encourage his disciples to practice earnestly, meditate, study the teachings, and carry out their chores diligently. A description of Buddha's daily life as a propagator of the Dharma begins with his morning hours:

Everyday, the Buddha rose before the break of dawn to brush his teeth and wash his face. In Buddha's time, the people cleaned their teeth by chewing on willow twigs in the form of toothbrushes used today. In *Vinaya in Five Divisions*, the Buddha spoke of the five benefits of chewing willow twigs: 1) aids with digestion, 2) clears phlegm, 3) enhances sense of taste, 4) eliminates bad breath, 5) clearer vision.

While washing up, the Buddha also intoned prayers. For example, when washing one's face, "As I cleanse my face with water, I wish for all living beings to find purity and never be tainted." When brushing one's teeth, "As I chew on the tooth stick, I wish for all living beings to tame and purify their minds, and eliminate all afflictions." These prayers serve the purpose of reminding spiritual practitioners to always pray and remain mindful.

Having woken and washed after a night's sleep, the mind is refreshed, devoid of worries and afflictions, and is clear. Thus, one is most aware in the morning hours. As the sky brightens and roads become visible, the Buddha would lead his disciples on alms processions in Magadha and Kosala, accepting offerings from people in an orderly fashion.

By "orderly fashion," it denotes that the bhiksus cannot choose between wealthy or poor households, or eschew the line. Regardless of the quality or content of the offering, they can only see the victuals as medicine that cures the weakening body. This is also the Buddha's way to demonstrate the spirit of equality.

During alms processions, not all devotees made their offerings at set times or always with the same contents. In the Buddha's time, the Indians had a tradition of setting a table of offerings at the door during funerals or festivities. When bhiksus passed their house, they would then kneel, join their palms, and respectfully offer a bowl of rice, a bowl of food, a flower or some fruits. Should the offering from one household be insufficient to sustain anyone for the rest of the day, the bhiksu could then beg from the second or third house for more food. Once finished, they immediately returned to the monastery to partake of their meal.

In the vast but sparsely populated land of India, bhiksus follow the rules of proceeding from adjacent to distant locations in an orderly fashion and dignified manner, so as to inspire respect in the devotees. When Sariputra saw Asvajit begging for alms in Sravasti, he was deeply moved by his demeanor and sacredness. Hence he approached him to ask who his teacher was, and what his teachings were about. A monastic's dignified demeanor thus became the cause for Sariputra taking refuge in the Buddha.

This practice of alms procession enabled people to come in close contact with Buddhism, whilst Buddhism was allowed to stay connected to society. In return for the devotees' material offerings, the Buddha and his disciples would offer gifts of Dharma by teaching them the Truth about life. As the saying goes, "The giving of Dharma differs not from the giving of money." Eating with a mindset of equality was the Buddha's intention behind establishing the rules of alms begging. This assisted greatly in the development of Humanistic Buddhism.

Considered in modern units of time, the practice of alms begging took approximately one hour from beginning to end. After that, the bhiksus returned to their quarters to wash their hands and feet, sit cross-legged, and eat their meals.

They also ate, through the procedure of alms begging, while being mindful of the Five Meal Contemplations, which are also commonly seen in contemporary monastery dining halls. Bhiksus of Buddha's time similarly followed these eating procedures.

After the meal, they washed their bowls, cleaned their feet, and straightened their robes. This was likewise Buddha's emphasis on chores and conduct. This showed that the Buddha taught by example and demonstrated the true form of spiritual cultivation.

According to the Sutras, eating was followed by walking meditation around the monastery. According to the *Vinaya in Four Divisions* (T22 No.1428), there are five benefits of walking meditation: 1) enhances stamina, 2) enables tranquil contemplation, 3) greater immunity to illnesses, 4) aids in digestion, 5) prolonged period of meditative concentration. Afterwards, the Buddha led his disciples back to their seats to meditate, followed by his teachings.

Buddha was not necessarily the one to initiate a teaching.

Whenever his disciples had queries about life, ideas, experiences, and cultivation, they went to the Buddha for answers and instructions. Thereafter, the bhiksus returned to their own abodes to meditate, contemplate, and reiterate what the Buddha had taught.

Having listened to the Buddha's teachings of the Dharma, the disciples would each return to their own place to practice. Following this would be time allotted for all people from society. At about ten o'clock, devotees would come to the Vihara to seek advice or pay respect to the Buddha. The Buddha would then impart his teachings to them. Sometimes he would speak on the Four Noble Truths, the Three Periods, or the cycle of rebirth through the Twelve Links of Dependent Origination. Sometimes, he would speak about ways to strengthen one's faith or eradicate afflictions. Other times, he would encourage devotees to observe the Five Precepts, and practice the Ten Wholesome Deeds, as well as kindness, compassion, joy and equanimity. These teachings were all memorized, then later compiled and recorded as the Tripitaka: Sutra, Vinaya, and Abhidharma.

Other than large assemblies, sometimes the Buddha also taught to individuals or small gatherings. For example, his teachings on the *Mahaprajnaparamita Sutra* took place at four different venues over sixteen gatherings. The *Avatamsaka Sutra* involved seven venues and eight gatherings. On the other hand, the *Lotus Sutra* involved a single gathering of over one million people and heavenly beings. The location and scale of each teaching varied. Today, when the Buddha's Light International Association (BLIA) organizes a variety of activities in different parts of the world, their purpose is to relive the moments of Buddha's Dharma assemblies.

After lunch, some disciples would prostrate, some would meditate, some would do walking meditation, some would be in meditative contemplation, and some would rest. Members of the Sangha community each had their own practices, and as long as they did not trespass on others, practitioners were free on their own.

The weather in India is mostly very hot as it was back then. Most people opted to stay indoors during noontime. When outdoors, bhiksus would disperse around nearby caves, in the shades of trees, or beside waters to debate and exchange thoughts. This is quite similar to modern day school group discussions yet with a rather different ambiance. Bhiksus lived a somewhat simple life and seldom lost their discipline to indulge in recreation. Most of them practiced diligently with right mindfulness, and strictly abided by Buddha's precepts and regulations to purify their bodies and minds, as well as improve their characters.

In the afternoon, Buddha would gather the bhiksus to discuss their realizations and questions regarding spiritual cultivation. The Buddhist sutras that we see today contain records of questions and answers raised by the Sangha community. Following this, Buddha would then reach out to society to propagate the Dharma. It is not difficult to see that Buddha focused on spreading the Dharma to the world.

Given the hot weather in India, all that bhiksus needed were their three robes. Their material needs were minimal so as to reduce their burdens. For Dharma Services, they would don their nine-striped robe, while the seven-striped robe was for daily wear. When doing chores, they would put on their five-striped robe. This is analogous to the different outfits worn by BLIA members for the different activities of Humanistic Buddhism. The designs and styles may differ, but when worn as a uniform, they carry the same significance as the three robes passed down by the Buddha himself.

At night, members of the Sangha community continued with

their respective practices, where most would meditate and connect spiritually with the Way taught by Buddha.

On the path of spiritual cultivation, there will be different levels of attainment. Be it the Four Stages of Arhatship, or the Fifty-One Stages of Bodhisattvahood, they must all be accredited by the Buddha to confirm their spiritual progress. Just as modern day schools are divided into different grades, the progress of spiritual attainment also involves different stages.

In the sutras, we can see how Buddha lived his days in meditative contemplation and the Way. He was constantly mindful of the Buddha, Dharma, and Sangha. In his interactions with disciples and devotees, he was always teaching, instructing, benefiting, and bringing joy to them. Thus at the end of his discourses, his disciples would always vow to "practice in accord with Buddha's teachings" before departing with a bow and joyful minds.

Bihar: Ananda Stupa and Asoka Pillar

The Buddha seemed to have lived a life no different from ordinary people. He likewise ate, slept, walked, and talked. Yet when observed carefully, the difference is rather profound.

Once, a man asked a Chan Master, "How do you cultivate?"

"I eat, and I sleep."

"We also eat and sleep. Does this not mean we too are cultivating?"

"No. On the contrary, when you eat, you pick and complain about your food. When you sleep, you toss around in bed with an agitated mind. This is very different from how I eat and sleep." replied the Chan Master.

The life led by Buddha was one that abided by the Six Paramitas and illuminated with the light of prajna wisdom. This differs greatly from that of ordinary people who are always comparing and competing. For example, in begging for alms, not only did Buddha provide opportunities for devotees to accumulate their merits, he also used this to teach them the Dharma, which is the Paramita of Generosity. When Buddha donned his robe, what he demonstrated was the constant practice of precepts, known as the Paramita of Discipline. When he begged house to house and deemed the rich and poor as equals, this is known as the Paramita of Patience. When he washed his own bowl, laid out his sitting mat, and practiced zealously, this is known as the Paramita of Diligence. When he practiced walking meditation, sitting meditation, meditative contemplation, and dwelled deeply in the Dharma, this is known as the Paramita of Concentration. All of the above illustrate how an enlightened practitioner lives his life, which is known as the Paramita of Prajna Wisdom.

4) Guiding Disciples

Since the Buddha's disciples each had their own character, their daily routine differed. Some preferred to meditate inside caves or beneath trees, while others preferred to reach out to people and spread the Dharma. No matter their choice, Buddha always encouraged and supported them, and taught according to their aptitudes and needs. To understand how the Buddha taught, we can begin by looking at his attentiveness, care and teachings towards his disciples.

Once, when Buddha was inspecting the Sangha community, he discovered Sariputra—one of Buddha's Ten Principal Disciples, an arhat, and a leader of the Sangha community strolling around the forest late at night when everyone else had gone to rest. When Buddha asked why he was taking a stroll instead of taking a rest, Sariputra told Buddha that it was a day when the monastery was crowded and lacking beddings; therefore he gave his bed to a young bhiksu to sleep in. The next day, Buddha gathered the assembly to instruct them on the importance of showing respect to Elders.

When Maudgalyayana realized the evil deeds his mother had enacted before she passed away, he sought advice from the Buddha on ways to pray for and redeem his mother. Buddha instructed him to arrange a vegetarian banquet as an offering to the monastics on the first day of their return from their summer retreat. The merits accumulated from the offering shall release his mother from hell. This was the origin of the Ullambana Festival, which was later advocated by Emperor Wu of Liang (梁武帝 , 464-549) and Chan Master Baozhi (寶誌 , 418-514), a tradition that thrives to this day.

Purna—the Foremost in Expounding the Dharma, was particularly passionate about propagating the Dharma. When he expressed his wish to return to his homeland, Sronaparanta, Buddha reminded him of the cruel nature of the kingdom's people. In reply, Purna told the Buddha,

"I shall have no regrets. If they berate me, attack me or even kill me, then I shall see it as an offering of my life to the Buddha."

"Very well. Since you are prepared to sacrifice yourself for the Truth, you have my blessings," said the Buddha.

Ananda—the foremost in hearing the Dharma, was the most loyal member of the Sangha community. His handsome appearance was cause for much troubles. For instance, by giving a maiden two pieces of rice-cake stuck as one, he was accused of being fond of women. In addition, Matanga's crush on Ananda also prompted many troubles. Each time the Buddha came to his aid and resolved these troubles.

The noble Mahakasyapa was well-cultivated and most respected for his practice of austerities. Once, when he returned to the Sangha community wearing a ragged robe, the Buddha vacated half of his seat for Mahakasyapa as a message to the assembly that he is just as respectable and noble as the Buddha himself.

Mahakasyapa never begged for alms from rich families, because he believed that wealthy people had already accumulated sufficient merits from the acts of giving in their previous lives, therefore the "field of merits" should be spared for the poor to cultivate their fortune. This is the reason he favored poor families when begging for alms.

Conversely, Subhuti—the Foremost in Expounding the Teaching of Emptiness, thought otherwise. Because he felt that the poor were already in need of food, how could he add to their burdens by begging from them? Instead, it is easier for the wealthy to give, therefore he chose to beg from the rich instead of the poor.

Being aware of these intentions, Buddha spoke to the assembly, "To favor either the poor or the wealthy over another is contrary to the spirit of equality. The Dharma should be practiced with an impartial mind. Regardless of all the existing discriminations and differences in this world, what is most important is that we abide by the spirit of equality if we wish to benefit ourselves and others."

Buddha was always caring and attentive towards his disciples. For the elderly and sick, Buddha helped them bathe, collect water, and wash their clothes. When Aniruddha fell asleep during a lecture, he was severely reprimanded by the Buddha. Feeling extremely ashamed, Aniruddha vowed to practice diligently, and consequently went blind due to lack of rest. One day, upon seeing him struggling to thread a needle bereft of eyesight, Buddha helped him and even mended his robe for him. (*Ekottaragama Sutra*)

To the extremely zealous Sronakotivimsa, Buddha taught him that "Spiritual cultivation is like playing the zither. When the strings are too tight or loose, the zither will not play. Thus it is best to follow the Middle Path." Following the Buddha's instructions, Sronakotivimsa felt more peaceful, and attained arhatship swiftly. This is how Buddha guided his disciples, with understanding and compassion.

For those willing to follow his instructions, Buddha taught with patience. To those who could not, Buddha taught by expedient means. To those who were lethargic and passive, Buddha encouraged them to be diligent. Towards those rigid or fierce, Buddha taught them the ways of gentleness and caution. Be it intelligent or foolish disciples, Buddha taught according to their aptitudes and needs to help the Sangha community improve and grow.

For example, Cudapanthaka had a very poor memory, therefore Buddha patiently taught him to recite the line, "sweep away the

Maijishan Grotto 133: Prophecy for Rahula; CHINA, Gansu, Tianshui;
Song dynasty (960–1279); Clay; H: 3.1 m (Buddha), 1.44 m (Rahula)

dust, and remove the dirt." Cudapanthaka abided by Buddha's instruction and recited the line daily whilst sweeping the ground. By doing so, he eventually became enlightened and highly respected.

In fascicle six of the *Sutra of the Wise and Foolish*, when Nidhi the dung carrier, too ashamed of his low social status, tried to avoid the Buddha, Buddha purposely detoured to run into him. As Nidhi knelt to apologize to Buddha for coming face to face with him, an untouchable, Buddha very kindly replied:

"Would you like to become renounced under me?"

"Am I worthy of becoming the great Buddha's disciple?" Nidhi replied, confused.

"In my teaching, there is no difference between wealthy or poor, noble or lowly, or caste rankings." said the Buddha. As a result, Nidhi became renounced, and eventually was well-cultivated.

The Buddha observed that, as long as you treat someone with respect, care, compassion, encouragement, and help them build self-esteem, they will surely improve and grow.

Buddha established each precept with careful deliberation, always ensuring that the precept was both appropriate and suitable. For example, Kalodayin was tall and had a dark complexion. One evening, he went into the village to beg for alms. A pregnant woman came to answer the door and thought this tall and dark bhiksu was a ghost. In utter shock, she had a miscarriage. For this reason, Buddha deemed it unsuitable for bhiksus to beg for alms after dark and established the precept for bhiksus to fast after noon.

On another occasion, an engaged lady planned to visit her future mother-in-law with some homemade cakes. As she was baking them, some bhiksus came to beg for alms, so she offered her cakes to them. The cakes were so delicious that many bhiksus returned for more. As the young lady was obliged to make more cakes, she failed to visit her fiance's family on time. The groom-to-be became furious and threatened to cancel the engagement. Having heard the news from the lady's parents, Buddha immediately called for an assembly to establish a precept that required bhiksus to refrain from greed when begging for alms.

Each precept established by the Buddha is a demonstration of the close relationship between Buddhism and daily life. For example, the procedures of posadha, repentance, and tripartite ceremony are similar to the establishment of laws in modern day congress halls, where a bill needs to be read out loud three times in order to be passed. The precepts system can be said to be the earliest form of democratic congress.

Examples of how Buddha taught the Dharma to the world are

Borobudur: Prince Sudana Jataka
INDONESIA, Central Java, Magelang; circa 8th–9th century; Andesite

countless. Regardless of nobility or peasantry, wealth or poverty, man or woman, career, race, or faith, Buddha treated all as equals. As stated in "Chapter on Suffering and Joy" of the *Ekottaragama Sutra*, "Once the waters from the Four Rivers flow into the ocean, they shall no longer bear their old names and instead, as one, all be called the ocean. The same applies to the caste system, be it ksatriya, brahmin, elder, or layman. Once shaven in the house of the Tathagata, all shall don the three robes, learn the monastic way of life, and relinquish their birth name." This was how Buddha challenged the caste system to achieve true equality.

Take Upali for instance. Though he was born a low rank, he was admitted into Buddha's Sangha community, renounced, attained enlightenment, and eventually became the Foremost in Upholding Precepts amongst Buddha's Ten Principal Disciples. When Upali first witnessed the royal princes each becoming renounced under the Buddha, he became saddened by his lowly upbringing, which eliminated his chances of doing the same. Aware of his thoughts, Sariputra said to him, "Buddha's Dharma is about the attainment of ultimate freedom, equality, and compassion. Regardless of one's intellect or profession, anyone who is willing to abide by Buddha's teachings is eligible to become his disciple and attain enlightenment."

Consequently, Upali received his tonsure from the Buddha, and was introduced to Prince Bhadrika and other royals, who were reluctant to greet him. Therefore the Buddha said, "The primary task for a renunciant is to subdue one's arrogance. Since Upali has renounced first, you shall all pay respect to him as your senior." Bhadrika and the others accepted Buddha's instructions and humbly paid respect to Upali. (*Abhiniskramana Sutra*)

In those days, Buddha would sometimes send his senior disciples to teach bhiksus living in remote areas, unable to abide by the rules and regulations of the Sangha. Upali was among the Buddha's first choices. When there were disputes in Kausambi and Saketa, Buddha would also send the calm and gentle Upali to resolve the conflicts.

Once, Buddha intended to send Upali to Saketa again, who uncannily declined.

"What is your reason for declining?" asked the Buddha.

"Dear Buddha, traveling during the rainy season would be rather uncomfortable if my only robe gets soaked by the rain. That is why I cannot oblige your request." replied Upali. Touched by Upali's honesty, Buddha amended the precepts so that bhiksus would be allowed to bring an extra robe with them when they travel.

Upali was respected by the community for his self-discipline and gracefulness so the Buddha also taught him how to visit the sick, as well as how to prepare food and medicine for sick bhiksus. (X44 No.744)

Buddha taught and guided all disciples equally, and always gave them fair chances. For example, he once allowed a drunken Brahmin to become renounced. Once sober, the Brahmin became frightened by his new appearance and fled the Sangha. Some disciples questioned Buddha's decision despite knowing the inevitable outcome. In reply, Buddha explained the extreme rarity for the Brahmin to even think of renunciation. That is why he created a cause for his future liberation.

Rahula, the Buddha's son, was a naughty and playful novice monk who often teased Buddha's visitors. One day, Buddha came to Rahula's living quarters, his demeanor stern. When he sat, Rahula collected some water to wash Buddha's feet, who remained silent until Rahula was done, and pointed to the basin:

"Is this water drinkable?"

"No, Buddha, this water is already dirty, and therefore not drinkable."

"Your mind is just like this water; originally pure, but now polluted. Despite your pure practices, your lack of verbal discipline and impure deeds are like water that is tainted and no longer pure." The Buddha then continued:

"Can this basin be used as an eating bowl?"

"No Buddha. A foot basin should not be used as a food bowl, because it is too dirty to contain food," replied Rahula.

"Rahula, you are just like this basin. Despite being a spiritual practitioner, your mind is filled with impurities. How can it contain the pure Truths?" Buddha kicked away the basin, causing Rahula to be frightened. He then asked Rahula,

"Are you afraid that the basin would be broken?"

Bharhut: Life of the Buddha - King Prasenajit Visiting the Buddha
INDIA, Madhya Pradesh, Bharhut; circa early 1st century BCE;
Red sandstone; H: 79.5 cm; Indian Museum, Kolkata, India

"No, Buddha, it would not matter for a dirty basin to be broken."

"Rahula, your lack of concern for this basin is similar to the community's lack of concern for you, because you have no regards for demeanor or respect for others. That is why you make fun of people. No one will care for someone like you," replied the Buddha.

His entire body covered in sweat, Rahula felt extremely ashamed and vowed never to lie again. Working very hard to correct his behavior, Rahula subsequently became known as the Foremost in Esoteric Practices. Not only was Buddha strict to Rahula, he also demonstrated compassion in his strictness.

Other than Rahula, Buddha also cared for other novices. One day, Katyayana, who was propagating the Dharma in a distant land, sent his disciple back to Jetavana Vihara to see the Buddha. Upon seeing Katyayana's disciple arriving from afar, the Buddha instructed Ananda to add an extra bed in his room for the young novice. For a great enlightened sage to show such delicate concern, how could this faraway disciple not be touched? This is the human empathy shown by Buddha the great sage.

There were times when members of the Sangha community failed to cope with the monastic lifestyle. The Buddha obliged their wish to return to their family and a mundane life though still as practicing Buddhists. This respected their wishes and self-esteem.

Not only did Buddha teach through example of his present life, he also used lessons from his previous lives. For example, the *Sutra of the Nine-Colored Deer* tells the story of betrayal that befell the nine-colored deer. In *Sutra of the Collection of the Six Perfections*, Buddha was the Deer King who took the pregnant doe's place as a sacrifice. In the *Older Sutra of Parables*, Buddha was the parrot that attempted to extinguish a forest fire by small mouthfuls of water. In the *Prince Sudana Sutra*, Prince Sudana vowed to practice generosity to help as well as liberate sentient beings, and had no regrets in undergoing extreme suffering. "Chapter on King Dighiti" in the *Madhyama Agama* records the story of Dighiti who returned anger with kindness. Many times, Dighavu the son of Dighiti had the chance to take revenge on Brahmadatta for his father, but each time he recalled how his father never held grudges against his enemies, and was always kind. Remembering how his father taught him never to make enemies, three times he withheld his desire to kill. Such thoughts of forgiveness touched Brahmadatta, who vowed to never cause harm on another. These exemplified the Buddha's teachings and compassion, which he bestowed to the world.

5) Benefiting and Serving All Beings

After attaining enlightenment Buddha traveled across the Five Indias, from Magadha in the South to Sravasti in the North, from Varanasi to Vaishali, along the Ganges, and across mountain ridges and steep cliffs. All for the purpose of propagating the Dharma and benefiting sentient beings without rest.

Throughout the forty-nine years of his endeavors in Dharma propagation, Buddha spent the first twenty-one days teaching the *Avatamsaka Sutra*. After that, he catered to the aptitudes of his audience and taught the *Agamas* for twelve years, the *Vaipulya Sutras* for eight years, the *Prajnaparamita Sutra* for twenty-two years, and then the *Lotus Sutra* and *Nirvana Sutra* for eight years altogether. These were teachings delivered in front of an assembly, coupled with the countless instances of individual teachings, through which Buddha changed the lives of innumerable people.

Other than leaders of other traditions, faiths, royalty, and wealthy elders, sovereigns such as Bimbisara, Prasenajit, Vaidehi, and Mallika were also among Buddha's followers. His teachings are like a boundless ocean that was home to every being, and alike the sun and moon that illuminate the Earth. To merchants, Buddha would speak of the ways of management. To farmers, he would teach them the ways of farming. To statesmen, he would speak of the ways of governance. He always taught according to the conditions of his disciples, caring for them equally. Markedly, Buddha did not just practice inside his Vihara, he also reached out to people in different places with his disciples, teaching them the Dharma, and even helping to resolve disputes.

For example, in the *Attadanta Sutta* from the *Samyuktagama*, Buddha helped settle a dispute between the Sakyans and the Koliyans by advising them to lower their clubs, and share the water resources peacefully as equals to survive the drought together.

Buddhism developed rapidly in India during those days. For this reason, kings and statesmen sought the Buddha for advice. The site where King Bimbisara parked his carriage on Vulture Peak still remains today.

When still Siddhartha, on his journey to finding a way to cultivation, he once passed the kingdom of Magadha. Being so moved by his demeanor and determination, King Bimbisara offered him half of his kingdom, but Siddhartha declined and instead promised to return to guide him if he ever attained enlightenment.

After becoming the Buddha, he kept his promise and returned to Magadha with his disciples to teach the Dharma to King Bimbisara, who in return built the Venuvana Vihara for the Buddha to settle the Sangha community and propagate the Dharma. Whenever Buddha stayed at the Vihara, the king would visit him for guidance.

Years later Devadatta incited Prince Ajatashatru, son of King Bimbisara, to usurp the throne by imprisoning his father. Not only did Ajatashatru feel sorrow in becoming King, when he thought of his father's love and kindness, he felt so much remorse and regret that he fell ill. Jivaka, the doctor, advised him, "Your Majesty, we doctors may cure your physical illness, but we cannot cure your spiritual illness. All this suffering is coming from your mind. If you are willing to see the Buddha, the supreme potentate of doctors, he will surely cure your illness."

When Ajatashatru willingly went to the Buddha, the Buddha said to him: "In this world, only two kinds of people are able to find true happiness. The first is one who practices virtuous deeds and never begets transgressions; the second is one who has created transgressions but is willing to repent. Now, if you are willing to repent and redress yourself, then you can still be a good person. From now on, you shall govern your people with righteousness instead of unwholesome deeds. Be benevolent in making policy, and not only shall your good name spread far and wide, you will also be respected by all."

Upon hearing Buddha's words, Ajatashatru fell to his knees and broke into tears. With much gratitude, he regained hope and faith in starting anew. (*Mahaparinirvana Sutra*)

In the *Varsakara Sutra* from the *Madhyamagamas* (T01 No.26), a story depicts Ajatashatru's intention to conquer Vrji. The king sent his minister, Varsakara, to inform Buddha of the plan. Knowing the minister's intentions well beforehand, Buddha turned to Ananda and spoke about the virtues of Vrji, "The people of this kingdom often gather to discuss good causes....the king and his ministers share a harmonious relationship, and people are always respectful to one another....it would be difficult to overcome such a great kingdom." Varsakara understood Buddha's intention and left without speaking further. Judiciously, Buddha was able to prevent a war and bloodshed from occurring.

Another who shared a deep connection with Buddha was King Prasenajit of Kosala. Being obese, the king was often troubled by shortness of breath. Thus the Buddha taught the following verse:

Dazu Rock Carvings Baodingshan Great Buddha Bay Niche 17: Illustration of the
Returning Favors Sutra - Sakyamuni Buddha Carrying His Father's Casket
CHINA, Chongqing, Dazu; Southern Song dynasty (1127–1279); Stone

One shall be mindful
In always dieting on food intake;
In doing so, all perceptions will be light,
With good digestion and longevity in life.

What this means is that we shall always remind ourselves to
control our food intake. Never overeat to add burden to the body,
so that one can stay light, comfortable, healthy, and long-lived
(*Samyuktagama*, T02 No.99).

When King Prasenajit was grief-stricken by his mother's death, Buddha said to him:

Ever since ancient times, humans have experienced the following four most horrifying matters:
1. Where there is birth, there will be death.
2. When sickness strikes, one's body becomes gaunt and unsightly.
3. Upon death, the consciousness will leave the body.
4. After death, one will be forever separated from loved ones.

No one can be exempt from the rules of impermanence. No matter how intimate, loved ones will eventually be separated. No one can escape death. Instead of grieving over someone's death, one may as well accumulate some merits for them, which will truly benefit the deceased.

This indeed opened up King Prasenajit's mind and helped him recover from his grief.

This story, told in the *Sutra on King Prasenajit Covered in Dust After His Mother Passed Away* (T02 No.122), points out the inevitable truths of old age, sickness, death, and rebirth. Whenever there is birth, there will be death; whenever there is arising, there will be extinction. No one is exempt from the rule of rebirth. Nevertheless, the Buddhist perspective on rebirth depicts an unending cycle of birth, death, rebirth, death, and so on, highlighting the fact that birth is not the beginning, whilst death is not the end. True wisdom is what enables us to discover an undying life within the continuously changing cycle of birth and death.

The compassionate Buddha never overlooked anyone who shared an affiliation with him. No matter how ignorant or stubborn, he always guided them through life with hope and Dharma. For example, using the parable of the Kusa grass, Buddha gracefully guided a woman out of her grievance over her dead son (*A Collection of Parables*, T04 No. 208).

Other than speaking to devotees to help resolve their problems, sometimes the Buddha also visited the homes of troubled families. The most well-known example was Buddha's teaching to Sudatta's daughter-in-law, Sujata. "True beauty lies not within a good appearance or a nice body. These are not worth being proud of. Only those with a graceful heart and conduct, womanly elegance, as well as respectability can be called a true beauty." Furthermore, Buddha also taught her the Five Virtues to adequately care for her parents-in-law. As a result, Sujata requested the Buddha to ascribe the precepts to her, vowing to always live as an Upasika who followed the Buddhist ways of family. Appreciative, Sudatta gave Sujata his blessings, and this became an exemplary story of how Buddha helped resolve family issues (*Sujata Sutra*, T2 No.142).

A happy family can only be created with the presence of a compassionate father, dutiful sons, loving siblings, a loyal husband and wife who are respectful, tolerant, and understanding as well as forgiving towards one another. Buddha always instructed his disciples and devotees with the use of parables and inspirations to help them realize that the right path can be trod without the need for punishments or reprimands. Not only does this preserve a person's dignity, it can also help avert wrongdoings.

Many women and children were also among Buddha's disciples. For example, Lady Mallika was a pious believer of the Three Jewels who strictly upheld the pure precepts. Together with her husband King Prasenajit, they took refuge under the Buddha and propagated the Dharma to their people. Their daughter, Srimala, made Ten Great Vows and sounded her lion's roar by speaking the Mahayana teachings. She too, took refuge and propagated the Dharma together with her husband, King Yasomitra of Ayodhya. Srimala paid special attention to children's education, and summoned every child above the age of seven into the palace on a regular basis for lessons (*Sutra on the Lion's Roar of Srimala*, T12 No.353).

Lady Visakha, mother of Migara and loyal patron of Buddhism, not only provided for the daily necessities of Buddha, bhiksus, and bhiksunis; she even gave away her pearl dress to build the Mrgaramatuh Prasada. It can be said that swift progress could not have been possible without the dedication of these Dharma patrons.

In the *Maharatnakuta Sutra*, the enlightened eight-year-old Naga girl became the teacher of Manjusri, the Bodhisattva with supreme wisdom. This little girl questioned the Buddha on how to eradicate delusion and attain enlightenment, astonishing the entire assembly. She thus inspired faith in sravakas and pratyekabuddhas to follow the Greater Vehicle.

Having spent his time teaching the Dharma in the human world, Buddha also valued children highly. When Buddha was out one day, he saw a few children playing with fish beside the river. Very gently, he reminded these children that animals have fear and pain just like human beings, that they should have compassion for all forms of lives by protecting and cherishing them.

Once impermanence strikes, it may be hard to be reborn as a human being. Thus Buddha told stories on the importance of diligently serving and helping others, and also to possess Right View and Right Thought.

In the *Sutra of Parables*, a man journeyed across the wilderness when, out of nowhere, came a charging elephant. Being very frightened and having nowhere to run, the man found a dry well and climbed down the well along an old vine. As he was about to reach the bottom of the well, four giant snakes suddenly appeared. Too afraid to descend any lower, he clung tightly onto the vine. Then, a white and a black mouse both began to nibble on the vine. At that very moment of life and death, five bees began hovering above the well and released five drops of honey into the traveler's mouth. Being so absorbed with the beautiful and sweet taste of honey, all the existing dangers had been precluded in the traveler's mind.

In this story, the elephant symbolizes impermanence, which follows us closely. The dry well represents the abyss of birth and death. The four giant snakes represent the Four Great Elements—earth, water, wind, and fire that comprise our physical body, threaded together by the line of life, that is, the old vine. The black and white mice are interchanging days and nights that nibble away our time, while the five drops of honey represent the Five Desires—wealth, lust, fame, food, and sleep. Indulgence in the small drops of sweet desire is enough to cause the traveler to forget the dangers that surround life. This indeed is a profound and astute story that calls for deep contemplation.

In addition, Buddha used the "Four Types of Friends"—that some friends are like a flower, like a scale, like a mountain, and like the Earth, to explain the types of friends one should have (*Commentary on the Foshuo Bei Sutra*, T17 No.790). He also used the story about the blind men and the elephant to show that ignorant sentient beings are like blind men touching an elephant. Their biased views only take them further from the truth about matters in this world, unable to see the whole picture. (*Dirghama Sutra*, T01 No.01). For this reason, the most dreadful nature in this world is neither poverty, hunger nor fear. It is ignorance making one unreasonable, have distorted and evil views, and do unwholesome deeds.

Not only do the ignorant suffer, their actions also affect others and the rest of the world.

Malunkyaputta, a bhiksu who was constantly perplexed by questions such as "Is the world permanent or impermanent?" or "Does life still exist after death?" went to the Buddha for answers. In reply, Buddha used the parable of a man who was shot by an arrow but refused to go to a doctor for treatment until he found out what material the arrow was made of, what shape the arrowhead bore, and what the name and physique was of the craftsman who made the arrow (*Sutra on the Parable of the Arrow*, T01 No.26).

Only fools would ponder over such metaphysical yet mean-ingless questions. The humanistic Buddha is more affected with issues concerning real life. Incidentally, parables such as the foolish doorkeeper, killing another son to balance the pole, yelling at water, the three-storied house, foolish man eating the salt, storing milk in the cow, and flogging oneself are all stories about the absurdity and folly of ignorant minds.

Ignorance is much more frightening than mistakes. The differ-ence is that a mistake can be corrected in the same way one gets back up when fallen; whilst ignorance is like walking in the dark without any light. Thus humans need the light of wisdom to dispel the darkness in their minds. Just as has been said, "A thousand-year dark room can be illuminated instantly with a single light; while endless kalpas of ignorance can instantly be enlightened with a single moment of wisdom."

Other than the above, did Buddha ever get aggravated? Did Buddha ever rebuke? Did Buddha lose his temper? We can find in the sutras that, occasionally, Buddha's compassion would be expressed in the form of anger and even reprimand. However, he reprimanded and got angry in a more refined way than ordinary people.

For example, Buddha admonished by using expressions such as "you have no shame," "you know not what afflictions are," "you have no respect," "kindness is absent in your mind," "you have no compassion," "you are inhumane." By 'inhumane' it is meant, "you are not acting like a human," or "you are unhuman." It can be forbidding to have this said to you by the Buddha, because as explained in the sutras, to be "inhumane" means one who is "not laughing when you are supposed to, not being joyful on joyful occasions, not being kind when kindness is needed, not correcting oneself in the face of evil, not feeling joy in seeing virtue."

The so-called 'dutifulness' in Buddhism is different from that in the mundane world, which is personal and limited. The act of renunciation is usually criticized by society on the assumption of negligence of one's duty towards parents, believing that, "One's body, hair and skin have been bestowed by one's parents, and therefore must not be harmed." This is untrue. In fact, the sutras have recorded stories about Buddha returning to the palace to teach the Dharma to his family and relatives (*Abhiniskramana Sutra*, T03 No.190).

"Chapter on the Mahaparinirvana of Mahaprajapati Gotami" of the *Ekottaragama Sutra* (T02 No.125) reveals records of the Buddha carrying his father's coffin and teaching the Dharma to his deceased mother. Even when his aunt Mahaprajapati entered nirvana, Buddha also led Nanda, Rahula, and Ananda in lighting the fire for her. These are all examples of Buddha's dutifulness to his family.

The *Ekottaragama Sutra* also emphasizes Buddha's continued love for his people, despite having relinquished his throne and becoming renounced. When King Virudhaka of Kosala set out to conquer Kapilavastu, Buddha attempted to stop his army by sitting in the middle of the road, beneath the scorching sun, reminding the King that only the shade provided by one's relations is greatest. This stopped the army and saved the Sakya clan from a bloodbath. From this, it can be seen that Buddha had not only never forsaken his parents and family, but that he was always loyal and protective of his motherland.

According to the *Xingqiji Jing* (T04 No.197), Buddha experienced ten calamities such as having his foot pierced by a wooden spear, bleeding caused by a rolling boulder, eating horse-grain, practices of austerity, headache, back pain, and joint pains. King Prasenajit once asked Buddha,

"Why is it that even someone of your unparalleled virtue and magnificence would still experience all such adversities?"

"Your Majesty, the Dharma-body of buddhas and tathagatas are their true eternal body. Such adversities as foot injuries, begging for milk, taking of medicine, and even nirvana, as well as distribution of relics to be enshrined in stupas are merely manifestations of expedient means to deliver sentient beings. By calling upon their awareness in the prevailing existence of karmic retributions that they may, out of fear, eradicate all transgressions and practice all virtuous deeds for the attainment of eternal Dharma body, longevity, and Pure Land." Replied the Buddha.

Upon hearing this, King Prasenajit's queries were thus answered and his mind filled with joy from gaining a deeper understanding of Buddha's profound compassion.

All of the viewpoints stated above bear the purpose of demonstrating Buddha's humanistic lifestyle. Nevertheless, it is natural for people to deify the human Buddha to illustrate his sacredness. For example, legends about Siddhartha being born through his mother's right armpit in Lumbini Garden, the marks of thousand-spoke

Dharma wheels at the soles of his feet, and how Buddha always lev-
itated three feet above ground. In theory and significance Buddha
is indeed liberated and has unified with the universe. But continual
emphasis on his supernatural powers does not necessarily aid in the
demonstration of Buddha's greatness.

The Buddha, as a being of the human world, has always
asserted the key tenets of normality, simplicity, impartiality, and
pertinence as well as humanism. In trust with these beliefs we hold
true to the original traits of Humanistic Buddhism, pertaining to its
relevance to all aspects of life as well as its universal propagation.
Through Buddha's chronicles we are able to perceive his self-
effacing way of life. This authenticity will not only aid to engender
greater faith but to also encourage, in the world of today, a greater
acceptance of him. My affirmation of the belief that Buddha is a
human being, not a god, and in his worldly allure is embodied in the
Buddha Museum. Ultimately, Humanistic Buddhism, as taught and
lived by the Buddha, is a truthful and genuine philosophy.

Chapter Three

Core Concepts of
Humanistic Buddhism

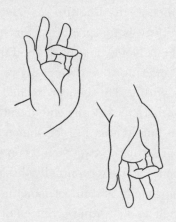

Summary of Chapter Three

Out of the Three Jewels—Buddha, Dharma, and Sangha—the Dharma is the most supreme, for it is what the Buddha relied on to attain enlightenment.

The Dharma can be categorized into "this-worldly" (conventional truths) and "other-worldly" (ultimate truths). The Buddha taught using "real teachings" as well as "provisional teachings." He was able to guide sentient beings through harmonizing the ultimate and conventional truths, using both real and provisional teachings.

Upon enlightenment, the Buddha realized that the truth of Dependent Origination was too profound for sentient beings. Instead, he spoke the Four Noble Truths at the First Turning of the Dharma Wheel. As suffering was more easily relatable, the Buddha began his teachings with it. He then proceeded with the cause of suffering, to inspire others to seek the end of suffering.

Additionally, he taught the Three Dharma Seals, explaining that all phenomena arise due to causes and conditions and are also bound by impermanence as they eventually dissipate. As conditions are unsubstantial, dependent, and impermanent, the Buddha taught the concept of non-self and emptiness. Since nothing is substantial, it is thus possible to transform affliction into Bodhi wisdom, ignorance into enlightenment, and ordinary beings into sages. It is also possible to attain the state of nirvana—absolute tranquility.

Unlike conventional Buddhist thought, which is passive, Humanistic Buddhism advocates harmonizing ultimate and conventional truths together. In this way, the Dharma is presented in a positive, optimistic, and joyful manner. To truly uphold the original intents of the Buddha, Buddhism must be a beacon of happiness for the world.

Core Concepts of
Humanistic Buddhism

When the Buddha taught, he constantly acknowledged the different aptitudes of his disciples and amended his approach. Yet, he always taught according to the same set of core concepts. For example, the teachings of suffering, emptiness, impermanence, and selflessness are commonly recognized as the earliest Buddhist teachings. In later periods, Buddhists were encouraged to practice the Six Paramitas, aspire to the Four Immeasurable States of Mind, and realize the Four Universal Vows.

Early Buddhism, as we understand it, ultimately concerned Buddha's perspective of the human world, which was expressed through the ideas of suffering, emptiness, impermanence, and selflessness. However, these teachings were later assimilated by Buddhists without depth, and were mostly interpreted from a negative perspective, leading people to assume that Buddhism embraced a rather passive and negative view on life.

It is a fact that the humanistic Buddha remained connected to society by living close to communities, begging for alms, speaking the Dharma, and delivering sentient beings. Regardless, modern day Buddhists choose to live secluded lives of spiritual cultivation, detaching themselves from society, and turning the proactive and soteriological concepts of Dharma into something passive and evasive of worldly matters, which is truly regretful. In this chapter, the fundamental teachings of Buddha are further elaborated on alongside their relation to Humanistic Buddhism.

1) The Ultimate Meaning of Suffering, Emptiness, and Impermanence

A large number of Buddhists portray life as an experience of extreme suffering, and further divide it into suffering caused by birth and death, the Three Sufferings, Four Sufferings, Eight Sufferings, and endless sufferings. The truth is, Buddha never taught about suffering to worsen our aversion to life and reality, treating the Saha World as the sea of suffering, regarding the Three Realms as a burning house, feeling that life is meaningless. Rather, his intention was to draw our focus onto suffering itself, and cultivate virtue to eradicate the causes of suffering and attain ultimate peace.

This is not how suffering should be perceived. Proactively, suffering can be regarded as a contributive factor to life. Suffering is a contributing condition, and a nutrient for life. Suffering causes

Life of the Buddha - Great Departure; MYANMAR; Early 19th century;
Ink and color on paper; H: 48 cm; British Library, London, United Kingdom

one to learn, work harder, improve, grow, and transcend. Suffering enables those with potential to endure hardship and strive harder, which are positive energies in life.

In terms of liberation from suffering and attainment of happiness, no student can pass exams without years of studious effort. No farmer will ever yield a good harvest without diligent cultivation. No soldier can emerge gloriously as a general without fighting hard battles. No engineers can become experts without years of research works. Without hard work, how can there be success? Without proper upbringing and education, how can parents raise their children well? Without caring and providing for one's parents, how can these children live an ethical life once they become adults? Without being subject to the harsh cold and bone-chilling storm, how can there be pleasant floral fragrances in spring? Without experiencing a long period of hibernation, how can animals exhibit the vibrant energies of life?

Suffering is our teacher, our strength, our factor of success, and what makes us admirable. Suffering is like clay, which, having gone through the furnace becomes solid and strong. Suffering is like asphalt, which once pressed hard into the ground becomes a firm path for travelers. Suffering is like gold, which must be subject to extreme temperature to become refined and pure.

Suffering trains us and makes us stronger, more determined, and more aspiring. Suffering is a path upon which we head towards a greater future. As the saying goes, "one becomes the best of the best by enduring the worst of the worst." Eminent Buddhist masters of the past all endured the greatest hardships in order to achieve spiritual attainment. Even the Buddha had to go through six years of austerity in order to become awakened. The Path is certainly not an easy one.

The Buddha Tending to the Sick

I) Suffering: Life, After Endless Hammering and Refinement, Becomes Full of Potential

After endless hammering and refinement,
it is ready to depart the deep mountains.
Having gone through the furnace of raging fire,
it is no longer linked to the ordinary.
Though its body is shattered and bones crushed,
it harbors no resentment.
All that is left behind in this world,
are the white colors of purity.

This poem by Yu Qian (于謙, 1398-1457), from the Ming dynasty, tells us that without excavation, high temperature, extreme refinement and chiseling, lime cannot become the pure white substance that beautifies the houses that people live in.

Suffering is indeed an inevitable truth of life. In Buddhism, there are the so-called Eight Sufferings: suffering caused by birth, old age, sickness, death, meeting with foes, separation from loved ones, unfulfilled desire, and burning of the Five Skandhas. Parents go through extreme hardship to give birth to and raise their children, the pain of which is certainly hard to imagine. When old age arises, the situation is worsened by loneliness, which is also suffering. Once sickness strikes, the torments of mental defilements such as greed, anger, and ignorance, added with the physical pains are indubitably oppressing. In addition, the fear of death certainly worsens life's bad reputation as one filled with nothing but suffering.

There are also the sufferings caused by loss of loved ones, meeting one's foes, and insatiable desires. These pains are certainly difficult to endure. Even everyday encounters can cause emotions of discomfort, fatigue, and hardship, which are also categorized as suffering in this world.

However, it is not entirely impossible to overcome such adversities and calamities in life. For example, despite the painstaking effort of having to raise one's children, when they hold their babies in their arms, the pain then transforms into the joy of hope. There are also dutiful children who offer constant care and love, which assuredly brings warmth to the hearts of the parents.

Old age may be suffering. However, there are also elderlies who enjoy a retired life in the company of their children and grandchildren. It is not a joy to care for one's spouse in old age and be in the company of one's offspring? When the elderly are respected, attended to, and provided for, old age certainly has its joys and splendor. Even when retired and alone, one still has a chance to start a second life and continue to expand life's horizons. Can you say that old age is truly nothing but suffering?

When we are sick, we can go to the hospital and find doctors of distinctive specialties to treat our illnesses. Concurrently, you must know your body well and give it sufficient nutrients, health care, and exercise in order to help it heal. Even bedridden patients are afforded various conditions and care. Therefore, sickness cannot be entirely regarded as suffering. Many are ultimately given the luxury of time when sick, and learn from the lesson of sickness. Some are able to retreat to quiet places to rest and enjoy natural surroundings by wandering in the wilderness, appreciating the flowers alongside the mountains and rivers. After the mind and body acquire deep relaxation and recuperation, they are able to start anew. In this way, illness has become a good cause.

As the saying goes, "the gift of food comes with a price." Sickness is not all bad for it can make us stronger. Buddhist masters view minor illnesses as companions for the Way, for they inspire us to improve and transcend life. In the sutras, suffering is categorized into: 1) Physical illness: old age, sickness, death, and rebirth 2) Mental illness: greed, anger, and ignorance. With the guidance of Dharma, you shall be able to train yourself in becoming mentally and physically free of suffering.

To those who lead a hectic life, the gains of minor illnesses are a few days of rest. Sometimes, through a minor illness, people come to understand the inspiration it offers. Illness is a reminder for us all that the world is not perfect, and no one can live forever. Illness shows the reality of life in helping us to become detached from it. "Illness is feared even by heroes," "Only with sickness does one come to realize that the body is a source of suffering." By embracing the suffering of illness, we will no longer become attached to it. It is usually upon the moment of sickness that people come to

Kushinagar: Mahaparinirvana Temple - Reclining Buddha
INDIA, Uttar Pradesh

realize the need to let go of the delusive joys of wealth and fame, and embark on the journey to finding life's true meanings. It is not a total loss if with illness come unique realizations.

Speaking of death, most people think the greatest suffering comes from death. Actually, not only can death be painless, it can even bring a sense of joy. Why so? An aging and dying body is compared to a dilapidated house that requires reconstruction in order for someone to live in it again. Death is similar to a rundown engine that needs to be replaced in order to get the machine running again. Death is also like a garden that needs to be trimmed and weeded, otherwise there is no hope for future blossoms. It is true ignorance to think that there is no hope or future beyond death. Just as the cycle of seasons continues to revolve, once winter is over, one need not be afraid that a spring full of blossoms will never come.

Death does not mean the end. Death is merely the sweet fruition of life. Once harvested, new seeds will grow and ripen for the next harvest. Once the cycle of old age, sickness, and death is complete, although the physical body dies, our True Thusness—buddha-nature lives on as the eternal life. Just as one log burns out after the other, what endures from the logs is the flame. From one stage to another, the flame of life continues to burn without end.

Consider chanting beads as another example. Each bead represents a single lifetime that is connected together by the thread of karma. From previous lifetimes to succeeding lifetimes, life continues in a cycle without end. It does not disappear when death occurs. It is only the disrememberment in-between lifetimes that cause one to feel separated by different bodies. When one migrates into a new body, it then symbolizes a new lifetime. Like a wall that places you on one side and I on the other, nothing beyond the present lifetime is remembered. What remains is one's wholesome and unwholesome karmas that keep us in the river of causes and conditions, floating on and on.

Death can be likened to migration to other places. Wealthy people have the capital to migrate to better places, while poor people are only able to reach the less affluent places. The same goes for rebirth, the forces of our good and bad karma guide us in great accuracy and fairness. Thus birth, old age, sickness and death are particularly natural processes, so there is no need to worry.

At one time, Buddhists explained the process of life by order of "birth, old age, sickness, and death," placing death as a final destination, which is rather passive. Imagine if the order were rearranged as "old age, sickness, death, and rebirth," though the contents remain the same, the new order now adds a sense of proactiveness to life. Since birth symbolizes a future, where there is a future, there is hope. Just as winter is followed by spring, is this not something good? Since the flame of life continues to burn, all we need is to do good to create good causes and good conditions; therefore there is no need to be so passive and negative about life.

We believe that Buddha intended for us to understand the natural process of life—birth, old age, sickness and death, and aspire for virtue and enlightenment, a broadened life, and an enriching future. Therefore, it is essential that we establish good affinities, and endeavor to do good so as to lead to a wealthy and joyful life, now and in the future.

Followers of the Buddhist faith will understand that life is made up of halves. If we adhere to Buddhist practices well-followed, we will find numerous solutions to our sorrows and sufferings. For example, the suffering caused by greed can be resolved by the contemplation of impurity. The suffering caused by anger can be remedied by compassion. The suffering caused by ignorance can be alleviated by understanding causes and conditions. In addition, lethargy can be relieved by diligence, and arrogance by respect. Henceforth, the remaining four of the Eight Sufferings—suffering caused by meeting with foes, separation from loved ones, unfulfilled desires, and burning of the Five Skandhas, as well as infinite types of suffering are not totally unsurpassable. Faith offers us so many wholesome solutions to life's problems and afflictions, and allows us to continuously grow and improve. How then can we not see the beauty of life?

Our fear of suffering is exactly what makes us vulnerable to it. Freedom from that fear will release us from the worries of hardship and suffering, which will enable us to confront life's challenges, overcome all adversities, and succeed in our endeavors. In the past, the key tenet within Chinese culture was the willingness to endure

Water-Moon Avalokitesvara
KOREA; Goryeo dynasty (918–1392), dated 1323; By Seo Gubang;
Ink and color on silk; 165.5 x 101.5 cm; Sen-oku Hakuko Kan, Kyoto, Japan

suffering, aggrievement, and hardships so as to attain greater strength to grow as a human being with a hopeful future.

We can also see that those who fear hardship, who are lazy and passive, are the ones who never succeed. Only those who are willing to confront adversity, overcome challenges, and strive hard will succeed. Hence, Buddha taught us suffering for the purpose of encouraging us to head for the Buddha path, to tread the untreadable, and endure the unendurable. To have no fear in suffering and adversity is what the Buddha wished to teach us.

In general, the statement, "life is suffering" is not wrong. Suffering connotes proactiveness and growth, and does not need to be interpreted as something passive and unendurable. As Buddhists, it is important for us to see austerity as a bridge that links us to spiritual cultivation and enlightenment. Nonetheless, austerity does not necessarily have to be the only path to success and accomplishment. Thus, we must understand suffering from a new perspective, that it is a contributing factor of growth, not our enemy. The spiritual practice of regarding suffering as joy, suffering as a blessing, and suffering as peace, allows us to enjoy life to the fullest.

2) Emptiness: What is Empty in this World Thereby Exists in this World

The greatest misunderstanding of Buddhism is the fear of 'emptiness.' Early translations of the Buddha's teachings on dependent origination rendered it as the word *sunya*, which was quite precise. However, *sunya* was also interpreted as 'nothingness' and 'emptiness,' thereby provoking even greater misconceptions of the Buddhist teaching on "Emptiness of the

Four Elements" as everything being nothing and empty. If anyone were asked to believe in Buddhism, they would feel as if they believe in a somewhat delusive life and empty world. When this misunderstanding worsens, in-depth understanding of the Dharma is thus hindered, which is a genuine pity.

The truth is, emptiness is not to be feared. Instead, it should be something we pursue. Imagine if there were no empty lands, where would I build my house? If there were no empty fields, where would I plant my crops? Without crops, how can there be a harvest? If my pockets weren't empty, where would I put my money? If my bowl were not empty, where would I place the rice and vegetables? Emptiness allows us to have and to hold something, which is said in the phrase, "Out of true emptiness arises wondrous existence."

Although Buddhism speaks of emptiness, it in fact gives rise to existence, helps us build our future, and enables us to succeed in life. For example, the often-misunderstood connotation of "Emptiness of the Four Elements" in fact means that everything in this world is comprised of the Four Elements—earth, water, wind, and fire. Since everything is a conglomerate of the Four Elements, everything is thus empty in nature. If the Four Elements disintegrate or cease to be empty, then nothing can be created or exist.

For instance, this universe is made up of the Four Elements. Without Earth, where can life grow? Without Earth, where can things be stored? Without the Earth, where can we stand and live?

Water is also as vital. Without water you would be dry and thirsty. Without water to cleanse you, you will be dirty. Without the nourishment and purification of water, do you think we would ever live happily?

Fire helps us cook food and keep warm. Is not the warmth of the sun truly wonderful? Imagine if there were no sunlight, no electricity, no fire, no warmth, or cooked food, would humans be able to survive?

The gentle breeze brings refreshing air to us. Wind is air that flows, and the air that we breathe. Imagine if there were neither wind nor air, how can beings survive?

Therefore, the Four Elements—earth, water, wind, and fire actually enable us to survive. It can even be said that the Four Elements represent existence, as emptiness and existence are one and the same. Without an empty pocket, you would have no space to carry your money. Without empty space in your organs, mouth, and nostrils, do you think you would be able to survive? Empty lands and empty space are indeed very precious! Even one square foot of open land can be worth millions of dollars, how can you say that emptiness is not good? Without empty space or land, where can houses be built? People fight over empty space. They would take each other to court for a single empty space.

Emptiness is the most ideal foundation of existence. Emptiness offers us the most bountiful riches. Therefore, there is no need to fear emptiness, because it gives us a chance to survive and prosper. For this reason, I have written the couplet:

> *The empty nature of the four elements manifest in existence;*
> *The incorporation of the five aggregates are ultimately*
> *unreal existence.*

In being empty, the Four Elements are in fact not empty. We all wish for our space to be as big as possible, because the greater the space, the greater the amount of matters we are able to contain therein. Those with big hearts embrace big things, and are more likely to succeed. Thus it must be understood that emptiness gives rise to existence, and existence depends on emptiness in order to be.

The Five Skandhas—form, perception, volition, mental formation, and consciousness, refer to our body and mind.

The Four Elements—earth, water, fire, and wind, symbolize our skin, flesh, bone, marrow, internal organs, tears, saliva, urine, body temperature, and breath. In Buddhism, these physical and astounding realities are generally referred to as form, while perception, volition, and mental formation are mental activities. Consciousness is the owner of this self, which directs our eyes, ears, nose, tongue and body. In addition, consciousness enables us to distinguish right from wrong, and even eliminate wrong by doing good.

Perceptively, it can be said that form is emptiness, and emptiness is form; the two are one and the same. This interpretation of life's truth will inspire in us wisdom, and provide insight to the ultimate meaning of life. Having understood that form is emptiness, and emptiness is form, one has understood the Truths, and will naturally be replete with the joy of Dharma and Chan. What reason is there for you to deny the wondrous meaning of emptiness? If you do, why would you desire more space?

The truths imparted by the Buddha in the *Treatise on the Perfection of Great Wisdom, Sutra on the Perfection of Great Wisdom, Diamond Sutra,* and the *Heart Sutra* can be abridged into the following: the non-duality of emptiness and existence. Since emptiness gives rise to myriad phenomena, existence, and matters, the phrase "form is emptiness, and emptiness is form" thus becomes such a wonderful truth! However, it is difficult for the world to understand this wondrous Dharma, and the word *se* (色) is even misunderstood as a tangible color or sensual pleasure. It is a real pity to see the profound wisdom of past great thinkers distorted in such a manner.

Sutra Cabinet; THAILAND; 18th century; Wood with lacquer and gold;
Chao Sam Phraya National Museum, Thailand

Emptiness embodies the meaning of causes and conditions, namely, the truth about everything in the universe. Frequently, we discriminate between the conventional manifestations of all matters instead of probing into the truth within them. As a result, we fail to understand the meaning of emptiness.

Take a table for example. The moment you call it a table, its conventional form traps you, because in fact it is timber. However, if you then call it timber, it is still conventional, because timber is obtained from trees, whose essence is actually a seed. Yet the moment you come to understand that the true form of a tree is a seed, you must also realize that this seed has gathered the conditions of soil, water, sunlight, air, and human labor in order to grow into a tree that is cut into pieces of timber, which are then made into a table.

For this reason, the Buddhist teachings often speak about an entire universe visible within a grain of sand. From a piece of timber, I am able to see the energy of the entire universe that brought it into existence. This is the meaning of causes and conditions. This whole connection explained in Buddhism can be expressed with one word, 'emptiness.'

Consequently, it can be said that emptiness is the foundation of all forms of existence, for it embodies the criteria of existence for all matters. Emptiness allows us to survive, and emptiness allows us to become prosperous. Thus, 'emptiness' should be praised, instead of misunderstood as something that is bad to us when it is actually beneficial. Why would you reject the treasure of emptiness?

The most unique part of Buddhism is that, unlike other religions that define the process of existence in a linear perspective with a single starting point and a single ending point, Buddhism explains the cosmology in an infinite and cyclical manner. Time is defined as beginningless and endless, while space is described as without inside or outside. Such an extremely wondrous and vigorous life brings so much hope and future to the human world. Why would anyone reject this teaching and taint the Truth?

Just as the seasonal cycle progresses from spring to summer, autumn and winter, what follows is not the end but the advent of spring yet again. When myriad phenomena go through the cycle of becoming, existing, deteriorating, and emptiness, emptiness does not mean nothingness. When a house is demolished, the empty land can make way for a bigger building. When the circle of life goes through old age, sickness, death and rebirth, death does not result in nothing. Like the arms of a clock, it merely means that the number twelve has been crossed and will start anew. Since the law of causes and conditions operates in a cyclical manner, then emptiness or the great void would be infinite and boundless. Such are the meanings of emptiness and conditions.

Since it is not easy to understand the concept of emptiness, reflected within the law of causes and conditions, even the Buddha went through painstaking efforts to realize this. Its full meaning cannot be described by words. For this reason, empty space has thus become a pragmatic method to teach the doctrine of emptiness.

It is often said that the more energy you possess, the greater the space you own. Modern day people define their wealth by the spacious mansions and lands that they own, yet they never realize that "a carefree mind sleeps on a spacious bed, while a troubled mind turns the Three Realms into the smallest spaces." Outwardly, one may seem as if he owns nothing, yet has the riches of the entire great chiliocosm. On the contrary, one with a narrow mind may look to enjoy a wealthy material life, but in reality he is nothing but a slave to his riches. Always fearing loss of his wealth, his life thus becomes meaningless. Such a person is ridiculed as the poorly wealthy. Furthermore, poverty is emptiness too, though one still lives in a confined space.

From this the proactive significance of emptiness can be understood. Emptiness gives rise to myriad matters. Emptiness is also a flowing river that enables us to cruise through the vast emptiness. Is this not a beautiful life? If the positive aspect of emptiness can be understood, then it shall no longer be misunderstood.

The meaning of emptiness, as explained by experts in Buddhist studies, may involve causes and conditions as supporting factors of all forms of existence. It also embodies the relationship between phenomena, and principle; effects result from causes. Emptiness is the foundation of existence. Form arises from the presence of conditions. Conditions comprise emptiness. The myriad matters are the same as emptiness. Without emptiness, how can there be room for any form of existence? Conversely, how can emptiness be conceived without existence of myriad phenomena?

As we are currently addressing Humanistic Buddhism, we should mention the contributions which emptiness, as taught by the Buddha, can offer us. That is, emptiness constructs existence for us. The greater our space, the wealthier we become. It is truly perplexing to see emptiness explained as 'nothingness' instead. Would this not create greater misunderstanding in the Buddha and his Dharma? Even more so, this not only does injustice to Buddhism, it is an even greater loss to all living beings, because they would misinterpret the Truth. What is worse, they may even be lost in delusive thoughts of themselves being correct, guiding the blind with their own blindness, causing many worries.

3) Impermanence: Everything Can Change

In the past, Buddhism was much feared for the constant mentioning of an impermanent world and a life that is short and full of suffering. In reality, impermanence makes life even more wondrous and infinite, because impermanence gives one a chance for change. Be it our daily life surroundings or future dreams, impermanence means changes and improvements are possible. On a different level, impermanence can be said to embody a positive and aspiring attitude towards life.

For example, impermanence means that poverty can be transformed into wealth through diligence. There are many real-life stories about students who have pursued their dreams of wealth and glory through studious efforts. We also see many aspiring youths who were promoted for their hard work and eventually became distinguished entrepreneurs or tycoons.

The world is impermanent. Swallows that have departed will return again. Wilted flowers will one day bloom again. Cold winter days will not be forever, for they will only remain temporarily. What follow would be warm springs and refreshing summers that offer the luxury of full blossoms and summer creeks. If this place is too cold, I can move to a warmer place. When a place is too hot, I can find a cooler summer abode. All of these are possible because with impermanence, everything is changeable. To be able to benefit so much from the ever-changing impermanent world, how can we not be content?

This world is filled with the continuous conditions of arising and extinction. Just as flowers bloom and wilt, the sun rises and sets, the crescent moon becomes full, the four seasons bring about warmth and cold, and day and night alternate. These are all the beauty of impermanence. Impermanence makes Mother Nature so much more wonderful and diverse. Impermanence also inspires us to strive hard. Therefore, there is no need to fear impermanence. Instead, we should be grateful of the wonderful prospects in life and the endless potentials to achieve greater success brought about by impermanence.

When perceived negatively, impermanence will bear a negative effect. However, impermanence can also help us improve. For example, being poor. If I work hard and broadly establish good affinities, then I would have a chance to succeed. Though being rich, without cherishing my blessings, even a gold mine will perish over time. I may not be smart, but if I study diligently, there is still the possibility of becoming intelligent as a result of my hard work. Imagine if poverty and dullness are set for life, then there would be no purpose in life.

A life filled with impermanence and ever-changing rules means just as long as we are willing to correct ourselves, refine our behavior, and strive hard; we can naturally turn our future and fate around. Thus impermanence teaches us to cherish our blessings, our conditions, and our relationships.

We should be grateful to impermanence for reminding us of the need to strive hard and work diligently, for life is transient. Impermanence reminds us of the need to cherish time and to protect our perishing environment. Due to impermanence, the beauty of spring blossoms and the autumn moon make this world so much more beautiful! Even if we were subject to the process of old age, sickness, death, and rebirth, we still have a chance to reinvent ourselves. Having shared with us such wondrous Truth of this world, which the Buddha awakened to, if we were able to believe, accept, and practice it, the resulting benefits would be worth more than the greatest wealth in this world.

4) Selflessness: From the Smaller Self to the Greater Self

In the past, the notion of 'selflessness' has created fear in people, causing them to feel that once the self disappears, life will no longer bear meaning. The truth is, this conventional body of ours is not worth coveting. The Buddhist doctrine of selflessness is not to deny ourselves but to teach us not to stick to that smaller and ignorant self. Instead, we should bring out that "true self" who makes us bigger, purer, greater, and more elevated. The Buddhist terms of True Thusness, intrinsic nature, tathagata-garbha, true form, prajna wisdom, and Dharma body all serve the purpose of helping us build a hopeful future, and strive for success. Therefore why would anyone define 'selflessness' as a form of annihilation?

The so-called Dharma body is omnipresent within the vast emptiness, and all-pervading within the Dharma realm. Life exists everywhere, and the vast emptiness exists within our minds. The self can be infinite and boundless. The self is eternity. The self goes through the cycle of old age, sickness, death, and rebirth with a predetermined life span and body. However, this is the same as changing from a ragged piece of clothing into a new one. When this body deteriorates, we then change into a new one. When the sun sets, it will rise again the next morning. Whilst sunrise has its glories, sunset is also filled with endless beauty. Are birth and death not just the same?

The story about two ghosts fighting over a body in Chapter Twelve of the *Commentary on the Perfection of Great Wisdom* is worth mentioning:

Once, a traveler missed his final chance to lodge before dusk fell, therefore he had no choice but to stay in a small abandoned temple. He cleared out a space beneath the altar table and decided to rest before resuming his journey the next day.

In the middle of the night, a small ghost suddenly entered the temple.

"Oh no! Am I in trouble now?" Thought the traveler. As he panicked, a taller ghost followed and yelled at the small ghost, "What do you think you are doing with my body?"

"What do you mean your body? It's mine!" Replied the small ghost.

"No! It's mine!" Said the tall ghost. The two began to fight fiercely over the body, causing the traveler to shake in fear. "Hey! There is a man here! Come out and be our witness. Tell us who came in with this body." Unsure of the consequences of telling the truth that it belonged to the small ghost, the man nevertheless decided not to lie, "I saw the small ghost come in with the body."

This made the tall ghost so angry that it ripped off the man's right arm and ate it. Not wanting to see the man who took its side suffer, the smaller ghost then ripped off the dead body's right arm and attached it to the man's body, causing the tall ghost to become even more angry. It then ripped off the man's left arm and ate it. Again the smaller ghost replaced it with the dead body's arm. It went on like this. Whichever part the man's body was ripped off and eaten, the smaller ghost would replace it with that of the dead body. In modern terms, this could be considered similar to an organ transplant.

After they had all the fun, the two ghosts ran off and disappeared into the distance, leaving the man in a serious dilemma, "Who am I? I used to be John from Broadway New York, but his body has been eaten away by the ghost, so to whom does this body belong?" A sudden realization came to him. The body was never really his, that it was just conventional existence. What remained uneaten and irreplaceable was his true nature. Thus his true self had finally been discovered.

"Who am I?" This is a question worth pondering for everyone. Is 'I' the conventional Four Elements? Is life measured by years? If so, then it would be a true pity to see life through such a narrow view. Humans are "eternal beings of the past and future, the ever-changing and prevailing beings across infinity." Humans are beings who pervade all directions and penetrate all three lifetimes. Human beings are made great from birth, which is why we endure the painstaking experiences of faith in pursuit of Buddhahood. Beyond the physical body is an eternal spiritual life that never dies. For this, life becomes extremely meaningful and full of hope.

For this reason, the 'I' within the question of "Who am I?" is not that physical body but a true self that must be understood and attained. Once we enter that state of eternal and undying self, we shall no longer fear or have delusive thoughts.

Thus it can be seen that the consequence of comprehending Buddha's early teachings of suffering, emptiness, impermanence, and selflessness with a passive mind would be unimaginable. On the other hand, when regarded with a positive mind, the teachings then become wonderful. Holding true to the original intent of Buddha, Humanistic Buddhism's interpretation of the Dharma offers hope to this world, and never provokes fear. By nature, every Dharma is meant to help and benefit us.

Buddha's teachings on life and the universe were later proven by scientists to be true. However, much of what Buddha awakened to still remains a mystery to even the most prominent scientists today.

For example, Buddha's awakened insight enabled him to realize that the Earth bears the same shape as that of an Amala Fruit. Indeed, the Earth was later proven to be round. Some sixteen centuries after the Buddha's declaration, Polish scientist Nicolaus Copernicus also proposed that the Earth was round. His theory was later supported by Italian astronomer Galileo Galilei who as a result, was tried by the Roman Inquisition for heresy. Almost a century later, English physicist Isaac Newton supplemented this theory by his laws of motion and universal gravitation. Based on the fact that Buddha's insights were slowly understood by the world through scientific proofs, it can be said that for any mundane knowledge to catch up to the level of Buddha's attainment would take an extremely long time.

Another of Buddha's insight from thousands of years ago was that he could already see within a glass of water the existence of 84,000 organisms. Thousands of years later, scientist were finally able to verify Buddha's claim through the use of microscopes. In Chapter Sixty-Five of the *Sutra of the Right Mindfulness of Dharma* (*Saddharma-smrty-upasthana-sutra*, T17 No.721), the Buddha explains that there are about eighty types of organisms that live on the human body. Modern day science has come to explain this with the term 'microbes.'

In addition, when the Buddha referred to the universe as "the three thousand great chiliocosms," he perceived the world as the greatest, boundless, and subtlest without any limits. According to the findings of modern day scientists, the Earth, which we live on, covers an area approximately one hundred and thirty millionth of the entire Solar System. Yet there exist two hundred billion suns within the entire galaxy, on top of which, millions of galaxies exist within the whole universe. The boundlessness of the universe is therefore exactly what the Buddha said.

Speaking from the perspective of the smallest of particles, modern day physicists have broken matters down to atoms, electrons, neutrons, and even smaller units. Yet by "micro dust," Buddha meant something even smaller than protons. This is similar to placing an animal hair underneath a microscope; you will be able to see even smaller particles within the hair. Reducing those particles ten thousand times into even smaller matters, we might come closer to what Buddha meant by "micro dust." Scientist have even discovered that 99.999999% of an atom is empty. What we perceive in reality are not what they are in essence. Instead, we are only perceiving matters from our own perspectives, under the control of our consciousness. True reality is like a sea of energy that is boundless and filled with infinite waves of change. Everything is a part of the whole, which holds us together by interconnectedness. Therefore, all the above conform to Buddhist concepts such as "the Three Realms are nothing but a creation of the mind, and all phenomena manifestations of the consciousness," "true emptiness give rise to wondrous existence," and "oneness and coexistence."

The Buddha claimed that the myriad phenomena in the universe all go through the cycle of formation, existence, disintegration, and emptiness, and that our mental process experiences the changes of arising, abiding, changing, and extinction. Scientists are yet to come up with an even more complete theory to surpass the Buddha who had already realized it all 2,600 years ago. No wonder Albert Einstein once said, "If there is any religion that would cope with modern scientific needs it would be Buddhism." Later facts have indeed proven that the more advanced science becomes, the closer it gets to the Truths expounded by the Buddha.

Buddha not only spoke in accord with the Truth, he also spoke in accord with the different aptitudes of living beings. To rulers, he spoke of the ways to govern and to love one's people. To entrepreneurs, he spoke of the proper means of business to benefit humanity. To the general public and even housewives, Buddha also patiently taught the ways to manage a household or to deal with people.

Buddha actively engaged in the activities of society. Other than teaching and developing the Sangha community, he spent most of his time traveling and teaching across along the shores of the Ganges River even at the age of eighty. For this reason, we are still able to discover the remains of those sites, which the Buddha had been to. For example, ruins of the Jetavana Grove still speak of the Buddha's teachings through every existing rock and brick, whilst conveying the Buddha's selfless and altruistic spirits.

2) The Mahayana Practices of Perfection

Mahayana Buddhism holds that in order for humans to be delivered, they must follow six practices known as the Six Paramitas: generosity, discipline, patience, diligence, meditative concentration, and prajna wisdom. On the surface, the Six Paramitas may appear to be nothing out of the ordinary, creating a rather mundane outlook of the Mahayanist teachings by simply telling us to share, abide by the law, work hard, be patient, focus, and have mental agility. If they were that simple, why would the Buddha have to teach these? Actually, what the Buddha had to offer was so much more and they are listed as follows:

1) Generosity
In the early days of Buddhism, the Buddha walked between Southern and Northern India across the shores of the Ganges River. In order to help people relate his teachings to their daily life, Buddha often used the river as an example. In the *Diamond Sutra*, Buddha taught that, if anyone were to "give away the seven jewels amounting to the three thousand chiliocosms as numerous as the sands from the Ganges River," he would accumulate innumerable merits. However, such merits would still be bound by form, by number, and by limit. True spiritual cultivation is to be able to

practice "formless giving" through the attainment of the "emptiness of the three aspects of giving." Anyone who has read the *Diamond Sutra* will see the immense heart of the Buddha that has room for the universe. He often taught his disciples to "give without becoming attached to form, and deliver sentient beings without become attached to the self." This certainly is the unconditional, altruistic, all-embracing, and non-dualistic trait of the Mahayanist teachings.

Therefore, does generosity actually mean giving to others or to self? If it were the former, people will find it hard to give away for a good cause. On the other hand, if generosity were taken to be an act of giving both to others and self, where benefit and honor is mutual, would you still hesitate to give? Just as farmers cannot harvest without sowing seeds, by giving you shall gain. Whenever there is giving, there will be gain.

The notion of generosity is frequently mentioned in Buddhism. On the surface, devotees give by donating money and materials to the Sangha community, while bhiksus and bhiksunis give back to the devotees by gifts of Dharma. Just as the saying goes, "the giving of money and Dharma are no different but one and the same." The Buddha continued to emphasize the quality between them, which is what makes the Dharma extraordinary.

In addition to the giving of money and Dharma, there exists an even more important form of giving—the giving of fearlessness. This means to protect people from worry and fear just as how a mother protects her baby, and how a nation protects its people. The greatest form of giving is to offer humanity a life filled with happiness and peace as well as freedom from fear.

In the process of giving, there may exist unwholesome ways such as giving with attachment, bias, greed for fame and benefit, or expectation of return, all of which have been mentioned in various sutras. Nevertheless, the most significant meaning of giving, according to the Dharma, should be remembered as: "the giver and receiver are one and the same."

In the act of giving, instead of just thinking about what merits we will have, we must also remember that those who accept our giving will receive just as much merits. This is similar to inviting guests to our house for dinner; at the end of the day, we as hosts must thank them for coming, for their friendship, and for coming all the way to our house to accept our offerings. In other words, we must thank people for eating our food. This indeed brings the relationship of the giver and receiver to its most profound level.

2) Discipline

People usually fear the word 'discipline,' because it carries the tone of restrictions on the self. Thus we must raise the question, "does discipline actually mean restriction or freedom?"

The answer is not difficult to see with a little deliberation. Discipline means to prevent wrongdoings and cease unwholesome acts. If you can achieve this, discipline is no longer a restriction but ultimately freedom. When we abide by the law, why would we be jailed? We can see that inmates of prisons in this world are mostly people who have violated the Five Precepts and broken the Law. Thus they are sanctioned for their crimes. If they never committed the acts of killing, stealing, sexual misconduct, lying, drinking or taking intoxicants, then why would they be anywhere but inside prisons? Just as trains must stay on track, and planes must fly on routes, long ago the Buddha had already pointed out a clear path for life.

For example, after the Vinayas came east into China, in order to become fully ordained, one must go through the Triple Platform

Full Ordination Ceremony. At the first platform, sramaneras and sramanerikas must take the Precepts of Rites, that is, to follow the discipline of demeanor in walking, standing, sitting, and reclining. Coming to the second platform, bhiksus and bhiksunis must take the Precepts of Virtues, that is, to practice all good deeds and actively reach out to teach sentient beings, and to serve society. Finally, at the Third platform, either lay or monastics must take the Precepts to Benefit Sentient Beings and to "deliver all beings from suffering and adversity with great loving-kindness and great compassion." To reach the state of "no concept of self, people, sentient beings, or lifespan" as said in the *Diamond Sutra* would be the ultimate practice of discipline and precepts.

3) Patience

On the path of spiritual cultivation, our most intimate companion is the paramita of patience. It is not easy for us to swallow insult and humiliation, endure suffering and adversity, or tolerate wrongful accusations and criticism, because we would feel as if we were disadvantaged. That is why people are able to endure hunger, suffering, or adversity, but are unwilling to endure insults. When confronted with aggrievement or grievance, most people tend to yield to the tendency to resist and fight back.

Furthermore, patience does not mean to simply endure physical discomforts such as harsh cold or starvation, nor does it mean to endure humiliation or insult, or to yield and swallow your anger. Patience as taught by the Buddha is a kind of strength. However much praise, ridicule, slander, honor, profit, loss, suffering or joy you are able to endure, however much stronger you will be.

The truth is, patience is a kind of wisdom and compassion. By enduring a situation, you will certainly come to know the causes, effects and stories behind it all, and then be able to transcend and rise above the situation. Just as the saying goes, "Endurance brings peace and serenity; compromise makes the world so much bigger."

In regards to patience, one question is worth pondering over, "Is patience really a disadvantage or advantage?"

For most people, the answer would be the former. However, one who endures places oneself at an advantage, and one who doesn't will be at a loss. The ability to endure makes us stronger and wiser. Never be a pot that calls the kettle black. Being able to endure, I should strive to rise above and be better than the perpetrators. That is why various Mahayana sutras encourage the practice of the paramita of patience in the practice of the Bodhisattva Path.

The importance of patience must not be overlooked. Disharmony in a family could turn members against each other, and ruin chances of happiness and peace. If we are always calculating and arguing with people, always being so stubborn and unwilling to endure, or lacking manners, then how would it be possible for us to survive in society?

The world today is filled with disputes, wars, crimes and murders. Lawsuits are endless. All of these are caused by people's unwillingness to endure insult or anger. Those who lose will become depressed, while those who win will continue to inflict pain and suffering onto others. Is this truly the happiness we want? If it is, how long would this happiness last?

The ancients used to say, "Only patience brings peace." In order to achieve world peace and happiness, it is essential to inspire mutual benefit and tolerance. Any moment we are able to endure a little misunderstanding, aggrievement, slander or insult; then the world will be at peace.

In the *Agamas*, patience can be divided into: Ordinary Patience,

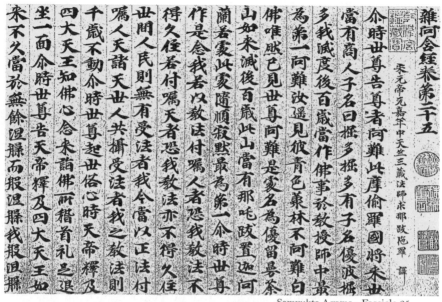

Samyukta Agama - Fascicle 25
CHINA; Northern Song dynasty (960–1127), circa 1008;
Regular script; Handscroll; Ink on paper; 24.4 x 662.3 cm;
Metropolitan Museum of Art, New York, USA

Dharma Patience, and Patience of Non-arising Dharmas. What this means is that the only way for us to survive in this world is through the wisdom and strength found within patience.

Ordinary Patience means the wisdom to see the good and bad of this world in order to survive. Patience is also a form of acceptance where not only are you able to take in all the humiliation, insult, merit, profit, as well as good and bad treatments but also to take these matters into your own hands and resolve them. One who is patient will find the courage to endure all suffering and adversity, and help people find happiness and peace.

Ordinary Patience is endurance and courage, which arises from our will to survive. It is also wisdom and strength, which is cultivated from our experiences resolving everyday matters and relationship issues. Therefore, whether we are able to endure any unfair treatment or adversity in life will depend on our ability to learn from these lessons, as well as our wisdom and strength within.

Dharma Patience is best represented by the phrase, "To remain unmoved against the Eight Winds." In other words, to remain unmoved by all matters in life, all phenomena in this world, all the sorrow, sadness, suffering, affliction, fame, gain, benefit, kindness and coldness experienced. In addition, Dharma Patience enables us to understand, confront, resolve, transform, and even purify these circumstances. Therefore, only patience will enable us to understand, accept, confront, and resolve life's problems.

Patience of Non-arising Dharmas is yet an even higher state, it means an insight into the reality that every phenomena intrinsically neither arises nor extinguishes, that everything is equal, non-dualistic in essence. To be able to go along with any condition and an enlightened mind to realize the theory of non-arising, then even the concept of patience would have no need to exist, as everything simply just is.

Therefore, does patience actually put us at an advantage or disadvantage after all? My eighty-years of experience as a monastic has taught me the true wonder and power of patience. The greater your patience, the closer you are to success.

4) Diligence

On the Bodhisattva path, not only are the practices of generosity, discipline, and patience important, diligence is also essential to the training of a bodhisattva. As the saying goes, "There is only benefit in diligence, not in play." The Buddha taught four ways to practice diligence:

1. To prevent evil from arising when there is none.
2. To eradicate evil when there is any.
3. To prompt the arising of virtue when there is none.
4. To enhance the growth of virtue when there is any.

In other words, the Buddha taught us to actively engage in acts of virtue when we have yet to engage in any, to eradicate and not repeat transgressions we have committed, to refrain from unwholesome deeds at anytime, and to discipline our minds from trespassing upon others by thoughts of greed, anger, or jealousy. In short, it is all about diligently engaging in the acts of stopping evil and doing virtuous deeds without lethargy and negligence.

While the wealth and luxury enjoyed by millionaires in this world may be attributed to their blessings and favorable conditions, most of them have earned it by hard work. Money will never fall into your lap while you are sitting idly at home; nor will it pop out of the ground at your disposal without toil. As the saying goes, "Even if there is gold flowing down along the stream, you still have to rise early to scoop it up." Scholars who are studious will succeed. Farmers who diligently cultivate their fields will not fear lack of harvest. Therefore, does diligence mean toil or happiness?

Laundry that is left unwashed will always be dirty, and only clean clothes will give us comfort. When your home is unclean and untidy, how will you be at ease living in it? In this world, parents raise their children, and teachers educate their students all for one purpose: to teach youngsters that good grades in school or success in one's career would not be possible without diligent effort. Therefore, is diligence actually hardship or happiness? Before you reap, you must first sow. How can there be a fruitful harvest in the vineyard without the diligent works of cultivation, weeding, and fertilization?

Humanity has evolved from the agricultural era to the industrial revolution, and then finally to the era of technological advancement. Although automated robots now largely assist our works, the human brain still plays a key role in designing the function and operation of even the most advanced computers. The most advanced robot still depends on humans to give it the power to move.

If all members of a family are united and cooperative, then there will be happiness within the family. An organization cannot progress if its members do not work as a team. If every person in this world strives hard to bring happiness to others, then how can this world be without peace and joy?

5) Meditative Concentration

Within the practices of the Six Paramitas, we see that it is important to learn the many ways of dealing with the world and people. In the process of liberating both oneself and others, the practice of meditative concentration is also essential to an aspiring bodhisattva. Most of the time, the unrest of our minds is caused by our afflictions. When our minds are filled with greed, anger, ignorance, resentment, and jealousy, there will be no willingness to do anything that is beneficial to others. If such unrest remains for as long as delusive thoughts of greed persist, then how can we help or be of service to others? Therefore, meditative concentration is a key practice to finding peace and purpose in life. It is also the driving force of the remaining five paramitas.

When Buddha held up a flower and smiled on Vulture Peak,

what emanated from his smile was a wonderful spark in the universe, the profound Truth of life, and the beginning of endless words of wisdom in Chinese Chan Buddhism. Let us ask a question: "Is Chan lively or rigid?" The answer is the former. Most people take meditation to be an act of sitting cross-legged with eyes closed. In reality, sitting meditation is merely a means and a process by which the development of wisdom through meditative concentration is assisted. The true way of Chan should be something active and lively. As has been said, Chan is found in collecting firewood and water; eating and drinking; when walking, standing, sitting and reclining; in silence and movement; and in a lifted eyebrow and blinking eyes. Chan is a smooth and carefree attitude used in dealing with the world.

6) Prajna Wisdom

In general, the first five paramitas—generosity, discipline, patience, diligence, and meditative concentration on their own are merely worldly teachings. Only in the presence of the Prajna Paramita do they then become transcendental teachings. Just as the saying goes, "The first five paramitas are like blind men awaiting the guidance of prajna wisdom." The worldly acts of giving and discipline are conducted with attachment, but when guided by prajna wisdom, these can then be practiced without attachment to form, attachment to dualistic stances, and without being comparative or calculative.

At this point, another question must be raised, "Can prajna wisdom be sought through the within or the without?" From without, you would need to consult science and philosophy, which are nonetheless mundane knowledge, and still far from the prajna wisdom which can only be sought from within. Prajna wisdom, attained by inner searching, is wisdom perfected by gaining an insight into the law of Dependent Origination and the nature of emptiness within all phenomena. With prajna wisdom, we will overcome all dualistic views between self and others, transcend all afflictions caused by ignorance, and thereby reach the state of perfect ease. Thus the Six Paramitas bear a much more profound meaning than what it simply exhibits in words.

Humans are Made Sacred through Life and Spiritual Cultivation

In the practice of Humanistic Buddhism, one must first elevate his character if he wishes to be a decent human being with a healthy mind. For example, to make oneself a better person than others, to strive for a better and greater personality in time. The Six Paramitas, as practiced by bodhisattvas, are the guides to our practices of Humanistic Buddhism. For example, a blueprint of Humanistic Buddhism on ways of dealing with family and relatives, friends, food, clothing, daily living, transportation, education, leisure, resources and spiritual cultivation is provided in the *Vimal-akirti Sutra*:

> *Wisdom is the mother of all bodhisattvas,*
> *Skillful means the father.*
> *Among all guides and teachers,*
> *None are not born from these parents.*
> *Joy in the Dharma is the wife,*
> *Compassion the daughter,*
> *Kindness and sincerity the sons.*
> *Ultimately, Dharma is the home.*

The *Lotus Sutra*, regarded by the Tiantai School in Chinese Buddhism as their primary text, advocates the ultimate teaching

Mogao Cave 158
CHINA, Gansu, Dunhuang

of the One Vehicle, which embodies the bodhisattva way. "The physical manifestation of an arhat with the inner quality of an altruistic bodhisattva" encourages people to deliver all living beings whilst benefiting the world. In particular, metaphors such as that of a conjured city used by the Buddha serve as a reminder for us to come to terms with our own mind, and to cultivate ourselves physically so that we will not leave our inner treasure hidden and lost. Most importantly, we must let our "True Thusness"—our intrinsic nature shine and guide us along the path of life.

Other than the *Lotus Sutra*, Chengguan (澄 觀 , 738-839, also known as National Master Qingliang) was a teacher to seven

Fahai Temple Great Hero Hall: Sudhana
CHINA, Beijing; Ming dynasty (1368–1644), dated 1443

Emperors during the Tang dynasty. He encouraged Buddhists to imitate Sudhana from the *Avatamsaka Sutra*, who embarked on a journey to visit fifty-three teachers who could mentor him. He reached out to people of all walks of life across all social strata. For example, Megha-dramida the linguist, Indriyesvara the mathematician who played with sands, King Anala who governed his state with strict law enforcement, Vairocana the voyager, and Jayottama the judge.

In my opinion, any young student who does not seek advice in at least fifty to one hundred great mentors, on ways of self-establishment and dealing with the world, throughout his entire life is unlikely to succeed. Has any king ever assumed the throne solely on his own individual effort? If you desire a noble rank, then you must have staff, people, and a team. The *Avatamsaka Sutra* mentions the "phenomenal dharma realm", the "principle dharma realm", and "mutually unobstructed phenomenal dharma realm." These are in fact teachings about how we can be wise human beings who deal with the world appropriately, and our interactions with daily matters.

We come to understand the truth about the interpenetrating dharmas of the world and live life in joy and perfect ease.

3) The Sacred Truth of Humanistic Buddhism

Certainly, it is not possible to perfect oneself in an instant. Based on my lifetime experience, we each have our own attainments, and each day's cultivation means each day's growth. By gaining thorough understanding of the Mahayana teachings such as prajna, Middle Path, or Dependent Origination, which embody the profound meaning of "oneness of self and other," we will also establish the sacred connection between Humanistic Buddhism and Buddha.

Therefore, can the sacredness of a bowl of rice be denied? Can the sacredness of the joy found in life or the support and help we are given be overlooked? Is not a smile, handshake, or a nod sacred? When I am willing to give others faith, joy, hope, and convenience, would this not be regarded as sacred?

The Three Acts of Goodness are promoted for the purpose of helping people do good deeds, speak good words, and think good thoughts. Therefore is this not regarded as sacred? Faith itself is sacred. Spiritual cultivation itself is sacred. The process of purifying ourselves and transforming ourselves into sages and saint is the power of our sacred faith.

Based on this, it can be said that Humanistic Buddhism is Buddhism. In fact, since Buddha taught the Dharma to human beings in the human world, Buddhism certainly is none other than Humanistic Buddhism. During Buddha's time, many yogis and shamans adopted odd and eccentric approaches of spiritual cultivation, which were in disaccord with ordinary human behavior. Out of his compassion, Buddha subdued ninety-six such 'heretics' and underwent the arduous journey of spreading the Dharma to enlighten sentient beings. Although he made tremendous progress, the large discrepancies in principles and habits among sentient beings were ultimately hard to unite. In particular, Devadatta's rebellion and conspiracy besides his propagation of austerity, all ill attempts to surpass the Buddha, in the end all failed.

Although Buddhism counsels against hedonism for it will eventually lead us astray, over insistence on austerity to win admiration and followers is not deemed ideal for the benefit of society either. True Humanistic Buddhism should advocate the Middle Path and practice in accord with what the Buddha taught and practiced.

In light of this, the future of Buddhism should certainly be a faith that follows what the Buddha taught to humanity. Just as the saying goes, "The attainment of Buddhahood is concurrent with the perfection of our human characters." Once we master our ways as humans, how can we not become buddhas?

Furthermore, Buddha taught us the Four Ways of Embracing and the Four Universal Vows as ways to deliver sentient beings. He also taught us to value every part of our daily life, discover true peace, and perfect ease by applying the transcending and profound meanings of the Dharma.

Buddha's sacred teaching of the age holds that our priority is to serve our nation, be dutiful to our parents, and regard all humans as equals. Both the Confucian thought of benevolence and Daoist principle of transcendence share a similar belief with Buddhism, although only in parts. Only the Buddhist Dharma is complete and all-embracing, and thus has prevailed over time as a unique teaching for humanity.

Humans Begin to Transcend in the Face of Equality

Equality is another teaching which makes Buddhism supreme. Within Vimalakirti's chamber, Sariputra was taught a lesson on equality by a young lady. From this it can be seen that even a great arhat must learn from the teachings of a female bodhisattva, which is equality. In the *Avatamsaka Sutra*, Sudhana was able to enter the realm of the Dharma under the guidance of female advisors such as Isana, Prabhuta, Bhadrottama, Maitrayani, Srimati, Simha-vijrm-bhita, Vasumitra, and Vasanti.

Thus to all bhiksus of today, is not the Guanyin Bodhisattva to whom you constantly make prostrations also manifested as a lady? I wonder why your so-called respect for women is often contradicted by your actions? Is this not ironic? This is the result of your lack of understanding in Buddha's teaching of equality.

Equality applies not only between men and women, it also applies to lay and monastic Buddhists; to past and present, and to phenomenon and principle. It can be said that Truth itself is equality. That is why I composed the BLIA verse:

> *May kindness, compassion, joy, and equanimity*
> *pervade all Dharma realms;*
> *May all people and heavenly beings benefit*
> *from our blessings and friendship;*
> *May our ethical practice of Chan, Pureland, and Precepts*
> *help us to realize equality and patience;*
> *May we undertake the Great Vows with humility and gratitude.*

The most important messages within the verse are equanimity and patience, which represent the ultimate teachings of the Dharma.

Living in the modern era, a majority of Buddhists aspire for nothing but transcendence of life and liberation from death. I wonder what this actually means? Has anyone ever been seen achieving this?

True transcendence of life means to remain unattached to life, to never compare, and to never cling to anything. It also means to have no fear of death or see it as destruction. In fact, death is just like moving places alike immigration; it is like buying a new car, or changing into new clothes, all of which are something worth celebrating. Moreover, death is preceded by birth, if there were no birth, would there ever then be death? In the moment we are born, we are already destined to die.

Not only should Buddhists stop pursuing only their own cultivation and liberation; the habit of praying, prostrating to, and chanting Buddha's name requesting his blessings and help should also be corrected, because these actions still come with the intents of greed and desire. What the Buddha taught us is to maintain a simple and pure mind. True faith is found in the motivation to spread the humanistic spirit of Buddha, that is, to follow the Bodhisattva path of aspiring for the willingness to sacrifice, to give, to serve, to propagate and practice the Dharma, and deliver all living beings. The path of Humanistic Buddhism is pursued through the development of the Bodhi Mind, only by which can the essence be truly reflected. Therefore, it is not enough to just beg or pray to the Buddha; instead, we should practice the Buddha's ways. Only the Bodhisattva path can pave our way to Buddha's humanistic spirits.

古寺天寒夜一宵不禁風泠雪霏霏蚝無奈勤何事特曲取堂中木佛燒

Master Danxia Burns Wooden Buddha Statues
CHINA; Yuan dynasty (1271–1368); By Indara; Ink on paper;
32 x 36.7 cm; Ishibashi Museum of Art, Kurume, Japan

4) The Omnipresent Humanistic Buddhism

All of the abovesaid harmonizes Early Buddhism with
Mahayana Buddhism, such is the original intent of the Buddha.
Buddhists today should never omit any single teaching. Should you
choose to retreat into the mountains, you will not be abandoned by
Humanistic Buddhism. Should you choose to cultivate and endeavor
to benefit humanity, Humanistic Buddhism will not reject you either.
The Buddha's original intent was to embrace the vast emptiness,
embrace all forms of existence, and encourage coexistence as well

129

as mutual respect. Nowadays, when I am writing my One-Stroke Calligraphy, I often choose words such as "co-own," "co-share," "co-exist," and "co-live" to explain Buddha's original intents in simple words and practical manner.

Throughout nearly eighty years of my life, I have gradually come to realize the importance of emptiness. If your mind is as big as the vast emptiness, how can you not embrace the entire universe and everything that the Buddha ever taught? The world exists in our minds. All sentient beings live as beings within our hearts. The myriad phenomena are also embraced as the myriad phenomena within our hearts. Since everything exists within our minds, why should we reject anything? Therefore, since emptiness is existence, what is stopping you from realizing all forms of existence within emptiness? If my mind is as vast as the emptiness, what is stopping me from becoming the master of the world?

As said in the *Avatamsaka Sutra*, "Shall one desire to see the state of the Buddha, he must first empty his mind like the great void." The void neither arises nor extinguishes. Realization of such nature of emptiness will enable us to also understand that life also neither arises nor extinguishes. In Buddha's explanation about life, he too mentioned that our Dharma body can be attained through the cultivation of our physical body. This Dharma body is omnipresent, all-pervading, and is that original face of ours which exists anywhere and everywhere. To realize this would be the goal of spiritual cultivation.

Today, if someone asks me where the Buddha is, the answer based on my personal experience would be: "The Buddha is in our hearts. The Buddha is in the vast emptiness within which we exist. The Buddha is in our faith."

Buddha is within our hearts. For this reason, there exist the common sayings, "Everyone has the buddha-nature," "Buddha is in my heart," or "I am a buddha." Nevertheless, it cannot be said that there will then be no *icchantikas* in this world. Would Buddha exist in the mind of an *icchantika*? Would Buddha exist in the minds of terrorists? Would Buddha exist in the minds of the bishops at the Vatican? Thus it is not entirely correct to say that Buddha exist within every one of our hearts.

In this case, where exactly is Buddha? Based on my more than seventy years of Buddhist practice, Buddha probably exists within the vast emptiness and dharma realms. Just as the sutras say, "The Dharma body of the Tathagata permeates the vast emptiness, and is omnipresent within the dharma realms." Where within the vast emptiness does Buddha not exist?

When you prostrate to a painting, for you, you are doing so not to a piece of paper but to Buddha. When you prostrate to a Buddha statue, you are not revering some substance of gold, silver, bronze, steel, concrete, or timber; your respect is fully directed at the Buddha. In the same way, we can regard everything in this world as Buddha.

> *The sounds of the creeks are voices spoken*
> *by your broad and long tongue,*
> *The mountains are none*
> *but manifestations of your pure body.*

Be it mountains, rivers, the sun, moon and stars, which of them is not a manifestation of Buddha? It can be said that the entire vast emptiness and Dharma realm are the Buddha's true body.

The Chan stories of Danxia burning a Buddha statue and the old lady who burns down the temple should make us wonder who truly has seen the real Buddha. Once, a monastic said during his Dharma lecture that Buddha's Dharma body is all-pervading and omnipresent, making his audience feel the greatness of the Buddha.

Suddenly a Chan Master began to cough and then spat at the Buddha statue, leaving the entire assembly speechless.

The Dharma lecturer became very angry and yelled at him, "How dare you blaspheme against Buddha?! You can spit anywhere you want, so why do it to the Buddha?"

The Chan Master coughed a few more times and replied, "Dear Venerable, I would like to spit again, please show me a place in the entire emptiness where the Buddha does not exist. I shall aim in that direction."

What the Chan Master pointed out was the segregation of theory and practice, which becomes a hindrance to the thorough attainment of Dharma. Nonetheless, it is not an easy task to see and realize the all-pervading and omnipresent true body of the Buddha.

Simply put, where is the Buddha? The Buddha is found in our faith. Since the depth of faith varies within each one of us, what the Buddha looks like to each one of us will subsequently vary too. When Bodhidharma (達摩) said to his disciples, "Dao Fu (道副, 464-524) has only received my skin, Zong Chi (總持) (Bhiksuni) my flesh, Dao Yu (道育) my bones, and Huike (慧可, 487-593) my marrow." It implies the same message that the depth of our faith will influence the way in which Buddha appears before us. It is hoped that Buddhists will not shirk their faith and allow their attachment and biases to block them from seeing the Buddha, thereby distancing themselves from him. Our glimpse of the Buddha is not found through an epistemological world based on discrimination but through the different depths of our faith. On the ultimate level of theory and practice, you will realize that you are already living in Buddha's Dharma body, which already exists in your mind. Buddha is not a deity who is based in a particular place, nor the lord of the Thirty-Three Heavens. Buddha was an awakened one who realized the Truth. Only by ultimately putting into practice your faith will you see the true abode of Buddha.

Humanistic Buddhism: Rediscovering the Original Face of Buddhism

The fundamental concepts of Dharma, as taught according to the principles of the Three Dharma Seals: 1) Everything is impermanent, 2) Nothing has a substantial self, and 3) Nirvana is the ultimate peace, can only be elaborated in general. The profound attainments of Buddha are in fact beyond words and perception. They are not to be understood or realized by conceptualizations. Not even the compiled Buddhist texts such as the *Agamas* or other teachings in words of any form can thoroughly explain Buddha's state of formlessness, without-abiding, mindlessness, and boundless wisdom. Only by reaching such states will Buddha truly exist in your heart. As we speak of Humanistic Buddhism, this is exactly the order by which we continue to broaden ourselves.

By broadening ourselves, it means to see oneself and others as one and the same, to see the unity of the self and all phenomena, as well as transcending past and future. Just as the saying goes, "Those from yesteryears may not be able to see today's moon; yet today's moon once shone on those from yesteryears." Would you refuse to become the sun, moon and stars? Would you not see life as akin to them? As the Chinese say that "Each generation outdoes the last," we cannot help but wonder where the new generations come from?

Are they not our spiritual essence in the cycle of rebirth? Why are you not able to see your past self or that "original face before your parents gave birth to you?" "Towards the east flows the spring river", but to where exactly is the water headed? Would they not come back after all? This concept of undying life and eternally rotating cycle within the dharma world is exactly what brings hope to the world. If our faith in Humanistic Buddhism were not established upon this supreme and unparalleled insight, where else would be a good place for it?

For this reason, Humanistic Buddhism is no different from traditional Buddhism. The only discrepancy exists in our discriminative minds that have divided Buddhism. Just as the Yogacarians say "The same water is perceived four ways." Heavenly beings see water as crystal, humans see water as rivers, fish and prawn see water as their palace, while hungry ghosts see water as pus and blood.

Are we able to truly understand the original meaning of the Three Jewels—Buddha, Dharma, and Sangha? Be it Humanistic Buddhism, traditional Buddhism, or any Buddhism, we shall nevertheless be able to, through our faith, realize that all is equal in the face of Truth. What makes it different is only our attachments and our soliloquy.

Humanistic Buddhism: Our Future Hope

In today's society, since people all yearn for a positive, happy, reassuring, and hopeful life; would Humanistic Buddhism not be worth spreading, practiced, and held true to Buddha's original intent? The propagation of Humanistic Buddhism will offer a future to Buddhism as a whole, and shine a ray of light onto the world. Let us not submerge in Buddhism of the past that was conservative, passive, biased, and distorted. Today, we are propagating Humanistic Buddhism to return Buddhism to its true face, that is a proactive, transcending, and self-fulfilling Buddhism.

To sum up, the concepts of Buddhism, whether taught to large audiences or individuals, to monastic disciples or lay devotees; the Buddha always emphasized simplicity, peace, oneness of all, bringing joy and happiness to humanity, as well as perfect ease and liberation. By purifying ourselves of afflictions, rising to a world above mundane matters, transcending the world of form to a Dharma realm of boundlessness, formlessness, and infinity, then we would uncover our true Dharma nature as that of the Buddha. This would be the Dharma body, which reflects our Wisdom of Great Perfect Mirror.

In closing, our only intention is to inspire a holistic view of modern day Buddhism where people are able to perceive both the principles and phenomenal aspects, to regard oneself and others as one, and respect man, woman, and all beings as equals. May we follow the footsteps of the humanistic Buddha in allowing the bond between oneself and the multitude to prevail. Even when we become awakened, as buddhas, the human world and the vast emptiness will still be our abodes.

Chapter Four

Development of Buddhism in China

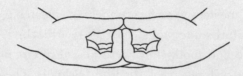

Summary of Chapter Four

Buddhism has exerted tremendous influence on countless facets of Chinese culture. Some of these include: politics, culture, art, fashion, and food.

The Chinese language evolved through Buddhism, not only by its contribution of new vocabulary, but also in enriching its existing literature. The beauty of the Chinese language can be attributed to the effect of Buddhist terminology.

The pride Chinese have for their culture, history and civilization is a result of the impact Buddhist practices and concepts had upon them.

Buddhist masters were forerunners in charitable, humanitarian and educational endeavors. Not only did they provide aid, infrastructure and food, they were also diligent in teaching, as shown by the development of the Eight Schools. The golden age of Buddhism, in the Sui and Tang Dynasties, is a direct consequence of all these efforts.

For over 2,000 years, Buddhism has endured in the face of adversity, and prospered. As it thrived, so did China prosper as well. Buddhist concepts such as dedication, peace, and compassion helped the country experience better social harmony, productivity, and stability. Catering to people's needs has resulted in Buddhism being one of the world's foremost religions. Moreover, this ability denotes that it is, in fact, Humanistic Buddhism. Through its propagation, we stay true to the Buddha's original intents.

Development of Buddhism in China

Humanistic Buddhism is not exclusive to any region or individual. As stated in previous chapters, it is what the Buddha taught to human beings. He was born, attained buddhahood, propagated the Dharma and benefited living beings all within the human world. The entire corpus of the Tripitaka and Twelve Divisions are his teachings for human beings. The Mahayana Buddhist Pure Land teachings which hold that the Saha World itself is Pure Land, affliction is in fact bodhi, or when the mind is pure, the land becomes pure, are all reminders that the Dharma is centered on human beings. It cannot be detached from the human world, and that attainment must be realized only within the human world.

After the Buddha entered nirvana, his disciples propagated his teachings in all directions, making Buddhism a common faith within Asia. In the 21st Century, Buddhism has become one of the biggest religions worldwide.

When Buddhism spread Eastward to China, Emperor Ming of Eastern Han Dynasty dispatched Cai Yin (蔡愔) in 64CE to the Western Region to search for the Dharma. He went to Dayueshi and brought two Indian monks, Kasyapa-Matanga and Dharmaratna, back to White Horse Temple in Luoyang. Thus, in China, the spread of Buddhism began from emperors to ordinary citizens.

Since the Eastern Han Dynasty, over a span of two thousand years, Buddhism exerted tremendous influence on Chinese politics, economics, literature, linguistics, art, music, and architecture. Buddhism's spread to other East Asian countries such as Korea, Japan, and Vietnam established the foundations of many East Asian civilizations.

The successful spread of Chinese Buddhism throughout society can be attributed to its key humanistic characteristics, inherited from the Mahayana and Theravada traditions. Societies as a whole, from emperors to ordinary citizens, were given equal chance to share in the rich and diverse elements of Buddhist culture.

Despite the rise and fall of Buddhism in various dynasties, monastic and lay disciples of the Buddha remained true to his original intents of teaching, benefiting, and bringing joy to the world. Examples include

Lingyan Temple Thousand Buddha Hall: Arhats
CHINA, Shandong, Jinan; Clay
Northern Song dynasty, dated 1066, H: 155 cm

benefiting rulers, society, and all living beings, as well as contributing to the fabric of Chinese culture. Eminent Buddhist masters, throughout history, have embodied the Buddha's spirit and teachings. Some taught emperors. Others traveled westward not merely to find and translate Buddhist sutras, but to promote cultural exchanges. Several built monasteries and established the pure regulations, while others excavated stone caves, planted trees, opened up mills, and set up Inexhaustible Treasure (*Wujinzang*) banks. Further endeavors involved constructing roads and bridges, providing shelters, engaging in relief aid, providing medical services, and education. A few conferred the precepts to ensure continuance of the Dharma. All the above undertakings subsist in their contemporary forms to ensure that both the spirit and the propagation of Humanistic Buddhism endure. This chapter provides an overview of such historical endeavors.

1) The Daily Routines and Practices of Humanistic Buddhism

Even the Buddha, an awakened sage, could not forego the basic necessities of life such as food, clothing, housing and mobility. Within the Five Vehicles, both human and heavenly beings depend on "this-worldly" needs, while the sravakas bear "other-worldly" minds. Bodhisattvas of the Mahayana path integrate the spirits of human and heavenly beings, sravakas, as well as pratyekabuddhas. Harmonized as one, this is the Bodhi Mind of the bodhisattva path, thus Humanistic Buddhism.

The development of Buddhism in China is elaborated below based on the premise of food, clothing, housing and transportation as the basics for life.

1. Food
As the saying goes, "Food comes before everything." Eating is integral to living. The vast influence of Buddhism can be seen in the culture of Chinese food. Its Eastward diffusion brought with it a majority of the fruits and vegetables eaten daily today. Some

include: barley, buckwheat, kidney bean, pea, eggplant, cantaloupe, grape, watermelon, pomegranate, tomato, cucumber, walnut, carrot, spinach, and jackfruit. All are main ingredients of customary Chinese cuisine. How inconvenient would life be for the Chinese without these produce?

Aside from vegetables, eating congee for breakfast is also a result of Buddhist influence. According to the Buddhist sutras, eating congee aids digestion, satiates hunger, and prolongs life. For this reason, congee has become a routine element of breakfast. To celebrate Buddha's [Enlightenment] Day (also known as the Laba Festival), every 8th December of the lunar calendar, Buddhist temples cook Laba Congee and distribute it gratuitously. To date, the Laba Festival is one of the most notable festivals in Chinese culture. Each year, Fo Guang Shan temples worldwide dispense over a million bowls of Laba Congee.

Chinese tea culture descends from traditional Buddhist monastery traditions. Tea was served in the reception halls of monasteries to welcome guests, while monastic assemblies for tea were called "Open Tea Session" (*pucha*). Particularly, tea was used to clear a weary and tired mind during long periods of sitting meditation. Subsequently, it is now a customary drink among meditation practitioners. Moreover, the drinking of tea, as a ritual duty, is included in the daily practices of Chan Monasteries. From Chan gongans such as Zhao Zhou Tea, the tremendous contributions through tea ceremonies of Chan practitioners to Chinese culture can be seen.

Today, many worldly renowned teas share a connection with Buddhist monastics. Examples include: Biluochun tea from Dongting in Jiangsu, Big Red Robe (*Da Hong Pao*) from Wuyi in Fujian, Longjing tea from Hanzhou Yuquan Temple, and Pu-erh tea from Xishuangbanna. All were cultivated in monasteries.

Toshodaiji Temple Founder's Hall: Master Jianzhen
JAPAN, Nara; Nara period (710–794); Dry lacquer; H: 80.1 cm

Without Pu-erh tea, the main Tibetan diet of beef and lamb would have been difficult to digest. Most tea plantations meeting the demands of tea drinkers in China are found near renowned Buddhist mountains and rivers. As a result, Chan and tea became one, and part of Chinese culture.

Master Jianzhen (鑑真 , 688–763) from the Tang Dynasty, known as the father of Japanese Tea, brought tea to Japan. Later, Japanese monk Myoan Eisai (榮西 , 1141–1215), studied in China, and introduced Japan to the tea ceremony. Buddhist monastics have exerted tremendous influence on the propagation of both Chinese and tea culture.

Other than the above, one of Buddhism's greatest contribution is the promotion of vegetarianism. In the Buddha's time, the Sangha community catered to the local customs when begging for alms. As convenience for the people offering whatever they had, coupled with the practice of impartiality, monastics did not differentiate between meat and vegetables.

However, after Buddhism spread to China, alms begging was deemed an unsuitable practice due to the local customs, climate, and the environment. Moreover, as Chinese monastics settled in monasteries to propagate the Dharma, kitchen and storage facilities became available. In Chinese Buddhism, vegetarianism advocates the spirit of compassion strengthened by the Confucian mindset, "Having seen [the animal] alive, how can one bear to see it die? Having heard its noise, how can one bear to eat its flesh?" Vegetarianism thus became a daily custom in practicing Chinese Buddhism. The integration of Buddhist and Confucian culture encouraged vegetarianism as a way of life and became a core concept of Humanistic Buddhism.

Although Buddhism is not against the consumption of meat, its advocacy of not killing demonstrates the equality, compassion, and oneness befitting all sentient lives. This is in perfect accord with the modern ideals of environmental and animal protection.

2. Clothing

After the Wei, Jin Northern and Southern Dynasties (3rd to 6th CE), Chinese clothing, due to the influence of Buddhism and Central Asian cultures, began to change markedly both in style and color. Considering the fashion of women's clothing in the Tang Dynasty, the convergence of Buddhist and Chinese culture is remarkably visible.

At that time, women were especially fond of the red skirts from the Western regions. The women of the palace favored the *feitianji* hairstyle, evolved from Sakyamuni Buddha's usnina, and sported by celestial beings in Buddhist paintings. The festoon of jewels worn by buddhas and bodhisattvas also became chosen accessories of palace women and musicians. Moreover, the Indian honeysuckle, lotus, and eight auspicious patterns all originated from Buddhist art.

Today, the *changshan* and *haiqing* robes worn by Chinese monastics, and those from India that bare the right shoulder, have all been recognized as the distinctive elements of Chinese robes. Contemporary Chinese Monastics, through their clothing, preserve Chinese culture in their own fashion.

3. Housing

Buddhists advocate a life of simplicity and proximity to nature. In Buddha's time, the hot climate made it possible for his disciples to sleep beneath trees and subsist on a single meal daily. Some bhiksus were able to lead communal lives in the mountains. However, in the cold climates of China, how could one live in the wilderness? For this reason, monasteries and temples were built.

The first Buddhist temple in China was Honglu Temple (also known as White Horse Temple) built during the Eastern Han Dynasty (58-75). Originally an imperial guest house, the arrival of two Indian monastics, Kasyapa-Matanga and Dharmaratna, turned it into a temple and place of cultivation for Chinese monastics.

Not only temples, other architectural designations such as monasteries, nunneries, and viharas were used as residences for Buddhist practitioners. Furthermore, the magnificence of Buddhist architecture became a feature of Chinese culture with palaces adopting such styles in their construction. The collective layouts of

Baima Temple: Main Temple Gate
CHINA, Henan, Luoyang

farmhouses were also influenced by monastic communities.

Later, Chinese temples were founded under the procedures of "Mazu's establishment of monastery" and the standards of "Baizhang's introduction of pure regulations." Rules and constitutions thus began as features of Chinese Buddhism. These influenced emperors of different dynasties in refining the laws of their kingdoms.

Some monasteries were built through the contributions of the common people. Others were erected by royal decree, such as Jiangtian Chan Monastery in Jinshan and Qixia Monastery in Nanjing. Both of these large and majestic complexes later became national temples. In the remote Western and Northern regions, temples were built in caves, serving as places of spiritual solace. They are now considered treasures of Chinese culture.

Historically, and unto today, the diversity of Buddhist architecture is the result of adapting to the requirements of the time. Each variance illustrates the historical development of Humanistic Buddhism.

4. Walking

Transportation is another valued component of Buddhist culture. At the time of the Buddha, when begging for alms, bhiksus maintained their demeanor by the following means: looking straight-ahead, keeping their minds focused, as well as maintaining a firm and steady stride.

In Chinese Buddhism, the "three thousand demeanors and eighty thousand subtle actions" denote the daily practices of appropriate conduct whilst walking, standing, sitting, and reclining. Particularly, to "walk like the wind, sit like a bell, stand like the pine, and recline like a bow" illustrates the proper demeanor of a spiritual practitioner.

Particular focus is placed on one's demeanor when lining up. In addition to one's bearing when walking, the formation of a line is as important. This is true whether it be for morning and evening chanting, and entering or exiting a shrine. A sense of space and timing, an essential cultivation in Humanistic Buddhism, is nurtured through the practice of lining up.

This custom of lining up should be re-established in modern society. Today, people shove each other, cut the line, and shout. They should follow the demeanors of Chinese Buddhists in speaking softly, walking and lining-up properly, as well as being civil. Coupled with the elegance and grace of the Chinese, greater harmony and order will pervade society.

Chinese Chan Buddhism split into five schools and seven sects. More schools meant further regulations. The bell and board signals, as well as the formalities of drum and bell varied according to each sect.

The rituals of the five sessions of practice and three daily meals demonstrate Humanistic Buddhism's emphasis on "life itself means spiritual cultivation." When monastics conduct themselves with good demeanor, they gain the respect of devotees. As the saying states,

> *Let the voice of the Buddha flow gently like water.*
> *Chant sutras and progress along the Way like orderly flying geese;*
> *Join palms at chest level as if carrying water.*
> *Stand tall and erect as if a bowl of oil is atop the head.*

Such elegant and upright practices were inspired by the Buddha's conduct. When Neo-Confucian philosopher Cheng Yi (程頤 , 1033-1107) of the Song era witnessed Dinglin Temple monastics entering a hall with such elegance, he exclaimed, "The joy of three generations of rites are displayed here." This demonstrates the general esteem for Buddhist etiquette. The daily necessities of clothing, eating, living and walking have all been tremendously influenced by Buddhism. Chinese culture and Humanistic Buddhism existed alongside the Buddha. Modern day monastics must recognize this to understand the fundamental daily practices of Buddhism.

The meaning of Humanistic Buddhism is that which human beings need. In this case, the needs are clothing, eating, living, and walking. Likewise, it is essential that it cater to the needs of people when establishing formalities and regulations. Such influences are now inseparable from Chinese culture. Thus, we Buddhists shall take on the duty of placing greater value on the development of Humanistic Buddhism within Chinese culture.

2) The Social Welfare and Charity Works of Humanistic Buddhism

Crucial factors in the global spread and acceptance of Buddhism are its dedication and support in helping people solve life's daily problems. The purpose of the Buddha's birth in this world was to benefit sentient beings. As one of the world's utmost philanthropist and volunteer, he was indefatigable as well as selfless.

The Buddha's disciples followed in his footsteps by teaching and benefiting both self and others. Exemplars abound, such as Upali, who not only visited the sick but brought them medicine. There were also Sudatta the Elder and Lady Visakha, generous philanthropists. Bimbisara inspired seven thousand of his subjects in taking refuge in the Buddha. King Asoka was tireless in providing meals, medicine, and lodgings for the sick and destitute. All were unprecedented Buddhist endeavors in charity and social welfare.

Subsequent to Buddhism's arrival in China, many Buddhist masters applied the Buddha's teachings through charitable activities. For instance, they planted trees, and dug wells in addition to providing water. Free porridge was offered for sustenance. Coffins were also freely provided. In terms of infrastructure, free schools were established; roads were paved, along with building banks, storehouses, pharmacies, and bridges. Any endeavor that benefits living beings is an instrument of the Bodhisattva path, which ties Humanistic Buddhism to society. Further examples of such undertakings are:

1. Free schools

The Sangha community established by the Buddha was the first free school in Buddhism. As he travelled to different places, he embodied the first Buddhist community school when he taught at these locations. In olden days, the people viewed Chinese monastics, being educated and knowledgeable, as teachers and sought them for answers. Buddhist temples provided free schooling, private tutoring, and learning centers, inviting distinguished teachers and masters as visiting instructors. Shrines served as classrooms, and sutra repositories as libraries. Temples and monasteries thus became locales for thinkers and the knowledgeable.

Nalanda: Sariputra Stupa
INDIA, Bihar

Throughout history, many outstanding scholars stayed at temples to study, some for the imperial exams. For example, Di Renjie (狄仁傑 , 630-700 CE) the Tang Dynasty minister, mandarinates such as Yang Zhen (楊禎 , ?-528), Li Duan (李端 , 743-782), Wang Bo (王播 , 759-830), ministers such as Li Shen (李紳 , 772-846), Xu Shang (徐商), and Wei Zhaodu (韋昭度 , ?-895). Lu Yu (陸羽 , 733-804), the sage of tea, having grown up in a temple, later wrote the all time classic—the *Classics of Tea*.

In addition, Song Dynasty minister Wang Anshi (土安石 , 1021-1086), Fan Zhongyan (范仲淹 , 989-1052), Hu Yuan (胡瑗 , 933-1059), and Lu Mengzheng (呂蒙正 , 944-1011) also spent time in temples as students. Even Chiang Kai-shek (蔣中正 , 1887-1975) lived in Zhejiang Xuedou Temple to study for the imperial exams. When Liang Shuming (梁漱溟 , 1893-1988) failed his Peking University entrance exam, he stayed in a temple to focus on his studies of Buddhist and Indian philosophy. His scholarly attitude was discovered by Peking University President Cai Yuanpei (蔡元培 , 1868-1940), who subsequently promoted him as honorary lecturer at the university.

Other than the above, academies were also influenced by Buddhist monasteries. For instance, the renowned Yuelu Academy was founded by Venerable Zhixuan (智璿). The most influential Neo-Confucian thinker, Zhu Xi (朱熹 , 1130-1200) once taught there. After the Yuan Dynasty, colleges were established in rural areas and nurtured many talents. All these efforts, under the affect of free Buddhist schools, were undertaken with the aim of assisting the development of education.

2. Environmental Protection and Forestation
Buddhists have always valued the protection of the envi-

ronment and contributed greatly to its preservation. As said, "Renowned mountains have been mostly occupied by monastics." Past generations of monastics have cultivated wastelands and built monasteries. For ecological preservation, they took to forestation, conserving sources of water, improving water and soil upkeep as well as natural disaster protection.

Among these monastics was Chan Master Zaisong (栽松) from the Linji lineage. He not only beautified his monastery but also set an example for his successors. Master Mingyuan (明遠) planted ten thousand pine, cypress, and camphor trees to prevent floods in Sizhou. Temples thousands of years old, such as Tantuo Temple and Jietai Temple in Beijing, are now surrounded by trees that reach up to the sky. They are classed as natural heritage sites today.

3. Turning Wastelands into Farmlands

After Buddhism's arrival in China, the Chan School observed "Mazu's establishment of monastery and Paichang's introduction of pure regulations." Monasteries transformed wastelands into farmlands as means of self-sustenance through agriculture. For example, Venerable Yongjing (永淨) from Xiangshan developed three hundred acres in the mountainous regions. Chan Master Fori Puguang (佛日普光) cultivated a thousand acres of fertile fields, increasing the annual harvest by five thousand litres. Chan Master Daokai (道楷 , 1043-1118) turned a dry lake into farmland and grew crops. Zhejiang Tiantong Temple cultivated reclaimed lands and increased the annual harvest by over fifteen thousand liters. Not only were these monasteries self-sufficient, they also contributed greatly to the growth of the surrounding townships.

Tiantong Temple: Buddha Hall; CHINA, Zhejiang, Ningbo

4. Oil Mills

China, as a nation, was built through agriculture, specifically rice farming. The staple diet of the people was rice. In olden times, farmers manually toiled the fields, which was both time and labor intensive. In the Tang and Song Dynasties, monasteries began building grinderies and rice mills. Hydraulic trip-hammers were found inside Mingzhou Tiantong, Maiji Mountain Shengxian, Chongguoyuan, Taizhou Huianyuan, and Lengqieyuan Temples. This greatly benefited not only temple residents but local farmers as well. As some temples set up oil mills to supplement the temple's incomes, this also benefited local farmers by raising the value of local agriculture.

5. Relief Aid

In the past, frequent occurrences of natural disasters, wars and

Mogao Cave 302: Illustration of the Sutra on the Field of Merits
CHINA, Gansu, Dunhuang; Sui dynasty (581–618)

man-made calamities caused poverty and distress. Not only did Buddhists act as spiritual mentors, they also provided assistance to the people. Buddhist temples spared no efforts to provide relief aid to the poor and needy.

For example, Master Tanyan (曇延 , 516-588), from the Sui Dynasty, gave away rice, and offered the poor shelter in his temple. He even helped the emperor resolve an issue of rice distribution. Tang Dynasty monk Zhicong (智聰) raised funds for rice storage to help the people. Other monastics such as Demei (德美 , 575-637), Huizhen (慧震 , 463-477), Fayun (法雲 , 467-529), and Lingrun (靈潤 , 590-682) established the "Fields of Compassion Funds" in addition to distributing free food.

Other Buddhist philanthropic undertakings include the "incalculable registry" (*Senqihu*) introduced by Tanyao (曇曜 , 407-463). He also utilized the provisions from the "incalculable grains" (*Senqisu*) storages to relieve people from famines. Furthermore, temple storages and pawnshops brought relief to those in poverty and distress.

In the Sui Dynasty, Chan Master Xinxing (信行 , 540-594) of the Teachings of the Three Levels (三階教), introduced the "Inexhaustible Storehouse" (*Wujinzangyuan*).This allowed people to pawn money, rice, food, lamp oil, and clothing interest-free. Mills that were built in later periods actually followed a similar principle. Similar to modern day farmer unions, cooperatives, and pawnshops, the Inexhaustible Storehouse was widely accepted for promoting compassionate charity by all levels of society in relieving the poor and needy.

Possibly the precursors to modern day pawnshops, Buddhists established loan centers (*Changshengku*) to provide financial aid to the people and state. The notable feature of these loan centers was their lack of pursuit for profit through high rates of interest. Their sole purpose was to give back to society what they had received. This exhibited the core spirit of Humanistic Buddhism by using society's generous contributions to help the people remedy their difficulties.

6. Medical services and support

The Buddha was regarded as the great king of doctors, whereas the Sangha was the nurse that cared for the people. In the past, many eminent monks such as Fotucheng (232~348), Zhufadiao, Zhufakuang, Tanyan (曇衍 , 503-581) and Tanluan (曇鸞 , 476-542) were skilled in medicine and used their expertise to treat the sick. During the Southern and Northern Dynasties, Buddhists established the "Houses of Benefit" (*fudeshe*), "Six Illnesses Center", and the "Guduyuan Asylum." In the Tang Dynasty, they set up infirmaries and treatment centers, whilst in the Song Dynasty the *Futianyuan* Welfare House was founded. Countless other examples exist. These were charitable undertakings helping the poor and sick.

7. Wells and water

Buddhists often volunteered to distribute water and lanterns to help passersby quench their thirst and continue their journey. To improve access to water, monasteries repaired as well as dug wells to provide drinking and washing water. Chan Master Deshao (德韶 , 891-972) from the Wu and Yue periods in the Five Dynasties excavated wells on Mount Wu, Hanzhou, to help people during droughts. In the Tang Dynasty, Venerable Hui Bin (慧斌) dug and built public wells in Wenshui as a show of gratitude to his parents. Venerable Chengguan (澄觀 , 738-839) at Puhui

Manpukuji Temple:
Master Yinyuan Longqi
JAPAN, Kyoto; Edo period
(1615–1868), dated 1671;
By Kita Genki; Ink and color on silk
138.4 x 60.2 cm

Temple in Jiangning provided public access to its water supply. All these efforts benefited the community.

8. Water resource development

Another act of philanthropy related to water, apart from digging wells, was the construction of irrigation works. In the Song Dynasty, Venerable Weixi (維溪) from Fuzhou spent nine years in Changle County to construct a twenty-seven-hundred meter embankment by intercepting twelve rivulets. This provided water for forty hectares of farmland. Venerable Shizhen (師振) took eleven years to fundraise for the construction of a thirty-thousand-meter levee. This irrigated over twenty hectares of farmland. Venerable Master Chuncui (純粹) from Hengyue Temple led the monastic order in digging canals to divert water into drought areas. At the renowned Westlake scenic area, embankments constructed under the supervision of Bai Juyi and Su Dongpo still exist. These infrastructures all share an affiliation with Buddhism today.

9. Paving roads and bridges

One of the most significant Buddhist contributions to local towns were the constructions of bridges and paving of roads. During the Song Dynasty, in the Fujian, Xiamen and Quanzhou regions, bridges funded and built by monastics numbered in the hundreds. Venerable Daoxun (道詢 , 1086-1142), in his lifetime, was said to have constructed over two hundred bridges. Venerables Puzu (普足), Liaoxing (了性 , 1222-1321), and Shouxing (守性) also erected numerous bridges. When added with those built by other monastics, the sum total was in the order of several thousand.

Others, such as Venerables Mingging (明 慶), Juexian (覺 先), Siqi (思齊), and Yunchang (蘊常) constructed street paths. Venerables Daoshen (道琛 , 1087-1154) and Wenda (文達) led monastics in carrying soil used to build roads. Venerable Daoyu (道遇) supervised the project of digging a pond near the Longmen Grottoes to build a watercourse. This shipping canal was a great boon for travelers and merchants, generating much local prosperity.

10. Hostels

In olden times, transportation and its related infrastructure were not as sophisticated. Thus, Buddhists erected pavilions offering refreshment and rest. They also hung lanterns to illuminate roads on the outskirts of towns. Monasteries, such as Baoshou Temple from the Tang Dynasty, and Putong Temple on Mount Wutai also provided lodgings for journeying merchants or imperial examination candidates. These were of tremendous convenience for travelers.

To propagate the Dharma, monastics would often travel by foot to faraway places. In doing so, they also brought with them various traditions and cultures. For example, many novices traveled between Chan Master Mazu Daoyi's (馬祖道一 , 709-788) monastery in Jiangxi and Chan Master Shitou Xiqian's (石頭希遷 , 700-790) monastery in Hunan. The two regions were thus collectively named *Jianghu* (lit. the World). Accordingly, travelers there were called "Jianghu roamers." During the Ming Dynasty, Chan Master Yinyuan (Japanese: *Ingen*) brought kidney beans and the Chinese tea ceremony to Japan. Thus the Japanese call the bean "Ingen mame" (Yinyuan's bean). He was also known as the father of the Japanese Way of Sencha (*senchado*).

Historian and professor Tang Degang (唐德剛) once told me that in the Eastern Jin Dynasty, a monastic named Huishen (慧深 , 436) had already traveled to spread Buddhism to Mexico, preceding Columbus' discovery of America. References to this can be found in Volume 54 of the *Book of Liang* and also Volume 79 of the *History of the Southern Dynasties.* According to him, residents of a Mexican town named Acapulco inherited their Buddhist faith from their ancestors. He also said that Venerable Huishen had left an anchor stone later acquired by a museum in San Francisco.

Originally an unknown religion there, Venerable Huishen's efforts brought monastics, sutras, Buddha statues, and the Dharma to the American continent. The propagation works of a Buddhist monastic thus connected China and Mexico, two of the world's greatest civilizations separated by the Pacific Ocean.

11. Emergency Relief

When wars occurred, temples would become grounds for army camps and refugee shelters. During the Anti-Japanese Resistance

Mogao Cave 302: Illustration of the Sutra on the Field of Merits
CHINA, Gansu, Dunhuang; Sui dynasty (581–618)

159

War, in 1937, Master Taixu (太虛 , 1890-1947) traveled to India to propagate the Buddhist doctrine of peace. He hoped to gain international attention for the anti-Japanese invasion movement. Venerable Leguan (樂 觀 , 1902-1987) organized a monastic rescue team to help the distressed. Venerable Jiran (寂 然) and Venerable Master Zhi Kai (志開 , 1911-1979) from Nanjing Qixia Monastery took in over two hundred thousand refugees. General Liao Yaoxiang (廖 耀 湘 , 1906-1968), a high-ranking commander who fought the Japanese, was hiding among the refugees. The monastics at Qixiashan helped conceal his identity to help him reach the frontlines and continue his defense of the country.

Soldiers and refugees were not merely provided with the daily necessities. Through the practice of Humanistic Buddhism, they were also offered comfort from distress, salvation from the cruelties of war, and ultimately a place to call home.

During the Northern Wei Dynasty, the establishment of Buddhist residences (*fotuhu*) allowed convicts to perform community service by farming temple lands, and digging canals. The wish of Buddhists to help not only the poor but also society and the state is evident in their charitable undertakings. Such compassionate efforts include bathhouses, winter aid relief, and free medical services as well as care for the elderly. In addition, releasing animals and nurturing gardens were means of caring not just for humans but also all flora and fauna. These are all Buddhist contributions to both country and society.

Prior to the establishment of a police department in China, temples assisted greatly in mediating disputes. For example, the Reception Hall of Putuoshan monastery served as a police station to help resolve disputes. Had Mazu not believed in Guanyin Bodhisattva, how could she have relieved people from distress and suffering? Chan Master Puzu (普足, also known as the Patriarch of Pure Water) is revered in Taiwan due to his rain prayers that nourished many lives.

Across different eras and societies, Humanistic Buddhism offered help and relief to the distressed. In this, Buddhists became self-sufficient through the unity of agriculture and Chan. The world must be made aware of this history. Where there is Buddhism, there will always be compassionate people to comfort and relieve people from sorrow and suffering. It is hoped that politicians, scholars, and social workers will contribute to the history of Humanistic Buddhism by recognizing its compassion and service to society.

The contemporary development of Humanistic Buddhism must ultimately be attributed to the Buddha's efforts and teachings. For this reason, as practitioners, we must never forget our gratitude towards the humanistic Buddha. We hope that when China promotes its culture, it also remembers the contributions and influence made by Humanistic Buddhism in shaping it.

3) Arts in Humanistic Buddhism

The archetype of Buddhist art would be the Ajanta Caves in India. In China, it took the form of architecture, carvings, paintings and calligraphy. Many examples of Buddhist art existing today are considered masterpieces. For example, the UNESCO has listed the Dunhuang, Yungang, and Longmen Caves as Cultural Heritage sites. These caves are said to be the greatest natural museums of oriental Buddhist art.

In the past, Buddhist temples seldom promoted Buddhist art.

Humanistic Buddhism: Holding True to the Original Intents of Buddha

Yet, in their talks on daily living, life, and the universe, mentions of aesthetic beauty are noticeable. In the *Avatamsaka Sutra*, the buddhas and bodhisattvas from the universe's three thousand great chiliocosms have inspired magnificent pieces of thousand-buddha caves in China. In the *Buddhacarita*, stories of the Buddha's life were written in beautiful poetic style, which consequently inspired Buddhist hymns and chanting in China. In the *Vimalakirti Sutra*, the witty dialogues between the celestial lady, Vimalakirti, and Sariputra shaped classic dramas and dances such as "The Celestial Rain of Flowers." The depiction of the Pure Land in the *Amitabha Sutra* was the basis for its majestic illustrations in other sutras. In fact, is the beauty of this world not a manifestation of the Pure Land itself? The paintings in the Dunhuang caves combining Chinese, Indian, and ancient Western Region cultures have inspired the world-renowned Dunhuang dance. These are not merely means of propagation used by past Buddhist masters but also priceless modern assets of the Dharma.

Such masterpieces showcased Chinese culture and Buddhism to the world. These honorable Buddhist masters dedicated their lives to Buddhism, and enabled the dissemination of the essence of Chinese culture and Buddhism. How can we not be grateful and value the scope of Buddhist art?

Just as our beauty is found in our character and wisdom, the greatness of a country resides within its culture and art. What people admire today at the Great British Museum, the Louvre, and the Art Institute of Chicago are collections of Chinese art and culture that have gained prominence amongst the originally dominant Western cultures. As much as we may regret the loss of such Chinese treasures, it probably is for the best. In the course of China's countless periods of war and chaos, doubtless many of

Sakyamuni Buddha; CHINA, Shanxi, Datong;
Northern Wei dynasty (386–534); Stone; H: 13.7 m

these artifacts would have been either damaged or destroyed. In the
end, these countries aid us not only in preserving Chinese culture,
but also showcasing it to the world.

1. Rock Carvings and Paintings

From the beginning, Buddhism exerted tremendous influence
on Chinese art and culture. The statues, paintings, manuscripts
and texts found in the Dunhuang caves eclipse the discovery of
Qin Shi Huang's Terracotta Army. Some universities have even
listed Dunhuang Studies as the focus of their professional research
programs.

For over a thousand years, rulers, ministers, Buddhists,
devotees and common people have regarded the Dunhang caves as
the greatest treasure of the world. Even the splendor of the Ajanta
Caves in India pales in comparison. It is certainly a miracle for
these vivid statues, extraordinarily beautiful reliefs, and carvings

Ajanta Caves: Cave 2 - Main Hall; INDIA, Maharashtra, Aurangabad

of Buddhist sutras to have survived the flames of war and remain well-preserved in the remote Gansu Province. To date, several hundred professionals at the Dunhuang Museum have taken on the responsibility to preserve, repair and maintain these artistic and cultural treasures, which are certainly not exclusive to just the Chinese but also for the whole world.

Other than the Dunhuang Caves, the Yungang Grottoes in Datong, carved by Tanyao, from the Northern Wei Dynasty are also of unparalleled magnificence. The majestic statue of Sakyamuni Buddha is often featured in magazines and other publications. It has also been listed as one of the most valuable art pieces in the world.

In the Longmen Grottoes in Henan, the elegant postures of buddhas and bodhisattvas remind us of Tang Dynasty ladies whose beauty were embodied in their vigorous and lush figures. The most iconic would be Yang Guifei (楊貴妃 , 719-756) and Empress Wu Zetian. Sculptures from the period portrayed buddhas and bodhisattvas with human statures, which is certainly the spirit of Humanistic Buddhism.

The fine carvings and elegant postures displayed by the buddha and bodhisattva statues at the Maijishan Grottoes are simply stunning. The serene and solemn Baoding Buddha Carvings of the Nirvana of Sakyamuni Buddha are also priceless treasures of Buddhist art. Other cave temples found along the Silk Road are also rich treasuries of carvings and paintings.

2. Calligraphy and Painting

The Buddhist influence on Chinese calligraphy is profound. For example, Wang Xizhi's (王羲之 , 303–361) *Preface to the Orchid Pavilion Collection* and even Huaisu's (懷素 , 737–799) *Diamond Sutra in Cursive Script* are both regarded as rare treasures. In the past, some Buddhist masters did not subsist on farming or chanting. Instead, they were recognized for their paintings and calligraphy, which allowed them to make a living while continuing their spiritual cultivation.

Seventy years ago, when I studied at Jiaoshan Buddhist College, aside from the Main Shrine, known as Dinghui Temple, there were also dozens of smaller temples each containing a studio and gallery, allowing collectors to purchase their favorite art pieces.

For this reason, Wu Daozi's (吳道子 , 685–758) portrait of Guanyin became a famous art piece. Other monastic artists such as Bada Shanren (八大山人 , 1626-1705), Shi Tao (石濤 , 1642-1707), Shi Xi (石谿 , 1612-1692), and Hongren (弘仁 , 1610-1664) also exhibited in their works the beauty of painting and elegant writing. These pieces elevated Buddhist calligraphy and art to higher level than even palace artists were capable of. In masterpieces such as *Along the River During the Qingming Festival* and *Dwelling in the Fuchun Mountains,* Buddhist temples and monastics often feature in the paintings. Evidently, these artists have a close affiliation with Buddhism.

Although some of these works gradually disappeared over time, some valuable pieces are now part of museum collections around the world. Renowned contemporary artist Zhang Daqian (張大千 , 1899-1983) spent almost three years at Dunhuang, copying the various painting styles. Others such as Pu Xinyu (傅心畬 , 1896-1963) created Buddhism-related pieces, all now priceless.

Speaking of Zhang Daqian, he once gifted me his work *Lotus,* which was auctioned at the Fo Guang University Fundraiser and acquired by the Hsu Family from The Far Eastern Group. Another of Zhang Daqian's piece, *Guanyin Bodhisattva,* is still at Fo Guang Shan among dozens of other artifacts. A man offered to buy it for fifty million Taiwan dollars, but we were unwilling to part with it.

3. Buddhist Chanting and Singing

Other than tangible creations of Buddhist art, intangible forms are also prized. For example, Buddhist chanting in Yushan and Tang Dynasty singing sermons are both unique features of Chinese culture.

According to a legend from the Three Kingdoms period, Cao Zijian (曹子建 , 192–232) perceived the sounds of waves and compared them to the sounds of heavenly beings. As a music en-

南无觀世音菩薩一軀

甲申六月寫燕京先居布
翔兵室記即贈五十九歲葉日
張大千記画

Avalokitesvara Bodhisattva;
CHINA; dated 1944;
By Chang Dai-Chien;
Ink and color on paper;
111 x 49.5 cm;
Fo Guang Shan Monastery,
Kaohsiung, Taiwan

167

thusiast, he composed these heavenly melodies, which later became a Buddhist chant known as "heavenly song" (梵唄).

Buddhist chanting contains the Four Main Prayers, and Eight Incense Praises that include the six-line verse short prayer— Incense Praise (爐香讚), and eight-line chant—Three Jewels Praise (三寶讚). The various tunes and intonations are profoundly emotive and beautiful. Regretfully, many such compositions were destroyed in the Taiping Rebellion, Sino-Japanese War, Civil War, and Cultural Revolutions. Fortunately, on the verge of being forever lost, some musicians brought them to Taiwan. I then cut recordings and produced cassette tapes to preserve the music. Today, they have been re-transmitted back to mainland China and can be heard all across the nation.

However, as these chants were only transmitted verbally, no music sheets exist. As the handbell and wooden fish were the only instruments available, only single chimes and double strikes were used to remember the following tempo, "three turns and nine twists, the one strong and three weak beats." Those who have heard these traditional Buddhist chanting would praise them as "sounds only heard from heaven and extremely rare on Earth."

Several years ago, Fo Guang Shan assembled the Chinese Buddhist Music Performance Group. It performed music from the Four Major Buddhist Schools, including Theravada, Chinese, and Tibetan traditions. Their world tour gained wide acclaim.

In the Dunhuang Caves, singing sermons are preserved in the form of sutra illustrations such as the Eight Stages of Buddha's Life, The Celestial Rain of Flowers, and Maudgalyayana Saves His Mother. As times changed, songs replaced these sermons. Fo Guang Shan has continued to hold Dharma Lectures mingled with Buddhist chanting at Dr. Sun Yat-sen Memorial Hall in Taipei for thirty consecutive years; likewise at the Hong Kong Coliseum for over twenty years. The propagation of Humanistic Buddhism through song has pervaded all levels of society and should certainly continue.

4. Sculpture and Architecture

Masterpieces of Buddhist architecture and sculpture are plentiful. However, it is regretful to see that most ancient Buddhist monasteries in Mainland China are listed only as tourist attractions. Moreover, by charging admission fees, these temples have become commercial ventures. If only these beautiful palace-style shrines, viharas, pagodas and pavilions were returned to their original purpose, the tranquil and serene ambience of Buddhist temples will perhaps be restored. Buddhist architecture in its myriad forms, such

Yulin Cave 25: Illustration of the Amitayurdhyana Sutra:
Western Pure Land - Music and Dance
CHINA, Gansu, Guazhou; Tang dynasty (610-907)

169

as gardens and landscapes has undoubtedly enriched the splendor of China's natural vistas.

Within the Buddha Museum, itself a representation of Fo Guang Shan's Buddha Gem, is a one-hundred-and-eight-meter seated Bronze Buddha. Flanked by eight Chinese-style pagodas, the Main Hall houses a dozen art exhibition spaces. Surrounded by a green garden landscape, the Museum has become a major tourist attraction visited by ten million guests annually.

Representing the Sangha Gem, Fo Guang Shan Monastery is an equally majestic complex that houses a Main Shrine, the Buddhist College, Pagodas, and garden landscapes. Embodying the Dharma Gem, the Sutra Repository is now nearing completion. Its grandeur has already left visitors in awe. These two complexes represent major contributions made by monastics and key members of Fo Guang Shan to Humanistic Buddhism.

5. Drama and Dance

With regard to Chinese opera, the most famous is the Kunqu Opera from Kunshan, in Suzhou. Other genres of opera such as the Peking Opera, and Yu Opera branched out from Kunqu and developed across China. Kunqu originated from the drama *The Mirror of Origin* (歸元鏡), written by Venerable Zhida (智達) in the Ming Dynasty, thus sharing a close connection with Buddhism.

Many of these dramas reflect the ideals of loyalty and dutifulness in tangible form. They are regarded as the best inspirations for moral ethics next to formal school education. This is one of the expedient means used in Humanistic Buddhism

Shuanglin Temple Sakyamuni Hall:
Avalokitesvara on a Lotus Petal
CHINA, Shanxi, Jinzhong; Ming dynasty
(1368–1644); Clay; H: 134 cm

to spread the Buddha's teachings. For example, *The Biography of Sakyamuni Buddha* has been adapted into musicals, movies, novels, radio shows, and stage plays all across the world. Other stories of loyalty, filial piety, moral integrity, and justice have also been portrayed in Buddhist audiovisual mediums to continue inspiring and purifying the people.

At Fo Guang Shan, Buddhist choirs spread the Dharma todifferent places around the world. The recently established Buddha's Light Youth Philharmonic Orchestra in Vienna has been composing and performing Buddhist songs. Of note, artists of the Guang Ming College Academy of Performing Arts in the Philippines created *Siddhartha: The Musical.* In Malaysia, eight thousand youths gathered to sing beautiful Buddhist songs, such as "I am the Future of Buddhism."

In addition, Dunhuang Dance Troupes in Taiwan alone number twenty-six, all performing on a regular basis. The tremendous influence of Dunhuang dance is thus evident. Furthermore, Disabled People's Performing Art Troupe of China has recently been performing *Thousand-Hand Guanyin,* to great acclaim.

6. Martial Arts and Chivalry

Shaolin temple has always been synonymous with martial arts. Legend tells that Bodhidharma, the patriarch of Chan Buddhism, invented the Shaolin Technique of Combat, thereby gifting martial arts a place and influence in China. The art lies not just within the expression of strength but in spirit and poise. The "One Finger Chan" and "Prajna Palm" are among the many kungfu skills that embody profound spiritual cultivation and chivalry. In the past, Shaolin monastics won the hearts of many for being chivalrous.

They upheld justice and protected their country. It is hoped that our inheritance of such spirit, as shown by our ancestors, can help us protect the people.

In brief, Humanistic Buddhism made tremendous contributions to the state, society and the individual. By enriching the spread of Chinese culture, it has made it globally respected. The abovementioned artistic achievements by Humanistic Buddhists are only a small part of a much bigger whole. They have been explored in the hopes of stimulating Chinese culture, itself enriched by Buddhist art.

4) Humanistic Buddhism and Literati

Since ancient times, poets and scholars in China held prestigious social standings due to the influence of their writings and opinions. With a single brush stroke, they had the power to bring down entire armies. This influence has prevailed even beyond their time.

The works of poets and scholars throughout the eras are key reasons to Buddhism's success. Through them, it was able to harmonize Confucian thoughts and become integral to Chinese culture. Buddhism's profound philosophy and its close connection with reality not only satisfied their pursuit of the Truth and life's numerous questions. It also inspired these writers and intellectuals into broadening their minds, leading to great creativity. One might say that under the influence of profound Buddhist teachings, these poets and scholars were thus able to create timeless classics.

Popular Chinese literature such as Gan Bao's (干寶 , 286-336) *In Search of Spirits,* Wu Chengen's (吳承恩 , 1501-1582) *Journey to*

the West, Cao Xueqin's (曹雪芹 , 1715-1763) *Dream of the Red Chamber*, and Liu E's (劉鶚 , 1857-1909) *The Travels of Old Decrepit* all exhibit Buddhist reflections. Not only have these literary masterpieces introduced Chinese literature to the world, they also aided the spread of Humanistic Buddhism. As Buddhism enriched the minds of literary writers, they in turn contributed to the dissemination of the Dharma.

Among the Eight Great Prose Masters of the Tang and Song dynasty, Han Yu (韓愈 , 768-824) and Ouyang Xiu (歐 陽 修 , 1007-1072) severely criticized Buddhism. However, their mindset drastically changed after making the acquaintance of Chan Master Dadian (大 顛 , 732-824) and Chan Master Mingjiao (明教 , 1007-1072). Realizing the ignorance of their past behavior, they repented sincerely and sought refuge in the Dharma. Others nurtured a close affiliation with Humanistic Buddhism, namely Tao Yuanming (陶 淵 明 , 365–427), Xie Lingyun (謝 靈 運 , 385-433), Wang

Departure at Huxi;
CHINA; Dated 1945; By Fu Baoshi;
Ink and color on paper; 136.5 x 36.4 cm;
Nanjing Museum, Jiangsu, China

Wei (王維 , 692-761), Liu Zongyuan (柳宗元 , 773-819), Bai Juyi (白 居 易 , 772-846), Wang Anshi, Su Shi, and Huang Tingjian. Markedly, Wang Wei, Bai Juyi, Su Shi, and Huang Tingjian even took refuge. The intimate relationship between Buddhism and literary writers remains till today. Some of these stories are mentioned as follows.

1. National Constitutions Based on Buddhist Thought

Xiao Tong (蕭 統 , 501-531), also known as Crown Prince Zhaoming (昭明太子), was the eldest son of Emperor Wu of Liang. Compassionate, kind, and extremely intelligent, he grew up under the influence of his father's devotion to Buddhism. Not only did he strictly observe the Bodhisattva Precepts, he was also well learned in Buddhist texts and teachings. Some of his works include: *Understanding the Two Truths* and *Thirty-Two Rules of the Diamond Sutra.*

Soon after Prince Zhaoming's death at the young age of thirty-one, without ever assuming the throne, Liu Xie (劉 勰 , 465-521), an acquaintance to the Prince took refuge in Master Sengyou (僧 祐 , 445-518). He assisted the Master in compiling the fifteen-fascicle *A Collection of Records on the Emanation of the Chinese Tripitaka*, which became the renowned *Catalogue of the Chinese Translation of the Buddhist Tripitaka.* In addition, he also wrote the ten-fascicle *Literary Mind and Carved Dragon* listed as one of the two most prestigious critiques of Chinese literature alongside Zhong Rong's (鍾嶸 , 467?-519) *A Critique of Poetry.*

Eastern Jin Dynasty poet Tao Yuanming, unwilling to "relinquish his dignity for five bushels of grain" (the official salary of low-rank officials), retreated to a country life. His poetic composition was natural, beautiful, and alive with Buddhist sentiments.

For example,

> *Glistening white moon in the clouds*
> *Resplendent flowers among the leaves*
> *Are such but transient beauties*
> *What shall become of them soon?*

Treating impermanence with such emotionality, the influence of Buddhism on him is clear. On one of his frequent visits to Master Huiyuan (慧遠 , 334-416) at Donglin Temple on Mount Lu, he crossed paths with Daoist priest Lu Xiujing (陸修靜 , 406-477). Upon seeing off his guests, Huiyuan almost broke his self imposed confinement by crossing the Tiger Creek, giving rise to the legend of the "Three Laughing Men at Tiger Creek."

Another close acquaintance of Huiyuan's was Xie Lingyun, a pious Buddhist and author of "Inscriptions of Buddha's Shadow." Inspired by Master Daosheng's (道生 , 355-434) "Theory on Gradual and Immediate Enlightenment," Xie composed *Discerning the Truth* to expound on the meanings of 'gradual' and 'sudden.' Moreover, having learnt of Venerable Huirui's (慧叡 , 355-439) knowledge in Sanksrit, Xie visited him at Wuyi Temple. There he acquired a profound understanding of the sound enabling a language to cut across boundaries.

Those were the days when the *Mahaparinirvana Sutra* had just reached China. The short and concise text, in addition to strange and difficult writing, made it difficult for beginners to understand. He therefore revised the text with Huiyan (慧嚴 , 363-443) as well as Huiguan (慧觀 , 366-436), and introduced the 36-fasicle "Southern Edition" of the *Mahaparinirvana Sutra*. This enabled wide dissemination of the Nirvana teachings as well as the theories of gradual and immediate enlightenment. As a poet, Xie Lingyun contributed tremendously to the spread of Buddhism.

2. Persecutors Inspired by Chan Masters to Repent

Han Yu was foremost among the Eight Great Prose Masters of the Tang and Song dynasties. His prose held the distinction of reversing the literary decline of eight dynasties. He advocated that "Writings should serve the purpose of carrying the Way," and critiqued Buddhism as well as Daoism. Later, when he wrote his famous *Memorial on Bone-relics of the Buddha*, he was demoted to provincial governor in Chaozhou. There, he visited Chan Master Dadian who, in deep meditative concentration, did not respond. An attendant, standing nearby, whispered into the Master's ear, "First you move [him] with meditative concentration, then you shall shake [his arrogance] with wisdom." Hearing this, Han Yu replied with admiration, "I have now received the message from your attendant." From then on, Han Yun continued to practice meditation and visit teachers. He also repented his past wrongdoings and became a pious supporter of Buddhism.

Ouyang Xiu, another opponent of Buddhism, received acclaim for his work *On Principles*. Chan Master Mingjiao Qisong (明教契嵩 , 1007–1072) wrote *Auxiliary Teachings* to refute Ouyang's work by advocating the integration of Buddhist, Daoist, and Confucian thoughts. His work transformed Ouyang's perspective, who exclaimed, "How could he be such an outstanding monastic!" He made a formal visit to the Chan Master to make further his enquiries. Afterwards, under the influence of Chan Master Zuying (祖印 , 1010-1071), he finally realized the profoundness of the Dharma and turned to Buddhism in sincere repentance for his previous behavior. Thereafter, his works frequently contained praise for the practice

傳来一鉢歲多
維思報勤勞句
槖饗千夜雄坊
妙軋響祖百腰
石重如山
福山
〔印〕

Sixth Patriarch
JAPAN; Kamakura period (1185–1333); Ink on paper;
83.7 x 34.7 cm; Masaki Art Museum, Osaka, Japan

of virtuous deeds. He also made acquaintances with many Buddhist masters.

Liu Zongyuan, founder of the Classical Prose Movement, grew up devoted to Buddhism and assisted in the spread of its concepts. His work *God of the Eastern Sea* is a commentary on Pure Land practices. In addition, a large number of plaque inscriptions such as that of Huineng the Sixth Patriarch have been attributed to him.

Known as the Three Literati of the Su Family—Su Xun (蘇洵 , 1009-1066) along with his two sons Su Shi (蘇軾 , 1036-1101) and Su Che (蘇轍 , 1039-1112) are counted among the Eight Great Prose Masters of the Tang and Song Dynasties. All family members were followers of Buddhism, despite Su Xun having a scholarly lineage in Confucianism. In fact, he was a close acquaintance of Chan Master Yuantong Juna (圓通居訥 , 1010-1071) and Baoyue Weijian (寶月惟簡 , 1011-1095). Though extremely talented, Su Shi nevertheless struggled through his career as an official and was exiled several times. For this reason, his poems are full of Buddhist realizations. His most famous story was that of Chan Master Foyin (佛印 , 1032-1098) who ridiculed him for being "the allegedly unmovable one who was blown across the river by a fart."

During his visit to Chan Master Changzong (常總 , 1025-1091) at Donglin Temple on Mount Lu, and gaining some realization conversing with the master, he wrote the following poem which later became the popular Chan verse,

> *The sounds of the creeks are voices spoken*
> *by your broad and long tongue,*
> *The mountains are none but manifestations of your pure body;*
> *Of the eighty-four thousand verses that we hear in the night,*
> *How are we to teach them to others in later days.*

Niaoke and Bai Juyi
TAIWAN, Kaohsiung, Fo Guang Shan

Furthermore, the *Summoning Words in the Yogacara Offering Service* was also composed by Su Shi, in which his compassion for living beings in the Six Realms and spirit of equality are characteristics of humanistic bodhisattvas.

3. Literary and Poetic Creations to Express States of Buddhist Attainment

Also listed among the Eight Great Prose Masters of the Tang and Song Dynasties was Wang Anshi, praised by Ouyang Xiu in his poem,

> *Above all verses from the imperial academy*
> *Excelling the Personnel Department's all time works*
> *Tis' time for this old man to retire now*
> *Because no one will ever surpass his [man].*

He took refuge in the Three Jewels at a young age, and was close to Chan Master Jiangsan Juehai (蔣山覺海 , 1069-1162). As a noble Prime Minister, he often spoke of the Dharma to intellectuals. Under the tremendous influence of Buddhism, he believed "there are no unchallengeable authorities or unchangeable rules; what is most important is to possess the right perspective of reality."

All Eight Great Prose Masters of the Tang and Song dynasties were demoted at one time or another and experienced great bitterness. When renowned Tang Dynasty poet Bai Juyi visited Chan Master Niaoke Daolin, (鳥窠道林 , 741-824) who lived in a tree, he shouted, "Chan Master, it is too dangerous to live in a tree!"

"Honorable Chief, you are the one who is in danger." Replied the Chan Master.

"I am a standing minister, what danger can there be?" asked Bai Juyi, disgruntled. "When sparks intertwine, ignitions are endless. How can you say that there is no danger?"

Having somewhat understood his intentions, Bai Juyi continued, "What is the essence of the Dharma?"

"To cease all evil, practice all good, and purify your own mind. Such is the teaching of all buddhas." recited the Chan Master.

Very disappointed, Bai Juyi replied, "This is too easy even for a three-year-old child."

"Sure. What is understandable to a three-year-old toddler is but impossible to an eighty-year-old man."

Fully inspired, Bai Juyi thus took refuge under Chan Master Daolin. He vowed to dedicate his literary talent to praising the Buddha's practice and to spread the Dharma. In his later years, he was fully committed to chanting Buddha's name, and composed a verse on "Chanting the Buddha":

> *At the age of seventy plus one,*
> *Poetry is what I no longer read or write.*
> *Reading too strenuous for the eye,*
> *While doing good deeds too much of a physical act.*
>
> *How can the mind then pass time?*
> *Amitabha is what I simply chant.*
> *I chant Amitabha while walking,*
> *I chant Amitabha while sitting;*
> *Even when buried in matters,*
> *Never forget Amitabha for a chant.*
> *Let those intellects ridicule me,*
> *And most of you skeptics of Amitabha.*

So what if you are an intellect?
So what if I ain't?

I urge all living beings in the Dharma realm,
To come together and chant Amitabha;
If one seeks liberation from the cycle of rebirth,
To chant Amitabha would be an essential act.

4. Family Legacy: Unshakeable Faith

Northern Song Dynasty poets such as Lu Mengzheng and Fan Zhongyan both lived in Buddhist temples at some point in their lives. Being the first scholar to top the imperial examination of the Song Dynasty, Lu assumed the post of Prime Minister to Emperors Song Taizong (宋太宗 , 939-997) and Song Zhenzong (宋真宗 , 968-1022) on three occasions, and was known as the "Eminent Minister" of his time. He resided in a Buddhist temple before his rise to success. Twenty years later, in gratitude, he returned to the temple. Each morning he payed respect to Buddha, praying that, "Let only pious believers of the Three Jewels be born into my family. May generations and generations of my lineage always be prosperous and supporters of the Dharma." This sense of gratitude and unflinching belief in the Three Jewels is one of the most valuable family legacy seen in Humanistic Buddhism.

Having sworn to "either be an eminent minister or a great doctor" and to "regard as one's top concern the state's affairs, and place as one's last goal one's own enjoyments," Fan Zhongyan spent his days studying in a Buddhist temple. After rising to fame, he made acquaintances with Buddhist masters such as Chenggu (薦福承古 , ?-1045), Yuanyu (圓悟 , 1063-1135). Subsequently, he became well-attained as a pupil of Chan Master Huijue (瑯瑘慧覺) from

Langya Province. In his lifetime devotion to the Three Jewels, he built temples to establish monastic communities everywhere he went, and even turned his own residence into Tianping Temple, as well as freely provided farmland to help his people.

Known as the "Poetic Buddha," Wang Wei was a pious Buddhist who observed vegetarianism. He was so devoted that he even bore the courtesy name Mojie, inspired by the name Weimojie (Vimalakirti). Having taken refuge and learnt meditation under Heze Shenhui (荷澤神會 , 688-758), he also sought instruction from Chan Masters Daoguang (道光 , 682-760), Puji (普寂 , 651-739) and Yifu (義福 , 658-736). The beauty and delicate style of his poetry also held a strong sense of Chan. For example, in his "Deer Enclosure,"

> *A secluded mountain with no one in sight*
> *Yet talking voices echo across the space*
> *Sunlight reaches into the deepest of woods*
> *As reflections on the ground's green moss*

His depiction of the subtle spread of sunlight and an empty mountain at nightfall is a reflection of the Buddhist mindset of quietude and impermanence.

Moreover, Wang Wei had a mother who was also a pious Buddhist. After her death, to commemorate her, Wang turned his house into a temple. He then spent the rest of his life as a monastic, diligently chanting and reading the sutras everyday. Upon the final moment of his life, he even foretold his death and sent out notices to his friends.

5. Writings are to Carry the Way and Deliver Humanity

Song Dynasty calligraphy master Huang Tingjian (黃庭堅, 1045–1105) also shared a special affinity with Buddhism. A prominent poet, his verses were widely circulated. One day, Huang visited Chan Master Yuantong Faxiu (圓通法秀, 1027–1090), who

Master Xuanzang
JAPAN; Kamakura period (1185–1333);
Ink and color on silk; 135.1 x 59.9 cm,
Tokyo National Museum, Japan

severely criticized him, "Are you no better than these convolutedly trivial writings of yours?"

There was an artist named Li Boshi (李伯時, 1049-1134) who specialized in painting horses. He always portrayed and imitated the movements of a horse. The Chan Master warned him that if he continued, the chances of him being reborn as a horse would be high. After, Li Boshi threw away his paintbrushes and never painted horses again. Hearing this, Huang ridiculed the Chan Master and said, "Are you going to warn me against being reborn as a horse too?"

"Your speeches of flattery have enticed the minds of many, I am afraid rebirth as a horse is too minor a consequence. You are more likely to fall into hell." Replied Faxiu. Taken Huang immediately repented himself.

Subsequently, having also

been inspired and taught by brilliant minds such as Chan Master Lingyuan Weiqing (靈源惟清 , d.1117), Huang became thoroughly reinvented and expanded his knowledge of Buddhism.

> *My flesh is the flesh of sentient beings;*
> *Though different in name, the essence remains the same.*
> *We all share in having the same nature;*
> *We merely vary in bodily form.*
> *If I leave others to suffer in pain;*
> *For the sweet and tender are what I want.*
> *There's no need to await Yama's judgment;*
> *I myself should already know the cost of such deeds.*

In this, his most renowned poem, one can clearly sense the Buddhist spirit of respecting all forms of life.

In the later years of his life, he built an abode in Peibin and focused on Pure Land practices. His poems were popular among monastics from the Five Mountains of the Muromachi Period, and had tremendous influence on the study of Chinese literature in Japan. When it is said that literature transcends borders, it is undoubtedly true.

Literature provides us with insights into the way human emotions and thoughts are expressed. A great work of literature is not merely beautiful, moving words or an interesting plot. It also needs to embody ideals and principles, such as morality, truthfulness, virtue, and beauty, that will inspire as well as cultivate human beings. The saying, "Writings should serve the purpose of carrying the Way," means that words carry the mission of teaching and transforming human minds.

That Dharma can be timeless, omnipresent, and inspire human

minds is because the literary works of great thinkers have been invaluable instruments in spreading the Dharma.

5) Humanistic Buddhism and Politics

After Buddhism spread to China, royal patronage enabled it to take root. Starting from Emperor Ming of Eastern Han (東漢明帝 , 28-75) to Sun Quan (孫權 , 182-252), Lord of Wu, Emperor Wu of Liang from the Southern Dynasty (南朝梁武帝 , 464-549), Emperor Xiaowen of Northern Wei (北魏孝文帝 , 467–499), Emperor Wen of Sui (隋文帝 , 541–604), Emperor Taizong of Tang (唐太宗 , 598–649), Empress Wu Zetian (武則天 , 624-705), Emperor Taizu of Song (宋太祖 , 927-976), even Emperors Kangxi (康熙 , 1654-1722), Yongzheng (雍正 , 1678-1735), and Qianlong (乾隆 , 1711-1799) of Qing, all greatly assisted dissemination of Buddhism in China. Particularly, Buddhism saw its golden eras in the Sui and Tang Dynasties.

Other royal patrons were Emperor Wu of Liang, Emperor Xuanzong of Tang (唐宣宗 , 810-859), and Emperor Shunzi (順治 , 1638-1661) of Qing who even abdicated their throne to become monastics. During the Nanzhao Period, King Longshun proclaimed Buddhism as the national faith. In the Dali Period, ten out of twenty-two emperors renounced. Buddhism was revered by the whole nation, from emperors to the common people. Empress Cixi (慈禧 , 1835-1908) preferred to be called the "Great Lord Buddha." A large number of emperors and kings ruled their kingdoms with Buddhist principles.

Buddhist monks, on the other hand, showed their patriotism differently. As imperial masters or counselors, they advised their

Emperor Wu of Liang; Hanging scroll;
Ink and color on silk; 76.8 x 56.4 cm;
National Palace Museum, Taipei, Taiwan

rulers in how to protect their country and care for people. Take Venerable Huilin (慧琳 , 385-485) for instance, known as the "black-robed prime minister" of the Southern Dynasty. He was summoned to the palace by Emperor Wendi to serve as counselor in decision making. Senior Monastic Officer Venerable Faguo (法果) from the Northern Wei Dynasty retained the trust of Emperors Taizu (太祖 , 371-409) and Taizong (太宗) of Wei. Chan Master Baozhi (寶誌 , 418-515) likewise counseled Emperor Liang of

Wu while Venerable Huizhong (慧 忠 , 675-775) from the Tang Dynasty was mentor to the Emperor. Countless monastics served as imperial masters, advising their rulers on how to develop their country. This would have been impossible if these masters were unwilling to engage in this-worldly matters whilst maintaining the other-worldly spirit.

"The task of Dharma propagation becomes difficult without royal patronage." Master Daoan (道安) believed that while politics needs the guidance of the Dharma, Buddhism is also in need of political protection. Righteous practitioners of Buddhism have never rejected politics, because only through a prosperous nation and righteous rulers can Buddhism continue to thrive. Throughout history, Buddhism's prosperity never occurred without a prosperous nation. Examples of the close relationship between Buddhism and politics are as follows:

1. Buddhist Masters as Imperial Counselors and Great Translators

The first emperor to exert tremendous influence on Chinese Buddhism was Emperor Ming of Eastern Han, who not only dispatched messengers to bring Buddhism into China but also decreed the construction of Buddhist temples. He demonstrated utmost respect for Buddhism.

During the Sixteen Kingdoms of the Five Barbarians period, Buddhism thrived in Northern China, under royal patronage inspired by masters such as Fotucheng, Daoan, and Kumarajiva. Using his supernatural powers, Fotucheng, revered as teacher to the king, transformed the barbaric natures of Shi Hu and Shi Le, and saved countless lives. Shi Le even sent the palace children to temples so they could learn Buddhism. He also visited the Buddhist temple on Buddha's Birthday, each April 8th of the lunar month, to bathe the buddha statue and pray. Under their reign, the whole nation followed the Buddhist faith.

Having convinced Fu Jian to cease battle, Daoan was escorted back to Changan to begin translating and writing commentaries on Buddhist texts. Another purpose was to establish the regulations and rules of monastic communities. The spread of Buddhism in Korea and Japan began when Fu Jian gave these nations gifts of sutras and Buddha statues.

Yao Xing (姚興 ; 366–416) the Emperor of Qin revered Kumarajiva as his teacher. The Emperor established China's earliest imperial translation court and pushed the spread of Buddhist doctrine to its zenith through the fluent and elegant translations of Kumarajiva. Yao Xing also decreed Kumarajiva's disciples to assume the posts of senior monastic officer (僧正) and secretary (僧錄) which marked the inception of monastic ministers in Chinese Buddhism.

The reason for the monastic ministry system came from senior monastics needing to assume official positions (with pay). They were entrusted to supervise and penalize any monastic displaying inappropriate conduct. Thus, they assisted in propagating Humanistic Buddhism. This position was known as senior monastic officer, meaning the duty of correcting self before correcting others. This system was inherited by the Southern and Northern Dynasties with different titles such as monastic officer, monastic secretary, senior monastic officer, left-wing monastic secretary, or right-wing monastic secretary. Each of these posts held authority and status.

During this period, Emperor Wu of Southern Liang (also known as the Bodhisattva Emperor) was China's first ruler to govern by the principles of King Chakravarti. His work "On

Refraining from Drinking Alcohol and Eating Meat" was the cause for Chinese monastics to practice vegetarianism. When he took and observed the Bodhisattva Precepts, forty-eight thousand people joined him. He was also the first Chinese emperor to renounce. Being well-versed in Buddhist doctrine, he often taught the Dharma to monastic and lay Buddhists, in addition to writing well over a hundred fascicles of commentaries on the *Nirvana Sutra* and *Vimalakirti Sutra*. The well-known Buddhist liturgies *Emperor Liang's Treasured Repentance Ceremony* and the *Water and Land Dharma Service Liturgy* are both his accomplishments.

2. Revitalization of Buddhism through the Creation of the Yungang Grottoes

Following the two persecutions that occurred during the Northern Dynasty, triggering catastrophic effects on Buddhism, rulers such as Emperors Wencheng (文成帝 , 440-452), Xianwen (獻文帝 , 454-476), Xiaowen (孝文帝 , 467-499), and Xuanwu (宣武帝 , 483-499) of Northern Wei Dynasty began the revitalization of Buddhism. Emperor Wencheng decreed for Tanyao to act as Senior Monastic Officer (沙門統) as well as to supervise the carving of the Yungang Grottoes. The first Buddhist cave temple in China, Yungang was listed as a World Cultural Heritage Site in 2001. Moreover, in the five years of Emperor Xianwen's short reign, he constructed temples and pagodas, creating a Buddhist city.

Emperor Xiaowen later relocated the capital to Luoyang. He decreed the large-scale excavation of the Longmen Grottoes, bringing Buddhist rock carving to its zenith. Added with the Maijishan and Dazu caves, Buddhism is said to make up a large part of Chinese culture. I still remember what Indian Prime Minister Nehru said to me during our meeting fifty years ago, "Both Indian

Longmen Grotto 140: Buddha Pentad (back wall)
CHINA, Henan, Luoyang

and Chinese cultures are listed as one of the world's greatest heritages, but without Buddhism, I believe India would fall off the list immediately." The significance of a rich culture to a nation must not be underestimated.

Chinese Buddhism reached its peak during the Sui and Tang Dynasties, where Emperor Wen of Sui was known as the Buddhist emperor who governed his nation by Buddhist principles. During his reign, he constructed temples and over eighty-three pagodas.

He also transcribed Buddhist sutras as a way of cultivation. His son, Emperor Yang was also a pious supporter of Buddhism who revered Master Zhiyi and observed the Bodhisattva Precepts.

3. The Thriving of the Eight Schools under Empress Wu Zetian's Imperial Patronage

Among emperors who supported Buddhism, Emperor Taizong of Tang was particularly pious. Among his contributions to Buddhism was the construction of the imperial translation court for Master Xuanzang (玄奘 , 602-664), who later translated Buddhist texts such as the *Yogacarabhumi Sastra, Mahaprajnaparamita Sutra*, and the *Heart Sutra*, all of which continue to exert tremendous influence on Chinese Buddhism. The emperor also sought the company and advice of Master Xuanzang in governing his kingdom.

Emperor Taizong was a magnanamous man with a big heart. His royal patronage nurtured outstanding monastics who propagated all schools of Buddhism, thereby bringing Chinese Buddhism into its golden age. The emperor himself was also well versed in Buddhist texts and actively practiced the Bodhisattva path. His foreword for the *Yogacarabhumi Sastra* was inscribed on the stele of "Foreword of the Holy Tripitaka Teaching of the Great Tang Dynasty."

Also a devout supporter of Xuanzang's translation works, Emperor Gaozong took the Bodhisattva Precepts under Venerable Xuanwan (玄 琬 , 562-636) and constructed Dacien Temple. He sought the company of Xuanzang on his imperial inspection tours and relied heavily on Buddhist teachings to rule his kingdom. When Xuanzang passed away, Gaozong was so grief-stricken that he was not seen at court for three days, having announced that "I have lost one of the nation's greatest treasures."

Master Xuanzang was the first "overseas student" in the history of Chinese Buddhism. He honored his country everywhere he went. Records of his travels to foreign nations are written in his *Great Journey to the West*, alongside *Records of the Buddha Kingdom* by Faxian (法顯 , 337-422) of Eastern Jin, as well as *A Record of Buddhist Practices Sent Home from the Southern Sea* and *Buddhist Pilgrim Monks* of Tang Dynasty by Yijing (義淨 , 635-713) of Tang. These are considered as the most valuable historical records of Central and Southern Asian, as well as Eastern and Western transportation and cultural relations.

The first Chinese Empress Wu Zetian inherited Taizong and Gaozong's (高宗 , 628-683) royal Buddhist patronage and elevated the status of bhiksus and bhiksunis. The opening verse found in almost all Buddhist texts continue to spread far and wide today. She founded the first imperial pharmacy managed by monastics, donated her own money to the carving of the Vairocana Buddha statue in the Longmen Grottoes, and enabled all Eight Schools of Chinese

Biography of Master Xuanzang - Scroll 10 (detail); JAPAN; Kamakura period (1185–1333); By Takashina Takakane; Ink and color on paper; Fujita Art Museum, Osaka, Japan

Buddhism to thrive during the Tang Dynasty.

Before assuming the throne, Xuanzong was once a monastic. After taking reign, he restored Buddhist temples that were destroyed during the Huichang persecution, and built precept altars across the nation to enable bhiksus and bhiksunis who had been forced to disrobe to renew their precepts and vows. He also bestowed the purple-golden robe to Master Wuda (悟達 , 811-883) and gave him the title "Master of the Three Teachings." The emperor dedicated himself to the restoration of Buddhism with tremendous success.

4. The Spread and Inspirations of the Dharma

Through generations of royal patronage, Chinese Buddhism was able to take root, bloom, and mature in the Middle Kingdom. Subsequently, it spread to countries such as Korea, Japan, and Vietnam. The Northern Mahayana tradition and a shared East Asian culture were thus formed.

- Buddhism believes in reason, not superstition.
- Buddhism believes in the greater good, not the lesser good.
- Buddhism believes in involvement with society, not seclusion from it.
- Buddhism believes in infinity, not limits.
- Buddhism believes in equality, not discrimination.
- Buddhism believes in self-reliance, not dependence.

Not only can Buddhism harmonize political powers, it can also serve to develop the norms of society through belief in righteous faith and wisdom.

In summary, Buddhism does not reject politics. The Buddha himself was born a prince of the royal family, who continued to teach in India after attaining enlightenment. Conscious of his political background, he also counseled rulers on how to govern their countries. Throughout Chinese history, the relationship between politicians and Buddhism, as well as officials and monastics, has been mostly harmonious. Consequently, one of the purposes of Buddhism is to be a faith for benevolent rulers as well as human beings.

6) Humanistic Buddhism and Language

After Buddhism's spread to the East, it gradually became acculturated to its new home. A unique result of this acculturation is the Chinese language.

Language is vital for communication. Through words and speech, human beings express and communicate their thoughts and views. Although the Chan School has advocated against the use of words, language is ultimately the core path through which people will come to understand the Dharma. Language should only be discarded when one reaches the ultimate level of attainment.

One sentence suffices to determine the fate of a nation. Likewise it is also sufficient to bring joy or hatred to a person. Therefore, how can one deny the importance of language? It is obvious that the spread of Buddhism depends on the use of language. As stated in the *Diamond Sutra*, "Not even the greatest treasure of the entire three thousand chiliocosm can compare to the merit acquired from upholding a four-line verse." Thus the emphasis of language in Buddhism is clear.

If Master Xuanzang had never brought the many texts back from India, how would Chinese culture have been enriched? Without such words of wisdom and truth, how would any Buddhist canon manage to express the Truth?

Deprived of language, communication between human beings would not be as graceful or pleasing. Without language, how could the works of ancient literati and philosophers be as profound? Thus, the spread of Humanistic Buddhism has contributed greatly to the spread of Chinese culture.

1. Chinese Language Enriched by Buddhist Expressions

In general, proficiency in one thousand expressions is sufficient to deem one as 'knowledgeable.' Narrowed down to hundreds, it is still sufficient to enable one to speak and write. Yet there are thousands of Buddhist phrases and terms, which have exerted tremendous influence on Chinese words and language.

In his *Eighteen Chapters on Buddhist Studies and Research*, Liang Qichao (梁啟超 , 1873-1929) mentions that, "After Buddhism was transmitted to China, translations of Buddhist sutras have added thirty-five thousand words to the Chinese language." Not only have these new words enhanced the beauty of Chinese literature, but their depth and meanings. Even daily speech became more elegant. In fact, the language of Humanistic Buddhism has long become part of people's daily usage. They simply do not realize that a large part of their language is actually Chan language.

Without the language of Humanistic Buddhism, I wonder if the Chinese could still speak as elegantly. For example, "May the Buddha's Light shine universally," "Let the stream of Dharma be everflowing," "the Four Elements are in essence empty," or "the Five Aggregates never truly exist." Each of these Chinese phrases is comprised of four characters. Once translated into English, they lose part of their meaning and elegance. This makes a translation that embodies both meaning and elegance challenging. Therefore, the Chinese language is not only profound in meaning, but its beauty and elegance is something that no other language can match.

Other Chan phrases such as "the Gate of Non-Duality," "True Thusness and intrinsic nature," "Field of the Eight Consciousness," or "Let the mind arise without abiding," are also rich in philosophical context and literary beauty. The task of translation into any other language would undoubtedly be extremely difficult. Four reasons as to why Chinese language stands out as most unique and profound are as follows:

i. Translation of Sutras and Integration of Languages

The spread of the Dharma would not have happened without the disciples. They held councils and compiled the Buddha's teachings and words after he entered nirvana. The world can now enjoy

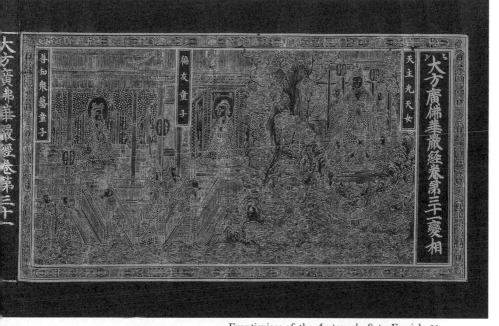

Frontispiece of the *Avatamsaka Sutra* Fascicle 31
KOREA; Goryeo dynasty (918–1392), dated 1337; Gold on indigo paper;
20 x 36.5 cm; Ho Am Art Museum, Yongin, South Korea

the eternal company of the righteous Dharma, which includes the writings and disseminations of the Tripitaka and Twelve Divisions of Buddhist Canon.

Monks originally from India, such as Kasyapa-Matanga, Dharmaratna, An Shigao, Lokaksema, Zhi Qian (支謙, fl. 222-252), and Kang Sengui (康僧會, d.280) took on the task of translating Buddhist texts into Chinese. Later, the Five Great Translators: Kumarajiva, Paramartha, Xuanzang, Amoghavajra (705-774), and Yijing translated a large corpus of Buddhist sutras, thereby completing the system of Buddhist thoughts. The task of translation not only enabled the spread of the Buddha's profound teachings but also allowed the Eight Schools of Chinese Buddhism to thrive during the Sui and Tang Dynasties. Translation also enabled Chinese Mahayana Buddhism to take form.

Translations done by Kumarajiva are regarded as "older translations" for his ability to grasp the meaning and transcribing them in fluent and concise writing. Four of his most prominent disciples—Daosheng (道生 , 355-434), Sengzao (僧肇 , 384-414), Daorong (道融 , 356-406), and Sengrui (僧叡 , 373-439) were all outstanding translators. With their participation, the *Lotus Sutra, Diamond Sutra, Vimalakirti Sutra,* and *Amitabha Sutra* were widely disseminated and extremely popular among Chinese Buddhists for the eloquent readability of the texts.

On the other hand, Master Xuanzang's insistence on remaining loyal to the original text increased the difficulty of his interpretations. He also established the rules pertaining to the "Five Untranslatables," the five instances under which only transliterations are rendered:

1. Secret: languages such as mantras or Dharanis.
2. Polysemy: words that contain multiple meanings.
3. Foreign: languages that do not exist in China.
4. Deference to the past: established transliterations from the past.
5. To inspire respect and righteousness: words such as prajna.

Certainly, the spread of a Buddhist text depended on the fluency of its translations. Translators from later periods followed Xuanzang's rules and rendered "new translations" remaining particular in their translation techniques.

Therefore, it is important that the language used in Humanistic Buddhism not be rigid. A reasonable level of adaptation to ensure the readability and fluency of the Buddhist language is necessary. Just as Chinese, Japanese, Korean, Theravada, and Tibetan Buddhism each developed their own unique languages and ways of practice, geographical and historical backgrounds were the major contributing factors.

Today, as we harmonize all forms of Buddhism into Humanistic Buddhism, not only are we integrating all Buddhist vocabularies throughout history; we are also reinstating the original intents of the Buddha. Our own resolve is to offer the world a unified teaching focused solely on the Buddha's intent at bettering society. Being what is essential to people, and in the belief we all can become buddhas, Humanistic Buddhism is certainly the Way.

ii. The spread of Buddhist texts

Throughout the two thousand years of Buddhism's spread in China, eminent masters went through painstaking efforts to translate Buddhist texts, which later became various editions of Buddhist canons such as the Kaibao (開寶), Khitan (契丹), Vairocana (毘盧), Qisha (磧砂), Koryo (高麗), Jiaxing (嘉興), Dragon (龍藏), Pinjia (頻伽), Tegen (鐵眼), Manji Daizokyo (卍字正藏), Manji Zokuzokyo (卍字續藏), and Taisho (大正) Canons.

Embodying profound literary and philosophical concepts, these canons have earned the world's respect and envy of Chinese culture. Not even Shakespeare's love stories or delicate portrayals of human nature and life can outshine these canons.

In Hu Shi's *History of Vernacular Literature*, he mentions that the *Gandhavyuha Sutra* from the *Avatamsaka Sutra* is itself a literary novel, while the *Vimalakirti Sutra* is the longest vernacular poem in history, exemplifying both philosophical attainments and literary beauty. Though certain Buddhists may not agree with such an approach to appreciating the Dharma, we cannot deny that literature and philosophy are the only ways through which the beauty of Buddhism and Buddhist literature can be comprehended.

While gratitude must go to the Chinese for developing printing techniques, the demand for these texts due to the spread of Buddhism, has advanced, perfected, and profited the printing industry as a whole. The benefits are undeniably twofold.

Today, books, magazines and even different editions of the Buddhist canon can be found in households. It can be said that the wide circulation of Buddhist texts has not only enriched the hearts and minds of the people, but also enhanced the spread of Humanistic Buddhism tremendously.

iii. Concurrent Sectarian Realities

Through the works of past eminent Buddhist masters, along with the Chan School separating into five distinct disciplines, and the Five Schools and Seven Sects, Chan Masters found an alternate way to the Truth. They did this through the mindsets of "pointing straight to the heart" and "attaining Buddahood upon seeing one's nature." Notably, they conveyed the Dharma to society in a manner that was acceptable and understandable by the people, from the children to the elderly. This is an important accomplishment.

Take Zhiyi (智 顗 , 539-598) for example. Having taught the *Lotus Sutra (Fahua jing)*, his school was thus known as the Tiantai School or Fahua School. Alternatively, in widely disseminating the *Avatamsaka Sutra*, Master Xianshou's (賢 首 , 643-712) school is hence known as the Xianshou School. Under similar circumstances, various schools took on names based upon where they were situated, what sutras were studied, or their founder.

The Pure Land School was otherwise known as the Lotus School, Pure School, and Chanting of Buddha's Name School. The Three Treatises School was also known as the Emptiness School, or Dharma-Nature School. The Faxiang School was known as the Mind-Only School. No schools were treated as equals, yet none rejected or excluded each other.

This is similar to the diverse Buddhist expressions used for the Tathagata-garbha, True-Thusness, intrinsic nature, and true reality in helping us understand the truth about our nature. Despite the distinction, there have never been feelings of contention or objection.

Just as it is fitting that the Buddha had ten epithets, so it was with elites and nobles in olden times. They had scholarly names, courtesy names, titles, and pseudonyms. Even the multitude has nicknames or alternative names. Regardless, they all refer to the same person.

For this reason, the propagation of Humanistic Buddhism requires the effort of all Buddhists around the world, for it embodies the Buddha's original intents. By acknowledging the term "Humanistic Buddhism," we already contribute greatly to the future of Buddhism worldwide. Conversely, deeming this term inappropriate or incorrect would only harm Buddhism and its dissemination.

iv. Common Expressions

Some say that the Chinese are the smartest people in the world, I wonder if many know how integral a part the Buddhist language was? The language spoken, written and used daily by Chinese is essentially derived from Buddhist texts. Buddhists and non-Buddhists alike are seemingly unaware that they are actually speaking the

Buddhist language.

The beauty of the Chinese language is said to be without equal.

1) Two-character terms

(online searchable version at: www.fgsihb.org/dictionary.asp)

一心	single-mindedly, wholeheartedly		入室	to enter the master's study for examination or instruction
一匝	to make a full circle		入門	beginner
一生	all one's life		入流	Srotapanna, stream-entrant
一向	one direction			
一劫	one kalpa		入滅	to enter into nirvana
一言	one word		入道	to enter the Way
一味	one taste		八苦	Eight Kinds of Suffering
一念	one thought		八難	Eight Difficulties
一門	one gate		力士	one of great strength
一流	of the same flow		十方	the ten directions
一音	one voice		三千	three thousand fold
一時	one time		三世	Three Periods of Time
一期	one moment of time		三生	Three Lifetimes
一路	all along the way		三劫	Three kalpas
人天	humans and devas		三災	Three Calamities
人生	life		三思	Three Mental Conditions
人身	the human body		三昧	samadhi
人師	a teacher of humans		三毒	Three Poisons
人間	human world		三界	Three Realms
入定	to enter into meditation		三乘	Three Vehicles

三時	Three Periods of Time	布施	generosity
三從	Three Obediences	平等	equality
三塗	Three Lower Realms	正命	right livelihood
三學	Threefold Training	正宗	authentic
三禮	Three Rites	玄關	entrance
三藏	Tripitaka	甘露	nectar
三寶	Three Jewels	生滅	arising and ceasing
上人	supreme teacher	示現	to manifest
上乘	superior vehicle	共生	coexistence
小品	short version	合十	to bring the ten fingers or two palms together
山門	mountain gate		
中道	Middle Way	合掌	to join palms
公案	gong-an	吉祥	auspicious blessings
分別	discrimination	同事	fellowship
化身	nirmanakaya	回向	dedication of merits
天眼	divine eye	因果	cause and effect
方便	expedient means	因緣	causes and conditions
止觀	calming and contemplating	地獄	hell
		如來	Tathagata
火宅	burning house	如是	thus, so
世間	world	如意	As one wishes
出家	to renounce	如實	real, reality, according to reality
出離	renunciation, transcendence		
		妄想	delusive thoughts
功德	merit	安住	to settle
加持	to bless	安忍	to bear adversity with calmness

成就	accomplishment		供養	offering
有情	sentient being		依止	to depend and rest upon
有緣	to have a cause, link, or connection		典座	temple chef
自在	perfect ease		初心	the initial mind
自覺	self-awareness		受持	uphold
行腳	to travel (by foot)		和尚	Most Venerable
行禪	to practice Chan		和南	A salutation, to pay one's respects to
衣鉢	robe and bowl		宗旨	cardinal meaning
伽藍	sangha community		居士	householder
住持	abbot		彼岸	the other shore
佛道	the Buddha Way		往生	to be reborn
佛學	Buddhology		往還	to depart and return
利行	altruism		念佛	to chant Buddha's name
劫數	inexorable fate		放下	let go
弟子	disciple		放光	to emit light
忍辱	patience		放香	free session
戒香	fragrance of precepts		法忍	patience attained through Dharma
投胎	to be reborn		法身	Dharma body
投機	to avail oneself of an opportunity		法乳	the milk of Dharma
抖擻	to shake off		法味	taste of Dharma
束縛	fetter		法舍	Dharma abode
沙門	sramana		法門	dharma-gate
沙彌	sramanera		法炬	The torch of Dharma
見道	to see the Way		法界	dharma realm

法師	Dharma master, Venerable	降伏	to subdue
法喜	Dharma joy	面壁	to face the wall in sitting meditation
法輪	Dharma wheel	首座	chief
法器	Dharma instrument	修行	spiritual cultivation
法寶	Dharma treasure	差別	discrimination
知客	receptionist	恩愛	affection
糾察	disciplinarian	悅眾	karmadana
糾纏	entangle	悟道	to awaken to the truth
舍利	relic	書記	secretary
金剛	diamond	根器	aptitude
長養	to nurture	殊勝	extraordinary
信仰	faith	浩劫	disaster, catastrophe
剎那	ksana	浮圖	Buddha
客塵	external taint	涅槃	nirvana
持戒	to uphold precepts	琉璃	lapis lazuli
施主	benefactor	真心	true mind
染汙	taint	真如	True Thusness
流通	to transmit and spread	真諦	truth
流轉	transmigration	神明	god, deity
相對	relative	神通	supernatural power
相應	response, correspond	素齋	vegetarian meal
紅塵	worldly affairs	般若	prajna
苦行	austerity	迷信	superstition
苦海	ocean of suffering	勘破	to penetrate

參學	travel and learn	報應	karmic retribution
問訊	half-bow	尊重	respect
問道	ask for the Way	悲觀	contemplation on loving-kindness
執著	attachment		
宿命	predestination	惡道	evil path
寂靜	tranquility	散亂	distraction
常住	monastery	普門	Universal Gate
惜緣	to cherish affinity	普度	universal salvation
掛單	lodging	普遍	universal
梵唄	Buddhist hymn	智慧	wisdom
淨土	Pure Land	朝山	pilgrimage
清淨	purity	朝暮	morning and evening
清貧	simple and frugal	朝露	morning dew
現在	now, present	棒喝	stick and shout
現身	manifest	無住	non-abiding
現象	phenomenon	無念	free from thought
眾生	sentient beings	無明	ignorance
罣礙	affliction	無畏	fearless
習氣	habitual tendency	無相	formless
莊嚴	solemn, majestic	無常	impermanence
袈裟	kasaya	無量	immeasurable
割愛	to relinquish	無盡	endless
善惡	good and evil	無緣	lack of connection
喜捨	joyful giving	發心	to resolve
單位	a single seat, or position	等持	holding oneself in equanimity

結緣	to develop affinity		煩惱	defilement
絕對	absolute		獅吼	Lion's Roar
菩提	bodhi		當下	immediate moment
菩薩	bodhisattva		當家	superintendent
虛無	nothingness, unreal		禁語	observation of silence
鈍根	dull aptitude		經行	walking meditation
開光	inauguration		罪過	transgression
開悟	to awaken		義工	volunteer
雲水	cloud and water		聖凡	sage and ordinary
雲遊	to travel freely		解脫	liberation
飯頭	rice chef		資糧	provision
傳法	Dharma transmission		遊行	to wander, travel
圓寂	perfect rest		遊戲	to be free and at ease
圓通	Universally penetrating		道場	place for spiritual practice
微妙	Subtle, profound		頓悟	sudden enlightenment
微塵	fine dust		僧伽	sangha
愛語	loving words		僧侶	monastic
感應	divine connection		塵勞	affliction
慈航	ferry of compassion		塵緣	worldly affinity
慈悲	loving-kindness and compassion		實相	reality
			對治	to remedy
敬信	respectful and faithful		慚愧	humility
業力	karmic effect		演說	to expound
業報	karmic retribution		福田	field of merit
業障	karmic hindrance		種子	seed
極樂	ultimate bliss			

稱念	to chant Buddha's name	諦聽	listen carefully
精舍	vihara	醍醐	clarified butter
精進	diligence	錫杖	staff
維那	karmadana	閻浮	Jampudiva
緇素	sacred and secular, monastic and lay practitioner	隨分	according to (one's) allotment
語錄	record of sayings	隨喜	To rejoice (in the welfare of others)
輕安	at ease	隨緣	to accord with conditions
障礙	hindrance	頭陀	austerities
增長	to increase, grow	應化	manifestation in response
彈指	to snap fingers	戲論	mental proliferation
慧命	wisdom-life	檀那	dana
摩頂	to lay the hand on the top of the head	禪心	Chan mind
樂觀	optimism	禪坐	sitting meditation
緣分	affinity	禪味	taste of Chan
緣覺	pratyekabuddha	禪定	meditative concentration
蓮社	Lotus Society	禪師	Chan master
調伏	to subdue	禪悅	joy of Chan
輪迴	rebirth	禪堂	meditation hall
遷單	to expel	總持	to hold to the good, total retention
餓鬼	hungry ghost	聲聞	sravaka
學人	student of the Way	講堂	lecture hall
導師	mentor	叢林	monastery
懈怠	laziness	歸命	to devote one's life
機緣	potentiality and condition	禮佛	to prostrate to the Buddha

繞佛	to circumambulate the Buddha		闡提	icchantika
翻案	to reverse a verdict		饒舌	chatterbox
薰習	influence		攝受	to receive, take in
轉身	turn around		灌頂	consecration
曠劫	since ancient times		纏縛	to bind
繫縛	tied to		魔障	mara-hindrance
羅漢	arhat		歡喜	joy
藥石	medicine meal		靈感	inspiration
證悟	to awaken (to the Truth)		靈驗	efficacious
顛倒	up-side down		觀音	Avalokitesvara
懺悔	to repent		觀想	contemplation
覺悟	to awake		觀照	careful consideration
警策	warning staff		觀察	clear perception
			讚歎	praise

2) Three-character expressions

一大劫	one great kalpa
一切法	all phenomena
一切智	wisdom of all
一合相	a composite
一味禪	Chan of one taste
一剎那	one ksana
一指禪	One-finger Chan
一食頃	The time of a meal
一微塵	a particle of dust
一彈指	a snap of the finger
七覺支	The Seven Factors of Enlightenment

九品蓮	Nine Stages of Lotus Incarnation
二六時	twelve hours
人中尊	The Honored One among humans
人我相	characteristics of the self and others
八福田	eight fields of merit
十法界	Ten Dharma Realms
三法印	Three Dharma Seals
三昧火	Fire of samadhi
三界外	outside the three dharma realms
三皈依	To take refuge in the Triple Gem
三摩地	samadhi
三寶佛	The Triple Gem Buddhas
上大供	great offering
口頭禪	lip service Chan
大和尚	master
大無畏	great fearlessness
大菩薩	great Bodhisattva
大導師	The great teacher
大醫王	Great Lord of healing
小沙彌	sramanera
不二門	The Gate of Non-Duality
不可得	unobtainable
不可說	inexplicable
不共業	individual karma
不自在	not in perfect ease
不放逸	no laxity
不思善	not thinking about the wholesome
不思惡	not thinking about the unwholesome
不思議	inconceivable

不倒單	Never laying down
不退轉	never regress or change
不動尊	Acala
不誑語	not lying
六和敬	Six points of reverent harmony
六齋日	Six Days of Purification
天人師	teacher of heavenly beings and humans
天地人	heaven, earth, and humans
天堂路	road to heaven
心意識	mind, thought, and perception
心解脫	liberation of mind
方便門	expedient means
日月星	sun, moon and star
比丘尼	bhiksuni
水上泡	bubble on the water
水中月	moon in the water
世間解	knower of the world
打禪七	meditation retreat
正遍知	correct peerless enlightenment
甘露水	nectar
光明燈	lamp of illumination
光明藏	treasury of light
共生緣	coexisting affinity
共命鳥	two-headed bird
吃十方	to live on offerings from the ten directions
吃早齋	vegetarian breakfast
因緣果	cause, condition, and effect
地藏王	Ksitigarbha
多寶佛	Prabhutaratna Buddha

好兆頭	good omen
如來佛	Tathagata Buddha
如意寮	sickbay
如實知	to understand things as they really are
存好心	Think good thoughts
安樂行	pleasant practices
自性空	emptiness of self-nature
西方船	Ferry to Western Pure Land
作麼生	why, how
妙吉祥	Wonderful and auspicious
弄猢猻	play with a monkey
戒定慧	morality, meditative concentration, wisdom
沙彌尼	sramanerika
走江湖	Jianghu roamer
來生緣	affinities in future lives
兩足尊	supreme among two-legged creatures
奈何橋	bridge to hell
居士林	Lay Buddhist's Association
念佛七	seven-day chanting retreat
所知障	cognitive hindrance
放生會	Life Release Ceremony
放焰口	Yogacara Dharma Service
明行足	perfected in wisdom and action
明鏡台	bright standing mirror
易行道	the easy path
法同舍	Dharma Abode
法如是	thus is the Dharma
法依止	rely on the Dharma
波羅蜜	paramita

盂蘭盆	Ullambama Festival
金剛心	Diamond heart
金剛身	The diamond body
門外漢	layman
阿修羅	asura
阿僧祇	asamkhya
阿羅漢	arhat
阿蘭若	aranya
非思量	not thinking
信願行	faith, vow, and practice
南無佛	namo buddha
帝釋天	Sakra Devanam-indra
度眾生	to liberate sentient beings
施無畏	bestowal of fearlessness
柔軟心	gentle and soft mind
香雲蓋	Incense cloud canopy
香積廚	Kitsch of Accumulated Fragrance
俱解脫	simultaneous liberation
海潮音	ocean-tide voice
消業障	to eliminate karmic obstacles
真實義	True meaning
臭皮囊	vile skin-bag
般若門	door of prajna
茶飯禪	Chan in tea and meals
鬼門關	the gate of death
做功德	to generate merits
做好事	Do good deeds
參話頭	contemplate the head phrase (of a gongan)
常不輕	Sadaparibhuta

接引佛	Welcoming Buddha
添油香	to make a donation
清涼月	pure and cool moon
清淨心	pure mind
現世報	karmic retribution in the present life
眾生相	characteristics of sentient beings
莫妄想	think no delusive thoughts
貪瞋痴	Greed, hatred, and ignorance
造口業	to commit verbal karma
善女人	good women
善男子	good men
善知識	virtuous companion
善護念	safeguard the mind
普同塔	Universal Unity Pagoda
普門品	Universal Gate Chapter
普陀山	Mount Putuo
普賢王	Samantabhadra
朝山團	pilgrims
無上士	unsurpassed one
無所得	nothing to be attained
無明火	fire of ignorance
無門關	Gateless Barrier
無為舍	the house of nirvana
無量光	infinite light
無量壽	infinite life
無盡燈	one lamp which is yet limitless
無盡藏	inexhaustible storehouse
無遮會	universal offering
無學位	stage of no more learning

發大心	generate great mind
紫竹林	Purple Bamboo Forest
菩提路	the Bodhi Path
菩薩心	a bodhisattva's mind
菩薩戒	Bodhisattva Precepts
開山門	to open the monastery gate
開眼界	to broaden one's views
雲門餅	Yunmen cake
須彌山	Mount Sumeru
微塵劫	kalpas as many as fine dust
慈悲心	compassion
獅子吼	Lion's roar
經律論	sutra, vinaya, and abhidharma
萬壽園	Longevity Park
解脫道	The path of liberation
滴水恩	gratitude for a water drop
福田衣	The garment of the field of blessing
種福田	to cultivate the field of merits
聞思修	hearing, contemplation, and practice
說好話	Speak good words
趙州茶	Zhaozhou tea
增上緣	contributory factor
增福慧	increase merit and wisdom
摩訶衍	mahayana
摩訶薩	mahasattva
撞頭鐘	strike the first bell
標月指	finger pointing to the moon
燒頭香	to burn the first incense
選佛場	Buddha selection court

閻羅王	Yama
優婆夷	upasika
優婆塞	upasaka
彌勒佛	Maitreya Buddha
禪和子	meditation-associates
藏經樓	Sutra Repository
轉法輪	To turn the Dharma Wheel
臘八粥	Laba congee
難行道	the difficult path
覺有情	awakened sentient being
露馬腳	to show the cloven foot
歡喜地	Ground of Joy
歡喜佛	Buddha of happiness
體相用	essence, function, and form
觀世音	Avalokitesvara
觀自在	Avalokitesvara

3) Four-character expressions

一心一意	Single-mindedness
一彈指頃	A snap of the finger
七情六欲	The seven emotions and six sensory pleasures
三生有幸	Blessings from the past three lifetimes
大慈大悲	Great compassion and great loving-kindness
不二法門	The Gate of Non-Duality
不生不滅	Neither arises nor extinguishes
不即不離	Neither close nor far
不增不減	Neither increases nor decreases
五體投地	Throwing all five limbs to the ground

六時吉祥	Auspicious blessings through out all six periods of the day
天女散華	Heavenly rain of flowers
心心相印	Heart-to-heart connection
心生萬法	All dharmas arise from the mind
心猿意馬	The mind is like a wild monkey and galloping horse
心隨境轉	The mind changes with the circumstances
本來面目	Original face
回光返照	Final radiance of the setting sun
因果報應	Karmic retribution
如影隨形	Like shadows following the body
安心立命	To find peace and attain enlightenment
有情世間	The sentient world
老婆心切	Like an old woman's ardent urgency
自作自受	To suffer the consequences of one's own actions
行住坐臥	Walking, standing, sitting and lying down
作繭自縛	To spin a cocoon around oneself
冷暖自知	The taste of the water in your mouth
坐斷十方	To sever all [delusions] in sitting meditation
拋磚引玉	To throw a brick to bring back jade
言語道斷	Beyond words
邪魔外道	Demons and heretics
事事無礙	Mutual unobstructedness among phenomena
事與願違	When things go against your will
味同嚼蠟	The taste of chewing candle
披星戴月	Under the moon and stars
拈花微笑	Buddha's flower and Kasyapa's smile
明心見性	To realize the mind and see one's true nature

泥牛入海	A mud ox into the sea
直指人心	Directly pointing to one's mind
虎嘯生風	Tiger howl with the rise of winds
返璞歸真	To recover one's true nature
金剛不壞	Indestructible diamond
剋期取證	To set a time limit for attainment
前世今生	Past and present lifetimes
剎那生滅	To arise or cease within a ksana
恆河沙數	As innumerable as the sands of the Ganges
洞然明白	Revealed in perfect clarity
風調雨順	Favorable weather
修成正果	To attain spiritual progress through the right path
留惑潤生	To preserve defilements to benefit beings
逆增上緣	Reverse contributory factors
動靜一如	Movement is the same as stillness
唯我獨尊	I alone am the honored one
將心比心	To see things through other people's eyes
教外別傳	Transmission apart from teachings
晨鐘暮鼓	Morning bells and evening drums
眼橫鼻直	Eyes are eyes, and nose is nose
通身手眼	Your whole body is your eyes and hands
逢場作戲	To play along for a little fun
單刀直入	To cut to the chase
智目行足	Eyes of wisdom and steps of conduct
無常迅速	Impermanence strikes fast
焦芽敗種	Barren seed
畫餅充飢	To try to satisfy hunger by drawing cakes
貴耳賤目	To trust one's ears rather than one's eyes

慈航普渡	The ferry of compassion
猿猴捉月	Like apes and monkeys trying to catch the moon in the water
當頭棒喝	Strike a telling blow
痴人說夢	To talk ignorant nonsense
葉落歸根	Falling leaves return to their roots
電光石火	Transient lightning and flint-fire
塵盡光生	When dusts are cleared light will shine
夢幻泡影	Dream, illusion, bubble and shadow
對牛彈琴	To play the lute to a cow
對機說法	Teaching in conformity with the mental capacity of listeners
滴水穿石	Constant dripping wears away a stone
端心正意	With a proper mind and regulated will
聚沙成塔	Sand grains accumulate to make a tower
蒸沙作飯	Steaming sand to make cooked rice
遠塵離垢	To be far removed from the dust and defilement of the world
廣結善緣	To broadly develop good affinities
撥無因果	To deny the rule of causes and effect
撥雲見日	To clear the clouds and see the sky
諸上善人	Utmost virtuous people
曇花一現	The night-blooming cactus
橫遍十方	Spanning the ten directions
磨磚作鏡	To polish a brick into a mirror
隨波逐浪	To drift with the waves and go with the flow
隨緣不變	To follow conditions while remaining unmoved
龜毛兔角	Turtle hair and rabbit's horn
擲地有聲	To make a loud statement

轉女成男	To be transformed from female in t
識心達本	To know the mind and penetrate t
嚴土熟生	Majestic (Pure)Land and well-atta
饒益有情	To benefit sentient beings
辯才無礙	Supreme eloquence

The following are some often used Buddhist

Most of these expressions originated fro
embody the profound philosophy and clever

which have made modern day Chinese more

一子出家，九族升天	When one ch kinsmen will
一切有為法，如夢幻泡影	All condition dreams, illus
一日不作，一日不食	A day witho without foo
一即多，多即一	One is many
一佛出世，二佛涅槃	When one will pass aw
一佛出世，千佛護持	The birth possible by buddhas.
一把鑰匙，開一把鎖	Each key
一言既出，駟馬難追	A word sp
一花一世界，一葉一如來	There is a buddha in
一報還一報	An eye fo

六時吉祥	Auspicious blessings through out all six periods of the day
天女散華	Heavenly rain of flowers
心心相印	Heart-to-heart connection
心生萬法	All dharmas arise from the mind
心猿意馬	The mind is like a wild monkey and galloping horse
心隨境轉	The mind changes with the circumstances
本來面目	Original face
回光返照	Final radiance of the setting sun
因果報應	Karmic retribution
如影隨形	Like shadows following the body
安心立命	To find peace and attain enlightenment
有情世間	The sentient world
老婆心切	Like an old woman's ardent urgency
自作自受	To suffer the consequences of one's own actions
行住坐臥	Walking, standing, sitting and lying down
作繭自縛	To spin a cocoon around oneself
冷暖自知	The taste of the water in your mouth
坐斷十方	To sever all [delusions] in sitting meditation
拋磚引玉	To throw a brick to bring back jade
言語道斷	Beyond words
邪魔外道	Demons and heretics
事事無礙	Mutual unobstructedness among phenomena
事與願違	When things go against your will
味同嚼蠟	The taste of chewing candle
披星戴月	Under the moon and stars
拈花微笑	Buddha's flower and Kasyapa's smile
明心見性	To realize the mind and see one's true nature

泥牛入海	A mud ox into the sea
直指人心	Directly pointing to one's mind
虎嘯生風	Tiger howl with the rise of winds
返璞歸真	To recover one's true nature
金剛不壞	Indestructible diamond
剋期取證	To set a time limit for attainment
前世今生	Past and present lifetimes
剎那生滅	To arise or cease within a ksana
恆河沙數	As innumerable as the sands of the Ganges
洞然明白	Revealed in perfect clarity
風調雨順	Favorable weather
修成正果	To attain spiritual progress through the right path
留惑潤生	To preserve defilements to benefit beings
逆增上緣	Reverse contributory factors
動靜一如	Movement is the same as stillness
唯我獨尊	I alone am the honored one
將心比心	To see things through other people's eyes
教外別傳	Transmission apart from teachings
晨鐘暮鼓	Morning bells and evening drums
眼橫鼻直	Eyes are eyes, and nose is nose
通身手眼	Your whole body is your eyes and hands
逢場作戲	To play along for a little fun
單刀直入	To cut to the chase
智目行足	Eyes of wisdom and steps of conduct
無常迅速	Impermanence strikes fast
焦芽敗種	Barren seed
畫餅充飢	To try to satisfy hunger by drawing cakes
貴耳賤目	To trust one's ears rather than one's eyes

慈航普渡	The ferry of compassion
猿猴捉月	Like apes and monkeys trying to catch the moon in the water
當頭棒喝	Strike a telling blow
痴人說夢	To talk ignorant nonsense
葉落歸根	Falling leaves return to their roots
電光石火	Transient lightning and flint-fire
塵盡光生	When dusts are cleared light will shine
夢幻泡影	Dream, illusion, bubble and shadow
對牛彈琴	To play the lute to a cow
對機說法	Teaching in conformity with the mental capacity of listeners
滴水穿石	Constant dripping wears away a stone
端心正意	With a proper mind and regulated will
聚沙成塔	Sand grains accumulate to make a tower
蒸沙作飯	Steaming sand to make cooked rice
遠塵離垢	To be far removed from the dust and defilement of the world
廣結善緣	To broadly develop good affinities
撥無因果	To deny the rule of causes and effect
撥雲見日	To clear the clouds and see the sky
諸上善人	Utmost virtuous people
曇花一現	The night-blooming cactus
橫遍十方	Spanning the ten directions
磨磚作鏡	To polish a brick into a mirror
隨波逐浪	To drift with the waves and go with the flow
隨緣不變	To follow conditions while remaining unmoved
龜毛兔角	Turtle hair and rabbit's horn
擲地有聲	To make a loud statement

轉女成男	To be transformed from female into male
識心達本	To know the mind and penetrate the root
嚴土熟生	Majestic (Pure)Land and well-attained sentient beings
饒益有情	To benefit sentient beings
辯才無礙	Supreme eloquence

The following are some often used Buddhist expressions.

Most of these expressions originated from Chan gongans. They embody the profound philosophy and clever wits of Chan masters, which have made modern day Chinese more artistic and elegant.

一子出家，九族升天	When one child renounces, nine clans of kinsmen will ascend to heaven.
一切有為法，如夢幻泡影	All conditioned phenomena are like dreams, illusions, bubbles, and shadows.
一日不作，一日不食	A day without work means a day without food.
一即多，多即一	One is many, and many are one.
一佛出世，二佛涅槃	When one buddha is born, the other two will pass away.
一佛出世，千佛護持	The birth of one buddha is made possible by thousand(s) of other buddhas.
一把鑰匙，開一把鎖	Each key opens up a lock.
一言既出，駟馬難追	A word spoken is an arrow let fly.
一花一世界，一葉一如來	There is a world in a single flower; a buddha in a single leaf.
一報還一報	An eye for an eye, a tooth for a tooth.

一朝被蛇咬，十年怕井繩	Once bitten, twice shy.
人生難得，大道難聞	It is hard to be born as a human, and hard to hear the Dharma.
人成即佛成	Buddhahood is attained the instant our characters are perfected
人命在呼吸間	We can only count on a single breath.
人要知道苦惱	It is important to feel pain and affliction.
八功德水，九品蓮華	The waters of eight merits and nine stages of lotus flowers
八風吹不動，一屁打過江	He who is allegedly unmovable even by the Eight Winds was blown across the river by a fart.
三千威儀，八萬細行	Three thousand demeanors and eighty thousand subtle actions.
三界似火宅，娑婆如苦海	The Three Realms are like a burning house; the Saha World is like an ocean of suffering.
三界唯心，萬法唯識	The three realms are only in the mind; the myriad dharmas are only in the consciousness.
上報四重恩，下濟三途苦	Have gratitude for the four kindnesses, and follow the Dharma to cross over the three lower realms of existence.
千生萬死，萬死千生	A thousand lives, a million deaths.
千錘百鍊才能成功	Success comes after endless hammering and refinement.
大地眾生，皆有如來智慧德相	All sentient beings possess the wisdom and virtues of the Buddha.
大地眾生，皆有佛性	All living beings possess buddha-nature.
大肚包容，歡喜自在	With great magnanimity comes joy and perfect ease.

山川異域，日月同天	Across the mountains, streams, and foreign lands, the sun and moon, all beneath the one sky.
不是冤家不聚頭	Destiny will make enemies meet.
不看僧面看佛面	If not for the sake of the monk, at least for that of the Buddha.
天外有天，人外有人	There are always people who are better than you.
天堂地獄，來來去去	We go back and forth between heaven and hell.
心如將軍能行令	The mind is like a general who takes command.
心如猿猴難安住	The mind is like a restless monkey.
水中撈月，空有歡喜	The joy of fishing for the moon in the water is a real as emptiness.
出汙泥而不染	To emerge from the mud untainted.
生不帶來，死不帶去	We come and go empty-handed.
生死輪迴，永無休息	The cycle of birth and death never ends.
因果業報，絲毫不爽	Causes, conditions, and retributions will never get it wrong.
因緣果報，絲毫不爽	There is no error in causes, conditions and retributions.
地獄不空，誓不成佛	I shall never attain buddhahood until hell is emptied.
好事不出門，壞事傳千里	For evil news rides fast, while good news waits later.
如人飲水，冷暖自知	Only you would know the taste of the water in your mouth.
如入寶山空手回	Never leave a treasured mountain empty-handed.

早知今日，悔不當初	It is too late to ever say "If only I had known..."
有佛法就有辦法	Where there is the Dharma, there is Way.
死了會生，生了會死	There is rebirth after death, and death after rebirth.
色即是空，空即是色	Form is emptiness, emptiness is form.
行如風，立如松，坐如鐘，臥如弓	Walk like the wind, stand like a pine, sit like a bell, sleep like a bow.
佛光普照，法水長流	May the Buddha's light shine universally and the Dharma water flow eternally.
佛在哪裡，佛在心裡	Where is Buddha? Buddha is in one's mind.
佛法在世間，不離世間覺	Dharma can only be found in the world, and enlightenment cannot be attained away from it.
佛觀一粒米，大如須彌山	The Buddha sees that a grain of rice is as enormous as Mount Sumeru.
佛觀一鉢水，八萬四千蟲	The Buddha sees 84,000 organisms in a bowl of water.
君子一言，快馬加鞭	A gentleman's word is as good as gold.
我不敢輕視汝等，汝等皆當作佛	I dare not denigrate anyone of you, for you are all going to become Buddhas.
我觀世界，如菴摩羅果	I see that the world is like an amala fruit.
求人不如求己	It is better to help yourself than to seek help from others.
放下屠刀，立地成佛	Lay down the butcher's knife and become Buddha on the spot.
泥菩薩過江，自身難保	Like a clay bodhisattva fording the river, even his own safety is in jeopardy.

花落春猶在，人死樓已空	Spring lingers even when flowers have fallen; a place becomes empty when someone passes away.
金剛不壞身	A body as indestructible as diamond.
既來佛會下，都是有緣人	All in the Buddhist community are friends.
是日已過，命亦隨減	Life shortens at the end of each day.
看破世間嚇壞膽	To see through the world and then be scared to death.
苦海無邊，回頭是岸	The ocean of suffering is boundless; only by turning back can one reach salvation.
飛蛾投火，作繭自縛	Like a moth flying into the flame, and a silkworm trapping itself in a cocoon.
冤家宜解不宜結	Better friends than foes.
做一日和尚，撞一日鐘	For each day that I remain a monk, I will continue my duty in tolling the bell.
救人一命，勝造七級浮屠	The merit of saving one human life outweighs that of building a seven-story pagoda.
清者自清，濁者自濁	A clean hand wants no washing.
無我相，無人相，無眾生相，無壽者相	No notion of a self, No notion of others, No notion of sentient beings, No notion of longevity.
發菩提心，成就佛道	To generate the bodhi mind and attain Buddhahood.
菩薩畏因，眾生畏果	Bodhisattvas fear causes while sentient beings fear effects.
須彌藏芥子，芥子納須彌	Mount Sumeru can contain a mustard seed, yet that same mustard seed can conceal Mount Sumeru.

飯來張口，茶來伸手	To be waited on hand and foot.
慈眼視眾生，福聚海無量	With compassionate eyes he gazes upon sentient beings; His merit as infinite as the ocean.
楊枝一滴，甘露法水	A drop from the willow is like the nectar of Dharma.
萬惡淫為首，百善孝為先	Sexual misconducts are the worst of all unwholesome deeds; filial piety is the foremost among all wholesome deeds.
解鈴還須繫鈴人	The knot can only be untied by the knotter.
道高一尺，魔高一丈	Virtue is one foot tall, the devil ten foot.
寧動江千水，不動道人心	It is better to stir up a thousand rivers than to disturb a practitioner.
慚愧之服，無上莊嚴	Humility is the most beautiful adornment.
種瓜得瓜，種豆得豆	Good begets good, evil begets evil.
遠親不如近鄰	Neighbors are better than distant relatives.
瞋拳不打笑面	No smiling face will ever be struck by a fist of anger
諸惡莫作，眾善奉行	Do no evil, practice all wholesome deeds.
豎窮三際，橫遍十方	Across all of time, and all of space.
擒山中之賊易，捉心中之賊難	It is easy to catch thieves in the mountains, but hard to catch the thieves in one's mind.
應無所住而生其心	To give rise to a mind that does not abide in anything.

4) Literary expressions

From these frequently used Buddhist expressions and terms, it is seen that Buddhist language has already blended into the lives of people and exerted tremendous influence on their way of life.

Single-character Buddhist terms that have become part of daily speech include:

1. **Karma:** deed or action that gives rise to retribution.
2. **Awakening:** to help the self and others realize or be clear about the Truth.
3. **Dissatisfaction:** a state of physical or mental dissatisfaction categorized into three, eight and mundane types.
4. **Kalpa:** an ancient Indian unit of time. In Buddhism this word bears the meaning of calamity.
5. **Condition:** the profound Truth, which the Buddha awakened to. Everything in this world is conditioned and interconnected. This interconnection cannot be severed.
6. **Emptiness:** the essence of being, and basis upon which matters arise.

For example, without 'purity,' how could homes be clean and minds untainted? Without the mention of affliction, how are we able to see its effect on us? Without "cause and effect," how can we comprehend the truth and law of life? Without 'humility,' how can we be moral? Without 'compassion,' would we not be surrounded by enemies?

Deprived of Buddhist thoughts and literature, how could works such as *The Water Margin, Dream of the Red Chamber, Journey to the West,* and the *Scholars* ever have been masterpieces?

While texts such as the *Lotus Sutra,* and *Diamond Sutra* may be poetic and legible, to fully grasp their profound meanings would be another matter. For this reason, the difficult terms used in the Buddhist language are said to have hindered its propagation.

Expressions such as "cause and effect" may seem easy to understand; yet their true meanings are hard to comprehend. Others such as nirvana, dhyana, prajna, sunyata cannot be understood without actual cultivation and experience. While these expressions are often used, few have grasped their true meanings.

Contemporary literary writers such as Lu Xun (魯 迅 , 1881-1936) and Ba Jin (巴 金 , 1904-2005) have espoused Buddhist thoughts in their works. When the 2012 Nobel Prize in Literature Laureate, Mo Yan (莫 言) visited Fo Guang Shan, he mentioned that the title of his work *Worn Out by Life and Death*, was inspired by the *Sutra of Eight Realizations of Great Beings*.

In summation, imagine the Chinese Language in its entirety bereft of Buddhism. Without Buddhism, would Chinese literary and historical expressions be as elegant and rich? With regard to revitalizing Chinese culture, we must be aware of the differencees Buddhist language has made to society and life. No matter your background or occupation, we speak the language of Humanistic Buddhism. As Liang Qichao (梁 啟 超 , 1873-1929) has stated, Buddhism alone contributed over thirty-four thousand words to the Chinese language. Without these contributions, the Chinese language would be ruined.

After long-term persistence in spreading the Dharma through culture and prizing the use of text, Humanistic Buddhism has indeed reached into society and assimilated with everyday life.

The Buddhist language contains only positive expressions. If we were to combine the beauty of the Buddhist language with the present era of instant communication, the possibilities are astound-

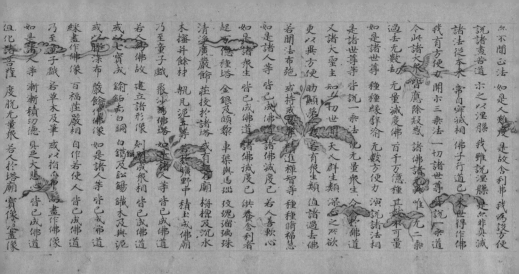

ing. Daily, we could share words of wondrous splendor, embracing the world in a warm spring breeze. As the saying goes, "a face devoid of anger is already a great way of giving, and to speak no words of anger is to emit wondrous fragrance from the lips." This is one of the most beautiful expressions in Humanistic Buddhism.

7) Causes of the Decline of Chinese Buddhism

Throughout the two thousand years of Buddhism's development in China, the golden eras of Humanistic Buddhism took place during the reigns of Emperor Ming of Eastern Han, the Wei and Jin Dynasties, the Northern and Southern Dynasties, and the Sui and Tang Dynasties. The efforts of Buddhist masters and devout lay patrons enabled the Buddhist doctrine of universal salvation to spread widely, highlighting the Buddha's focus on liberating people from life's difficulties. Nevertheless, mistakes in the propagation of the Dharma were eventually made and gave rise to unorthodox and inept teachers. Some of the causes for the decline of Chinese Buddhism are as follows:

1. Resistance and Exclusion by Local Religions

The transmission of Buddhism into China began precariously. Severe cultural clashes, Confucian persecutions, and Daoist resistance eventually led to the greatest disaster in the history of Buddhism—the San-Wu Yi Zong (三 武 一 宗) Persecutions. Oppression of Buddhists were perpetrated by Emperor Taiwu of Northern Wei (北魏太武帝 , 408-452), Emperor Zhouwu of Northern Zhou (北周武帝 , 543-578), Emperor Wuzong of Tang (唐武宗 , 814-846), and Emperor Shizong of Later Zhou (後周 世 宗 , 921-959). Another disaster for Buddhism was the Taiping Rebellion. The mandatory transformation of temple property into schools and the Cultural Revolution damaged Buddhism severely. But its doctrines of universality, equality and timelessness, coupled with its pure and righteous faith enabled Buddhism to survive. It did so by transcending religious and geographical boundaries. For these reasons, Humanistic Buddhism still exists today.

The first persecution began when devout Taoist Prime Minister Cui Hao (崔浩 , d450) and Daoist priest Kou Qianzhi (寇謙之 , 365-448) incited Emperor Taiwu of Northern Wei, also a pious Daiost, to execute all monastics in Changan, abolish Buddhism by burning all temples and Buddha statues, as well as forcing all monastics to disrobe. Even the Prince's teacher, Xuangao (玄高 , 402-444), was executed. This utterly devastated Northern Wei Buddhism and lasted for two years until the next dynasty emerged and gave Buddhism a chance for revival.

The second persecution followed some one hundred years later, when Emperor Wu of Northern Zhou was similarly encouraged by

Daoist priests Zhang Bin（張賓）and Wei Yuanson（衛元嵩）to order the abolishment of Buddhism. This was done by confiscating over forty thousand properties belonging to the temples and forcing over a million monastics to disrobe. In defiance of oppression, and in attempting to convince the Emperor of the depravity of his edict, Venerable Jingai（靜藹, 534-578) was executed. The following year, the Emperor died suddenly of an illness, thought by the people to be an immediate karmic retribution of his own doing.

Two hundred and sixty years later, in 845, Emperor Wuzong of Tang ignited the third disaster that nearly brought Buddhism to its extinction. A devout Daoist, the Emperor was influenced by Daoist priest Zhao Guizhen（趙歸真, ?-846) and decreed that over forty six hundred temples were to be abolished and properties seized. Two hundred and sixty thousand monastics were forced to disrobe. Iron Buddhist statues were remolded into farming tools, while bronze statues, instruments and artifacts were remolded into coins for currency. Perhaps it was karma yet again, for the Emperor died of poisoning the following year by ingesting medicine brewed by a Daoist priest, bringing his short six-year reign to an end.

The fourth persecution was initiated by Emperor Shizong of Later Zhou, who ordered the abolishment of Buddhism by destroying over thirty thousand temples and prohibiting the creation of Buddhist statues and instruments He also ordered that all bronze artifacts be smelted into coins for currency.

The orders for the abolishment of Buddhism and its oppression, as listed above were due to several causes. One such cause was malicious Daoist advice to the Emperor. Another was the ruler's own opposition to a foreign religion, and fear of the thriving influence of Buddhism.

In the early periods, Daoism was the national religion of China, and thus Buddhist-Daoist conflicts began. A Daoist priest named Chu Shanxin (褚善信) boasted to Emperor Ming of Eastern Han about the greatness of Daoist powers. He claimed that they could fly, and, as the supreme texts of the world, the Daoist sutras could not be burnt. However, in a disagreement with Kasyapa-Matanga and Dharmaratna, the Daoist sutras instantly caught fire and burned to ashes. Even worse, their artifices of flying, walking on water, and invisibility all failed. In contrast, the Buddha's relic brought forth by the monastics shone in bright colors. Kasyapa-Matanga uttered the following verse, later remembered as the greatest Buddhist-Daoist quarrel:

Foxes were never of the same kind as lions,
and lamps do not shine the true lights of the sun and moon,
Ponds have no capacity of boundless oceans,
and hills cannot peak the height of lofty mountains.
The cloud of Dharma now ascends into the world
And fertile seeds shall be inspired to sprout.
The rare Dharma will be made clear
To deliver sentient beings in all corners.

(*Comprehensive History of the Buddhas and Patriarchs*)

No less a tragedy when compared to the four imperial persecutions was the Taiping Rebellion. In the name of the Lord, Hong Xiuquan (洪秀全 , 1814-1864) the leader of the rebellion established the Taiping Heavenly Kingdom, and claimed to be "the Heavenly Lord." He issued "Heavenly Decrees" to suppress traditional beliefs by burning statues of Buddha and deities, as well as

Confucian and Mencian classics. Taiping rebels set fire to temples and destroyed statues everywhere. Buddhist temples in the Jiang-nan region (known as the Garden of Buddhism) as well as Yunnan, Guizhou, Guidong and Guanxi were severely damaged.

Fortunately, after ten years of resistance by imperial forces, led by Zeng Guofan (曾國藩, 1811-1872) and Zuo Zongtang (左宗棠, 1812-1885) sworn to defend Chinese culture, the Taiping army was finally defeated. Buddhism was thus able to rise once again.

During the late Qing and early Republic of China eras, in-tellectuals and government officials had little understanding of Buddhism. Moreover there were also covetous local despots and immoral gentry who not only confiscated temple property in the name of education, but also destroyed Buddhist architecture, and forced monastics to disrobe.

During the Kuomingtang Northern Expedition, Christian warlord Feng Yuxiang (馮玉祥, 1882-1948) destroyed Buddhist assets on a large scale, forced monastics to disrobe, and join his army. Temple properties were confiscated and turned into schools, shelters, and even entertainment houses. This was yet another disastrous episode for Buddhism in Northern China.

The Cultural Revolution brought about the largest persecution of Buddhism to date. Fortunately, the leaders of the Communist Party ended the revolution and redressed the situation. Coupled with the opening up of China by Deng Xiaoping (鄧小平, 1904-1997), Chinese culture and faiths were finally given a chance to renew.

2. The Prosperity of Buddhism as a Cause of Apprehension

In the early days of Buddhism in China, imperial and executive patronage led to the establishment of Buddhist temples, temple storages, Incalculable Registries and Inexhaustible Storehouses. At certain times, large areas of farmland were also offered to Buddhist temples, and their ability at self-sufficiency substantially developed.

The three hundred years of the Sui and Tang Dynasties witnessed the golden era of Chinese Buddhism. Whether academically, exegetically, or its propagation, Buddhism thrived. Monastics of different schools established various charitable endeavors. They planted trees, dug wells and offered water. They paved roads and built bridges. Practitioners of Humanistic Buddhism focused on any activity that helped society, the nation's financial burdens, and people with their daily needs. The bond between Buddhism and the people was already indivisible.

As Buddhist undertakings continued to develop, devotees were inspired and offered more donations. Temples became as wealthy as the nation and had extremely large followings. This caused anxiety at the imperial court and triggered envy in weak and incapable emperors. They resented Buddhism's prosperity in their failure to do likewise for their own kingdom. Fearing that Buddhist communities threatened the existence of their sovereignty, some ordered the suppression of Buddhism. This was certainly one of the causes for the imperial persecutions.

3. Seclusion from Society

Having lived as a novice monk when young, Emperor Taizu of Ming-Zhu Yuanzhang (朱元璋 , 1328-1398) was well aware of religious influence on the people. Thus, he ordered that monastics withdraw to the mountain forests, and forbade people from entering Buddhist temples or speak to monastics. Particularly, during the Yuan and Qing Dynasties, imperial patronage favored Lamaism, and thus Buddhism and Daoism suffered. The Qing government even banned women from visiting temples and monastics from alms-begging. As a result, most monastics led lives of secluded cultivation in deep mountain forests, with the goal of transcending life and death. Buddhism became disconnected from society and the people.

Some monastics even insisted that lay Buddhists follow their examples. They taught them to fear money for it was said in the sutras that gold is like a poisonous snake. Also, that betrothed couples were enemies in their previous lives, and that children were debt collectors. Such biased and distorted view caused severe aversion towards Buddhism.

The over-emphasis on suffering, emptiness, and impermanence pushed people away, denying them the proper understanding and positive attitude of Buddhism This caused people to think Buddhism was a faith with no connection to reality and no concern for human life. Quite the contrary, Buddha had originally intended to be actively interacting with the world. Unfortunately, spiritual practitioners were concerned only with their own salvation, and had little willingness to practice the bodhisattva path. As a result, Buddhism still had to contend with conflicts and tragedies.

The passive and evasive attitudes of those monastics resulted in little concern for daily life's issues or the need to improve its quality. Neither was there much bother to teach the Dharma as a way to purify human minds, nor to participate in the betterment of society. All they cared for was liberation from birth and death. They taught people to chant the Buddha's name only so they could be reborn in the Western Pure Land of Ultimate Bliss. This conflicted greatly from the need to seek happiness and peace in present life. The parting of Buddhism and humanity was made worse.

In those days, Buddhists lacked the ability to guide people towards a life found in peace and stability, creating a contrast between what people really needed and what Buddhism had to offer. Monastics were unable to embrace suitable means of teaching that fit intellectuals. As such, how could Humanistic Buddhism ever reach into families and people's hearts? Due to such reliance on passive, negative interpretations of the Dharma and lacking the bodhisattva spirit to help people, it is no wonder Buddhism declined.

4. Emphasis on Metaphysical Investigation over Human Concern

Many monastics spoke, in their teachings, of metaphysical explorations. They delivered overly philosophical and orotund sermons boasting of their knowledge. As a result, their teachings were found to be irrelevant to real life. Buddha's original teachings are meant as instructions for life. The claim that "the gift of Dharma excels all other forms of giving" means for Buddhists that the Dharma applies, enriches and assists to a better life. Believing in Buddhism without attainment of the Dharma is truly sad. In their dialogue, Chan master Niaoke and renowned poet Bai Juyi both consider that Buddhism carries the meaning of purifying the mind. As we passively prevent unwholesome doings, we should also actively do good deeds by practicing the Three Acts of Goodness, Four Givings, and Five Harmonies. Only then can we realize a life that is perfect and complete.

The Buddha established the Sangha community for the purpose of guiding people away from complex and profound metaphysical investigations, including usage of difficult and incomprehensible language. Other than the Buddhist schism that occurred in India, another reason for Buddhism's decline was the feud between Hindus and Muslims. In addition, academic studies of Buddha's teachings have also diminished the Dharma's function in helping people solve their problems. How could Buddhism not decline when the emphasis was on the division between Buddhist schools and classification of their teachings?

Another example is the sermon on the *Lotus Sutra* delivered by the Taintai patriarch Master Zhiyi. He was said to have expounded on the meaning of 'wondrous' (*miao*) over a period of ninety days. Subsequently, he established the entire Tiantai system of thought, and was much celebrated by traditional Buddhists. Looking at this from today's outlook, if a single word takes ninety days to be fully explained, then how many kalpas of lifetimes would be required to cover the entire Buddhist sutra? The only result of speaking in a metaphysical sense is a greater separation between Buddhism and the people.

Living in an era of speed and efficiency, any study and task that requires a long time for completion is viewed as unimportant. Such abstract and impractical ways of teaching can never suit the needs of today, let alone be relevant. No matter how great a philosophy or teaching may be, if disconnected from the needs of reality, even Buddhism will decline.

5. Chanting and Repentance Services Leading to the Decline of Moral Ethics

During the Tang and Song Dynasties, some temples made a living collecting land loans, while others survived on devotees' donations. Following the Ming and Qing Dynasties, Buddhist persecutions caused a large fall in income. Monastics were thus forced to conduct chanting and repentance services in the homes of devotees. Consequently, temples turned into chanting service centers or merely shrines receiving offerings for incense and candles.

That is not to say that chanting and repentance services are unacceptable, for they also represent means to help people through the stages of old age, illness and death. They are equally as important as teaching the Dharma. To benefit both the living and the deceased is also a way for Buddhism to contribute to the world.

Nonetheless, chanting and repentance services should not be regarded as a business. For some monastics, it was much easier to receive offerings by conducting chanting services than delivering Dharma lectures, which seldom inspired people to make offerings. The pursuit for profit thus caused certain monastics to neglect spiritual cultivation.

As the saying goes, "Being able to chant [an incense anthem], one will not be without food anywhere he goes." All monastics needed in order to make a living was the ability to chant, and it is certainly easier than being a missionary. However, a true missionary needs to do more than just being able to chant. Without being of service and contribution, how can you be valued by society?

Tantric Buddhism is not viewed as inappropriate either. Tibetan Buddhism already had its own doctrinal system, while Japanese Esoteric Buddhism also has its established tradition. On the other hand, Tantric Buddhism in China seemed less organized and focused on accepting offerings, ignoring Buddha's will by underlining mystical teachings. In particular, during the Yuan and Ming Dynasties, the royals neglected the importance of mind purification and turned the imperial palace into a place of Tantric practices that indulged in pleasures. The people imitated this behavior, halting the spread of righteous Dharma and led Buddhism further into decline.

6. Troubles Caused by Beliefs in Deities and Spirits

The Chinese revere spirits and immortals. Such beliefs are re-

Buddhaisawan Chapel: Life of the Buddha - Return from Trayastrimsa Heaven
THAILAND, Bangkok; Bangkok period (1782–present), dated 1782–1809;
Bangkok National Museum, Thailand

flected in many literary works that contain parables or reflections. For example, popular works of fiction such as *In Search of Gods*, *Extensive Records of the Taiping Era*, or *Strange Tales of Liao Zhai* all had the objective of admonishing people to do good. The Chinese have held to the belief that deities watch them from above.

The original purpose was one of restraint, making people fear the consequences of their wrongdoings. However, such emphasis resulted in people fearing gods and deities. So, to gain their blessings or have their own wishes fulfilled, people would slaughter animals as sacrifices. In other cases, some emphasized punishments that would follow bad deeds, such as falling into hell or karmic retributions. As a result, people came to fear Buddhism.

The notion of turning to gods and deities for answers is done out of the need to find mystical alternatives in resolving life's issues.

Although Buddhism accepts the existence of traditional deities or gods, they should be regarded as figures of belief or refuge. Since Buddhism follows the teachings of Sakyamuni Buddha, himself a human, and not a God; what he taught are teachings to help us better our lives.

Humanistic Buddhism values a happy and peaceful life, right livelihood, proper means of entertainment, compassion and loving-kindness, and mutual respect. Regretfully, Buddhists seldom advocate these. Intellectuals and the public still regard Buddhism as superstition, due to the faulty practices of fortune telling and divination erroneously attributed to it. Due to this reason, movements against superstitious beliefs also included Buddhism.

Truth is, not only does Buddhism dispense with superstition; it strives to eliminate it. In Buddhism, neither the practices of astronomical observation nor those of time calculation are practiced because each day can be a good day. In Buddhism, the practice of fengshui is not followed because with a peaceful mind, any place can be a good place. Buddhism advises people against blindly following superstitious beliefs and instead live a life of moral ethics and righteous faith. Should monastics not teach the Dharma in accord with life's ways, Buddhism would again be destined to decline. That is why all Buddhists must remain rational in this regard.

7. Distorted Views on Buddhism Caused by Heretics

"What eats into the lion's flesh are those bugs living on it." When Mara resorted to all means to sabotage the Buddha, the

Buddha nonetheless remained unmoved. Mara threatened him, "I shall dress like monastics but act otherwise by breaking all of your precepts." Upon hearing this, tears rolled down the Buddha's cheek. Before bugs are able to eat into flesh, first the flesh itself must be rotten. Internal corruption and dysfunction can be more damaging than external forces. Therefore, as monastics, we must ask ourselves, "Are we pious Buddhists? Do we all possess the right view and right understanding of the Dharma within ourselves?"

The development of Buddhism was always burdened by heretical disruptions. For example, the fall of Buddhism in India was mainly the result of interference by Hindus. Buddhists resorted to Hindu mantras and mystical beliefs to defy them, thereby losing ground both spiritually and literally.

They spread unrighteous thoughts in the name of Buddhism, and provoked unwholesome actions under the guise of cultivation. They sought to acquire money, profit, fame, and women under the pretext of religion. Even the government was powerless to stop such behavior. They deceived people through flaunting their supposed supernatural powers. They took advantage of people's weaknesses and misunderstandings in the pursuit of wealth and power. Such heresy at the expense of Buddhism should have been stopped. Yet, no Buddhists of righteous belief were able to do this. So how could Buddhism not have fallen?

8. Buddhism Replaced by Neo-Confucianism

Ever since Dong Zhongshu (董仲舒, 179–104 BCE) persuaded Emperor Wu of Han (漢武帝, 156-87 BCE) to "dismiss all schools of thoughts and revere only the Confucian," Confucianism was the mainstream belief in Chinese politics and culture. After Buddhism's transmission to China, it gradually harmonized with initially con-

flicting Confucian thoughts. Further integration with the philoso-
phies of Laozi and Zhuangzi resulted in the vast development of
Chinese Culture.

During the Tang Dynasty, Buddhism reached the peak of
its popularity in China, and saw the establishment of the Eight
Schools. Continuing onto the Song Dynasty, each of these schools
remained. Of note, the Chan School was especially popular among
the literati; almost all of them converted from Confucianism to
Chan Buddhism. For example, former self-proclaimed Confucian
thinkers and politicians such as Fu Bi (富弼 , 1004-1083), Fan
Zhongyan, Wang Anshi, Su Shi, and Su Che were all attracted
to Buddhist thought. A mindset that integrated this-worldly and
other-worldly thoughts was innovative and monastics were widely
sought after.

As a result, Zhou Dunyi (周敦頤 , 1017-1073), Cheng Hao
(程顥 , 1032-1085), and Cheng Yi (程頤 , 1033-1107) pioneered
Neo-Confucianism in an attempt to create a more rational and
secular form of Confucianism. While these intellectuals recognized
Chan Buddhist thoughts, they also criticized Chan and Buddhism
separately. For example, Ouyang Xiu's work *On Principles* was popular among those who opposed and critiqued Buddhism.

What possible reasons were there for Neo-Confucians to partial-
ly accept Buddhism yet at the same time partly reject it? Confucians
believed that Buddhism, as a foreign religion, couldn't compare with
the orthodoxy of Confucianism as mainstream Chinese culture.
The strong sense of duty in defending Confucianism was carried
by those from Mencius (孟子 , 372-289 BCE) to Hanyu, and then
onto generations of gentry and elites. Their prejudice towards
Buddhism as a foreign religion, and a sense of Confucian superior-
ity instigated the debate between Chinese and foreign cultures. The

insular interpretations of the Confucian perspective, coupled with a lack of understanding in Chan Buddhism meant they were looking at Buddhism from an extremely narrow viewpoint, and omitted much.

For example, Zhu Xi, a leading figure of Neo-Confucianism, remained acquainted with Buddhists and extensively studied the Buddhist sutras. His story is even recorded in the *Record of Lay Buddhists.* He had assimilated Sangha regulations and Chan Monastery rules into his Confucian Academy. In one way, Neo-Confucianism can be said to have been a branch of Buddhist thought. Conversely, Neo-Confucians, in essence, also strongly opposed Buddhism.

The main reason for the decline of Buddhism was the absence of leaders or paragons able to inherit and carry on the lineage. Remaining Buddhists were outnumbered by Neo-Confucians, who remained skeptical of Buddhist teachings. Their skepticism stemmed from the fact that the large corpus of Neo-Confucian text provided more agreeable answers to their investigations.

9. The Inevitable Influence of Western Culture

During the late Qing Dynasty, Westerners opened up the gate into China through use of force and canons. Missionary groups entered the country en masse. Hong Xiuquan, the self-proclaimed "Heavenly Lord," initiated the Taiping Heavenly Kingdom movement.

In 1850, Hong took advantage of the Chinese defeat in the Opium War. Fuelling people's hatred towards imperialism and their admiration for foreign religions, they started a war. Using the name of Jesus, they called upon people to join the Congregation of God-Worshippers and banned all faiths other than Christianity.

令太子射此鐵鼓太
子又言此弓弱更求
如是七弓將來師即
喚與太子便執七弓
以射一箭過七鐵鼓
時彼射師注白王言
太王太子自知射藝
以一箭力射過七鼓
閻浮提中无能等者
爾時白淨王聞此語
心大歡喜而自念
云何令我為作師耶
言我子聰明書論筭
藝四方人民未有知
者即勅太子及提婆
達多等五百童子又
復繁敲唱令國界大
子薩婆悉達却後七

Illustrated Manuscript of the Sutra of Cause and Effect in the Past and Present
Scroll 3 (detail); JAPAN; Nara period (710–794); Ink and color on paper;
26.4 x 1,036 cm; Jobon Rendaiji Temple, Kyoto, Japan

Everywhere they went, Buddhist, Daoist, and Ancestral temples were burnt and ruined. Statues and sutras were also destroyed. Not only did Chinese culture suffer greatly, any traditions respecting idols or ancestors were banned. Buddhism in particular, suffered greatly.

In 1953, when the Taiping Heavenly Kingdom occupied Nanjing, all other religions were forbidden. The Manchurian government lacked the power to resist. Buddhism, always advocating against force by promoting compassion and peace, was likewise powerless. Buddhism, already much weakened, was dealt another blow through an ominous absence of leadership.

10. The Intimidating Large Corpus of Buddhist Texts

A common reputation of Buddhism is that it is a religion that taught old ladies how to chant in order to be reborn in the Western

Pure Land, or that it has a large corpus of the Tripitaka divided into twelve canons containing countless terminologies and profound theories.

Without Buddhism, what would remain of Chinese culture? Buddhism has shaped everything, from our clothing, food, lifestyle, transportation, calligraphy, painting, music, dance, art, and architecture. Even the way we speak takes its roots from the Buddhist language. For example, "Are you having afflictions?" "Do you believe in cause and effect?" "Know of wholesome and unwholesome deeds." "Do you see the importance of developing affinity?" "This deed is meritorious." "Stillness is the same as movement." "Follow the conditions." 'Compassion.' Removal of the Buddhist elements would mean little vocabulary left in our speech. Chinese culture itself is Buddhist culture.

To ensure localization of Buddhism in the East, Buddhist mas-

Wutaishan Nanchan Temple Main Hall; CHINA, Shanxi, Xinzhou

ters made arduous attempts to translate Buddhist texts. Although editions of Buddhist canons from the Song, Yuan, Ming, and Qing Dynasties remain today, portions of these large corpuses of texts remain unedited and hard to read. The journey into the profound ocean of the Dharma has been rendered potentially more difficult due to the huge variety of titles and profundity of the teachings. Unlike Buddhism, there is only the Bible for Christians, and the Koran for Muslims. The more texts there are, the less one is willing to read.

In the past, Buddhist temples had no financial burdens owing to royal patronage. However, if monastics did not reach out to teach or spread the Dharma, in a way suited to the needs of the people, they gradually detached from the world. The situation was worsened by the absence of imperial protection during the Yuan, Ming, and Qing Dynasties. Any time an oppressive force fell upon Buddhism, it was ready to decline and fall.

In conclusion, the success of Buddhism in China can be attributed to its promotion of moral ethics through the teachings of the Five Precepts and Ten Wholesome Deeds. It, in turn, contributed to keeping order in society through the teachings of cause and effect, which rewards good and punishes evil. In fact, the Five Precepts can be regarded as equivalents to the Five Constant Virtues:

1. No killing equals benevolence
2. No stealing equals righteousness
3. No sexual misconduct equals propriety
4. No lying equals integrity
5. No intoxicants equals knowledge

Mathura: Standing Buddha; INDIA, Uttar Pradesh, Mathura;
circa 5th century; Commissioned by Yasadinna; Sandstone; H:
220 cm; Government Museum, Mathura, Uttar Pradesh, India

Furthermore, other Buddhist doctrines such as the Four Ways
of Embracing, Six Paramitas, Eightfold Noble Path, and Four
Universal Vows are teachings that have no equal in other religious
doctrines.

Many Humanistic Buddhist undertakings have been established
in service to society and benefit of the country. Of note, knowl-

edgeable Buddhist masters won the respect and support of kings and emperors. For catering to the needs of human minds as well as society, Humanistic Buddhism thus pushed the development of Buddhism to its pinnacle.

Regretfully, those who followed did not inherit these outstanding accomplishments and virtues. Many monastics were people who, having failed at a career or relationship, decided to escape to monastic life and simply live off Buddhism. The inherent qualities of these monastics were somewhat uneven. As a result, the humanistic quality of Buddhism gradually waned alongside Buddhism's decline.

Other than the above, internal disputes and opposition resulted from an emphasis on the division between schools and regions. Each school claimed preeminence and disapproved of the others. This led to the deterioration of Buddhism. It is similar to how scholars in Buddhist studies scrutinize and then judge Buddhism based on its flaws and mistakes. It is as if they believe their scholarly endeavors give them the legitimacy to do so. Under such circumstances, Buddhism can only but decline, and eventually end.

It is with mixed emotions and a feeling of inadequacy that I have methodically elaborated on the rise and fall of Buddhism over the two thousand years of its existence. Fortunately, Buddhism is now generally recognized and accepted in Mainland China. With the support and assistance of the Buddhist Association of China and the State Administration for Religious Affairs, the development of Humanistic Buddhism is successful and certain. I am filled with hope that Chinese Buddhism has a bright future ahead.

Chapter Five

Contemporary Development of Humanistic Buddhism

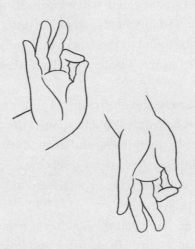

Summary of Chapter Five

India may be the birthplace of Buddhism, but Indian Buddhism has sadly waned. In contrast, the ascent of Humanistic Buddhism in China through active social participation has enabled Buddhism to spread globally. Its propagation worldwide has gained popularity and recognition.

In the past century, Master Taixu and Venerable Tzu Hang have advocated "Life Buddhism" and "Humanistic Buddhism," to affirm the link between Buddhism and everyday life. It is the same spirit Chan masters advocated when promoting "a day without work means a day without food." Also Master Huineng's saying, "Dharma can only be found in the world, and enlightenment cannot be attained away from it." These ideas have slowly gained prevalence.

The contemporary development of Humanistic Buddhism comprises five aspects: cultural publications, education, propagation societies, charitable activities, and internationalization. The influence of Buddhism lies in its doctrines; its true role is to offering spiritual guidance, ethics, social harmony and stability, and striving for world peace.

Particularly, the evolution of Buddhism resides within culture and education. That is why Humanistic Buddhism caters to needs of differing eras. Translation work and sutra printing, as well as publications in all mediums are used as contemporary instruments to continuously spread the Dharma. By offering education for monastics, devotees, and the public, Buddhists are better able to uphold the spirit of the Buddha and promote Humanistic Buddhism globally. Only through continuous progress, can there be new life for Buddhism. Only by holding to the Buddha's original intents can the Dharma truly be realized.

Contemporary Development of Humanistic Buddhism

Buddhism was founded in India and flourished in China. With the active propagation of Humanistic Buddhism in recent decades, Buddhism spread from Taiwan to all five continents of the world similarly to how Buddha journeyed across India to spread his teachings. Humanistic Buddhism has now taken root in different parts of the world.

In ancient times, numerous monastics from India and Western regions transmitted Buddhism to China by transporting abundant Buddhist texts via the Silk Road both on land and by the sea. The early editions of translated Buddhist texts from the Western regions also inspired monastics from China to travel westward to India in search of the Dharma. Among these nearly one thousand monastics were: Zhu Shixing (朱士行 , 203-282), Faxian (法顯 , 338-423), Xuanzang (玄奘 , 602-664), Yijing (義淨 , 635-713), and Dharmodgata. The texts brought back by these monastics conveyed to China the Buddha's thoughts of Humanistic Buddhism.

With regards to Chinese Buddhism's development, I had previously published an article, in 2001: "The Stages of Development of Chinese Buddhism" in the *Universal Gate Buddhist Journal*, dividing it into six stages:

1. **Qing, Han, Wei, and Jin eras:**
    The eastward spread of Buddhism through translation of texts
2. **Sui, Chen, Li and Tang eras:**
    Founding of the Eight Schools
3. **The Five Periods, Zhao and Song eras:**
    Competing positions of the Chan and Pure Land Schools

4. Yuan and Ming eras:
Royal patronage of the Esoteric tradition
5. Manchurian, Qing, and Republic of China eras:
Repentance services and worships period
6. 20th Century till present:
Humanistic Buddhism period

The particulars of each stage will not be further expounded here. To understand Humanistic Buddhism's contemporary development, this chapter details its propagation in the following five categories:

1. Cultural publications
2. Educational endeavors to nurture talents
3. Dharma propagation activities and organizations
4. Charitable undertakings to aid society
5. International propagation for the globalization of Dharma

1) Cultural Publications

In the Buddha's time, the Dharma was transmitted orally. Later, it was disseminated through the means of texts, art, sculptures, and paintings. In particular, texts played the most prevailing and influential role in the propagation of Dharma. Having elaborated briefly on the spread of Chinese Buddhism above, this section will focus on the revival of Buddhist culture through the efforts of Yang Renshan (楊仁山 , 1837-1911) from the late Qing and early Republic of China eras.

Recognized as the Father of Modern Buddhist Renaissance,

Yang Wenhui (楊文會, 1837-1911), courtesy name Renshan, dedicated his abode for the establishment of the Jinling Sutra Publishing House to produce and disseminate Buddhist sutras. Subsequently, the Tianjin Sutra Publishing House, Beijing Sutra Publishing House, and Yangzhou Tianning Temple Kunlin Sutra Publishing House were founded. Furthermore, publishing houses were also set up in locations such as the Fuzhou Gushan Yungquan Temple and Hanzhou Manao Temple.

Of import concerning the Jinling Sutra Publishing House is that, according to Zhao Puchu (趙樸初, 1907-2000), during the

Cultural Revolution, Premier Zhou Enlai (周恩來, 1898-1976) actually ordered the safeguard of Jinling to be top priority. To date, Jinling still continues to print and publish sutras. These publishing houses have played a vital role in the preservation, proofing, printing, and dissemination of Buddhist texts.

With regards to contemporary Buddhist publications, as early as the Guangxu period, Master Zongyang (宗仰, 1865-1921) was already publishing the *Pinjia Canon* in the Shanghai Hardoon Garden. Sadly, this publication was lost during the war. This dissemination of texts was sustained by the free distribution of books. For example, Master Yinguang's (印光, 1862-

y Free in the Sky; By Feng Yiyin

Haeinsa Temple: Printing Blocks of the Tripitaka Koreana
SOUTH KOREA, South Gyeongsang, Hapcheon;
Goryeo dynasty (918–1392), dated 1251; Wood

1940) *Selection of Works,* Master Hongyi (弘 一 , 1880-1942) and
Feng Zikai's (豐 子 愷 , 1898-1975) work on *Illustrations on Life
Protection,* Venerable Yuan Ying's (圓 瑛 , 1878-1953) *Complete
Collection of Venerable Yuan Ying,* and *The Xuyun Almanac* edited
by Cen Xuelu (岑 學 呂 , 1878-1959) from Guangdong. All these
works are prodigious contributions to the spread and development of
Humanistic Buddhism.

As Western philosophy began ascending in the East, the
exchange of thoughts kindled the publication of various Buddhist
publications. The earliest in Mainland China was the *Buddhist*

Studies Journal published by Di Baoxian (狄葆賢 , 1873-1939) and Pu Yicheng (濮一乘) in 1912, followed by Master Taixu's (太虛 , 1890-1947) *The Buddhist Monthly, Ocean Waves Magazine,* and *Awaken the Masses Weekly*; *Inner Learning* by the China Inner Studies Institute founded by Ouyang Jingwu (歐陽竟無 , 1871-1943) ; Venerable Rensan's *Dharma Waves,* and *The World Buddhist Lay Association Magazine*; and Kang Jiyao's (康寄遙 , 1880-1968) *Buddhistic Occasional, Great Hero Monthly, Prayer Magazine,* and Taixu's *Dharma Propagation Journal,* respectively exerting great influence in China. Other publications such as the *Buddhist Daily* in Shanghai, *Awakening the World News* in Beijing, and *Buddhist Paper* in Hankou were subsequently published.

Moreover, publications in the Southeast Asian region include: *Lamp in the Ocean of People Monthly* by Venerables Chi Chern (寄塵 , 1886-1938) and Tong Yi (通一) from Guanzhou Kaiyuan Temple, *Humanistic Buddhism Magazine* by Venerable Tzu Hang (慈航 , 1893-1954) in *Southeast Asia, Endless Light* by Venerable Zhu Mo (竺摩 , 1913-2002) in Macau, *Hong Kong Buddhism* by Venerable Kok Kwong (覺光 , 1919-2014), and *Inner Illumination* by Miao Fa Temple. These numerous Buddhist publications were of tremendous influence in the propagation of Humanistic Buddhism.

At that time, the inclination to Buddhist studies thrived, the most famous example being Ouyang Jingwu from the China Inner Studies Institute, and Han Qingjing (韓清淨 , 1884-1949) from the Three Times Association in Beijing. A variety of Buddhist dictionaries and books were published, such as:

- Ding Fubao (丁福保 , 1874-1952) *Dictionary of Buddhist Studies,* the first dictionary of Chinese Buddhism

- Liang Qichao (梁啟超 , 1873-1929), *Eighteen Papers on Buddhist Studies*, a pioneering work in Buddhist Studies Methodology
- Jiang Weiqiao (蔣維喬 , 1873-1958), *History of Chinese Buddhism*, a selected text by the Wuchang Buddhist College
- Wang Jitong (王季同 , 1875-1948), *Comparative Studies of Buddhism and Science*
- Lu Cheng (呂澂 , 1896-1989), *Methodology of Buddhist Studies*
- Tang Yongtong (湯用形 , 1893-1964), *History of Han, Wei, Eastern and Western Jin, and Northern and Southern Dynasty Buddhism*
- You Zhibiao (尢智表 , 1886-1948), *The Science of Buddhism*, and *Reports of Buddhist Studies by a Scientist*

These works of monastics and lay Buddhist intellectuals have empowered the philosophy of Humanistic Buddhism to blossom.

Later, when the Cultural Revolution ensued, elements of Buddhism and Chinese culture were utterly ruined. I clearly remember Yan Foon Gu (嚴寬祜 , 1924-2014) telling me that his Buddhist Publishing and Distribution Center was established, in Hong Kong, for the sole purpose of preserving texts salvaged from the flames of the Cultural Revolution. These texts were transported to Hong Kong and reissued for publication. Renamed the Hong Kong Buddhist Sutra Publishing Center, Mr. Yan willingly acquiesced any request to secure overseas Buddhist texts and instruments. Through his willingness to salvage Buddhist texts at any cost, Mr. Yan is as admirable a protector of the Dharma as Yang Renshan.

Amidst the Civil War, numerous Buddhist masters and intellectuals turned to Taiwan, Hong Kong, Singapore, and

Bodhedrum Magazine   *Human Life* Magazine

Malaysia to maintain their propagation efforts of Humanistic Buddhism, thus safeguarding Buddhist culture. To name but a few, in 1948, Venerable Tzu Hang came to Taiwan from Southeast Asia. The following year, Venerables Ta Hsing (大醒 , 1900-1952), Nan Ting (南亭 , 1900-1982), Dong Chu (東初 , 1907-1977), and Pai Sheng (白 聖 , 1904-1989) also arrived in Taiwan, followed by monastics from Hong Kong such as Venerables Tai Tsang (太 滄 , 1895-1968), Cheng Lien (證 蓮 , 1893-1967), Yin Shun (印 順 , 1906-2005), Yen Pei (演培 , 1917-1996), Tao An (道安 , 1907-1977), Jen Jun (仁俊 , 1919-2011), Hsu Ming (續明 , 1918-1966), and Ta Pen (大本).

1. Wide Circulation of Buddhist Publications at Rock-Bottom Prices

Concerning Buddhist publications in Taiwan, the initial recurrent publications were *Buddhism Taiwan*, and also *Ocean Waves Magazine* founded by Venerable Ta Hsing and inherited by Li Zikuan (李子寬 , 1882-1973). Established by Master Taixu, *Ocean Waves Magazine* was later reinstituted by Venerable Ta Tung (大同 , 1289-1370) under the new title *Awaken the Masses Weekly*, and later managed by Lin Ching-tung (林錦東 , 1924-1976) (also known as Venerable Chung Hsin 宗心). As for *Human Life Magazine*, founded by Venerable Tung Chu, I assisted as Editor-in-Chief for six years.

Others include:

- *Awakening Living Beings Magazine*, later retitled *Bodhedrum Magazine*, was founded by Li Bing-nan (李炳南 , 1891-1986) and Chu Fei (朱斐)
- *Chinese Buddhism*, founded by Venerable Pai Sheng
- *Buddhist Youth*, founded by Venerable Lien Hang (蓮航)
- *Awakening the World Periodical*, founded by Chang Shao-chi (張少齊), his son Chang Juo-hsu (張若虛), and myself as Editor-in-Chief. The magazine, later entrusted to me, continued for forty years, never an issue having been postponed. The periodical was later converted to the *Merit Times*, a daily newspaper.
- *Buddhism Today*, founded Venerable Kuang Tzu (廣慈)
- *Wisdom Torch*, founded by Chou Hsuan-te (周宣德 , 1899-1989) and Cheng Chen-huang (鄭振煌)
- *Lion's Roar* by Venerable Tao An

Journalists Chu Jing-zhou (朱鏡宙 , 1889-1985) and Chou Chun-hsi (周春熙) established the Taiwan Buddhist Text Circulation Center, not for profit, but to promote Buddhist culture. Popularly priced, Buddhist texts and books were widely circulated. Other devoted Buddhists such as Hsu Yen-tun (許炎墩), Tung Cheng-chi (董正之, 1910-1989), Zhou Bang-dao (周邦道, 1898-1991), Lee Heng-yue (李恆鉞, 1910-1998), Chen Hui-jian (陳慧劍, 1925-2001), Liu Guoxiang (劉國香), Chu Chiang-yuan (朱蔣元)and son Chu Chi-chang (朱其昌), Lee Shih-chieh (李世傑), Yue Chong-hui (樂崇輝), Li Tian-chun (李添春), and Tseng Pu-hsin (曾普信, 1902-1977) all contributed to Buddhist publications. Some edited magazines, others wrote books, and several established publishing houses to give voice to Buddhism, enabling both stability and continuity. As Buddhist publications and magazines have become diversified, I shall not elaborate on them further here.

2. Touring Taiwan to Promote the Tripitaka

Bookshops such as Zi You Book Shop in Keelung owned by Huang Kui (黃奎), Jui Cheng Bookshop in Taichung by Hsu Yen-tun (許炎墩), Nan Yi Book Shop in Tainan by Hsu Shao-tian (蘇紹典), and Ching Fang Book Shop in Kaohsiung by Lee Ching-yun (李慶雲) were all centers for the circulation of Buddhist writings. Layman Chang Shao-chi, a pious Buddhist, also established Chian Kang Book Shop to publish Buddhist books and duplicate the Tripitaka for circulation. Venerable Sheng Yin (聖印, 1930-1996), a student of mine at the Taiwan Buddhist Seminar in Hsinchu, established a Buddhist Artifacts Center in Taichung. Venerable Tung Chu similarly established the Chinese Buddhist Artifact Center in Peitou. All such locales greatly contributed to the enrichment of Buddhist artifacts.

The Sin Wen Feng Company, founded by Madam Sun Chang Ching-yang (孫張清揚 , 1913-1992), her son, Chang Shao-chi, as well as myself, was handed over in its entirety to Liu Hsiu-chiao (劉修橋) (Kao Pen-chao 高本釗). For decades, Sin Wen Feng has continued to publish Buddhist canons and books, assisting in the spread of Humanistic Buddhism.

In Taipei, executive government officials such as Chu Yung-kuang (屈映光 , 1881-1973), Zhao Heng-ti (趙恆惕 , 1880-1971), Ting Jiun-Sheng (丁俊生 , 1924-2010), Tsai Nien-sheng (蔡念生 , 1901-1992), and Chung Pai-yi (鍾伯毅 , 1880-1962), all Buddhists, co-initiated the Chunghwa Tripitaka Revision Association to produce the *Qisha Canon*. Alas, due to the lack of human and monetary resources, the project came to a halt after merely a few copies were published.

Revision and editing of the Buddhist canon is no simple matter. I had the opportunity to attend some of their meetings in Taipei. Once, I visited Tsai Nien-sheng, Assembly Representative of the R.O.C., at his home in Taichung. Seated behind stacks of objects that occupied his small Japanese style house, he carried out the task of proofreading, bared and perspiring on a summer day. The aspirations and vows of these great elders are truly admirable.

Speaking of the Tripitaka, under the patronage of Madam Sun Chang Ching-yang, Venerable Tung Chu initiated a duplication project of the Taisho Tripitaka brought to Taiwan from Japan by the Minister of Foreign Affairs—Yeh Kong-chao (葉公超 , 1904-1981). Later, he established a Tripitaka Reprinting Committee Tour directed by Venerable Nan Ting and led by Venerables Zhu Yun (煮雲 , 1919-1986), Kuang Tzu and myself. The tour was joined by youths from Yilan such as Tzu Hui (慈惠), Tzu Jung (慈容),

Tzu Lien (慈蓮), Tzu Fan (慈範), and Lin Sung-nien (林松年). Throughout this eighty-day tour, we managed to promote some hundred sets of the Tripitaka, and the minutiae of that tour were chronicled in "The Tripitaka Reprinting Committee Tour Diaries" penned by Venerable Tzu Hui.

3. Reader-Friendly Books on Buddhism to Assist in Greater Dissemination

Having never received a formal education, or ever been taught to write, I nevertheless was chiefly influenced by Hu Shi (胡適之 , 1891-1962) who said, "Writing is like talking, you write in exactly the same way as you talk." Hence, I abided by his instruction and promoted a vernacular Buddhist language movement by continually writing in a straightforward and easy-to-understand manner.

In the 1950's, I established the Buddhist Cultural Service Centers in Sanchongpu near Taipei and on Zhongshan 1st Rd. in Kaohsiung, offering novel ways to promote Humanistic Buddhism. Not only did we publish the first *Bilingual Buddhist Series: Sutras & Scriptures,* as well as *Doctrines of Buddhism,* we also introduced Buddhist literature such as *The Life of Su Dongpo, Buddhist Stories for Children, A Complete Collection of Stories on Buddhism, Buddhist Novels,* and so on. Particularly, publications of the *Sutra of the Month* series, reformatted and reedited, were essentially given away at below cost, a single dollar apiece, for the singular aim to establish Dharma affinities with readers.

These popular, vernacular, and accessible books on Buddhism were a resounding success. Consequently, Buddhist publications were widely circulated and were as prevalent as Amitabha Buddha and Guanyin Bodhisattva found in family homes.

During my early days in Taiwan, Venerable Hui Jui (慧瑞) from Hsinchu was advocating the publication of books on Buddhism, and thus my translation of *A Commentary on Avalokitesvara Bodhi-sattva's Universal Gate Chapter* was widely promoted. Moreover, my book *The Biography of Sakyamuni Buddha* was the first hardback Buddhist publication available, and has been distributed, in over one hundred editions, in Taiwan, Mainland China, Malaysia, Singapore, Japan, Korea, and Vietnam.

The youths who followed me from those days such as Venerable Hsin Ping (心平, 1938-1995), Tzu Chuang (慈莊), Tzu Hui, and Tzu Jung aided at these centers aimed at people from around the world. For example, Sung Fu-ting (宋復庭) from Brazil, Liao Cheng-hsiang (廖振祥) from Bangkok, Shen Chia-chen (沈家楨) from America, and Yan Foon Gu from Hong Kong have all been friends with us since.

Upon founding Fo Guang Shan, I listed "To propagate Dharma through culture" as one of the Four Objectives of Humanistic Buddhism. Ensuing the publications of *Awakening the World Periodical*, and *Universal Gate Magazine*, I founded the *Merit Times Newspaper* in 2000, which later was listed among Taiwan's Four Major Newspapers, bringing Buddhist beliefs of truth, virtue, and beauty to society and families on a daily basis.

As cultural publications in Taiwan continued to thrive, Buddhist magazines also became available in Mainland China one decade after the Cultural Revolution. For instance, *Dharma Voice Magazine*, founded by my good friend—Zhao Puchu, President of the Buddhist Association of China, is also a publication aimed at promoting Buddha's Humanistic Buddhism.

At present, the development of Buddhist culture in Mainland China is similarly seeing brighter days. On an annual basis, there are, on average, two hundred academic conferences held by institutes and temple organizations, each publishing a variety of journals, magazines and books.

Furthermore, *365 Days for Travelers: Wisdom from Chinese Literary and Buddhist Classics*, a conception fifty years in the making, was published by the Beijing People's Publishing House. My sixteen-volume narrative *Buddhist Affinities Across 100 Years*, published by the Shanghai Sanlian Publishing House, was widely read, according to what President Xi Jinping (習近平) said at our meeting, "I have read all your books." In addition, Citi Press Group also published my latest narration in 2015—*Hear Me Out: Messages from a Humble Monk.*

4. Catering to the Needs of the Time with Suitable Means of Propagation

All of the aforementioned publishing houses are eminent institutions under the Communist Party. In spite of Buddhism's devastation throughout the Cultural Revolution, the Party's contemporary leadership and committees are now expressing greater thoughtfulness towards Buddhism. Considerable appreciation goes to their vision and support for Chinese Buddhist culture. This greatly enhances our hope for the future of Buddhism and Chinese culture, as well as affirms our mutuality for the Cross-Strait propagation of Humanistic Buddhism. Of note, Venerable Xuecheng (學誠), current President of the Buddhist Association of China, now utilizes Internet technology and promulgates Buddhist culture in a dozen languages. The future of Humanistic

Buddhism is undoubtedly infinite.

In its efforts on cultural publications, Humanistic Buddhism caters to the need of different eras by developing from the earliest translations of Buddhist texts etched on wood or stone, to publications of magazines, journals, newspapers and digital mediums. The key lies in spreading information in the most suitable form in the given extant era. The books not only consist of fine printing quality and clothbound hardcovers, but their foci are of literary quality written in vernacular and easy-to-understand languages, as well as being pertinent to life. By instructing and enriching our minds, we are inspired to cultivate ourselves and reach out to help others. These are all expedient means through which Humanistic Buddhism holds true to the original intents of Buddha to cater to the aptitudes and needs of all living beings.

2) Educational Undertakings to Foster Talents

During the late Qing and early Republic of China periods, Hu Shi, Chen Duxiu (陳獨秀 , 1879-1942), Lu Xun (魯迅 , 1881-1936), Cai Yuanpei (蔡元培 , 1868-1940) were among those who initiated the May Fourth Movement in protest against Confucian religion and values, exalting science and aesthetics instead. Resultantly, Chinese culture, Confucianism, and Buddhism all suffered collateral damage. At that point, only intellectuals such as Zhang Taiyan (章 太 炎 , 1869-1936), Liang Qichao, Xiong Shili (熊 十 力 , 1885-1968), Lu Cheng (呂 澂 , 1896-1989), and Jiang Weiqiao were left, defenseless without the protection of both political and military authorities, and resulting in a lack of defenders of Buddhism. In such chaotic times, resistance was

Dinghui Temple, CHINA, Jiangsu, Zhenjiang

unfortunately rather weak.

At such a critical juncture, Master Yin Guang spoke up and proposed the remedy of the Three Abuses: 1) Abuse of access to full ordination, 2) abuse of the right to accept disciples, and 3) abuse of open monastery accommodation services, in order to revive monastic ethics. Concurrently, Master Taixu also proposed the Three Major Buddhist Reforms: 1) reform of Buddhist asset management, 2) reform of Buddhist systems, and 3) reform of Buddhist teachings. He published the article: "On Cleaning Up the Sangha System" and advocated *Rensheng* (Life) Buddhism as a way of Buddhist reform. Under his influence, Buddhists suddenly realized the need to revitalize Buddhism by propagating Humanistic Buddhism to remain true to the Buddha's original intents. Consequently, education and talent cultivation in Buddhism began to thrive.

The earliest Buddhist College in the Twentieth Century was the Monastic College founded, in 1906, by Venerable Wen Xi (文希) in Yangzhou Tianning Temple. Later, when Yang Wenhui picked up a copy of the *Shurangama Sutra* at a bookstall, he declared, "An encounter with the *Shurangama Sutra* has purged my willingness

to touch the world's vulgar works." Having developed such faith in Buddhism, Yang hence relinquished his home residence for the establishment of the Jinling Sutra Publishing House, Jetavana Vihara, and Buddhist Studies Association. Simultaneously, he promoted various cultural and education endeavors, which fostered paragons such as Master Taixu, Ouyang Jingwu, Venerable Ren Shan, and Mei Guangxi (梅光羲 , 1880-1947).

Successively, institutions such as the Huayan University founded by Venerable Yue Xia (月霞 , 1858-1917) in Shanghai Hardoon Garden, Guan Zong School founded by Venerable Di Xian (諦　閑 , 1858-1932) from the Tiantai School, China Inner Studies Institute, Wuchang Buddhist College, Minnan Buddhist College, Bolin Doctrinal Institute, Chongqing Han and Tibetan Doctrinal Institute, Lingdong Buddhist College, Jinling Buddhist College, Jiaoshan Buddhist College, Qixiashan Vinaya College, Pilu Buddhist College, Yufo Temple Shanghai Buddhist College, Fazang Buddhist College, Shanghai Jingan Temple Buddhist College and Huanan Buddhist College were established across the nation.

Rapidly, the Yogacara, Tiantai, Huayan and Pure Land Schools, as well as monasteries and meditation halls blossomed.

Particularly, Buddhist colleges in Wuchang, Minnan, and the China Inner Studies Institute were quite outstanding. Elites who graduated from there include: Venerables Hui Jue (會覺), Fa Fang (法舫 , 1904-1951), Fa Zun (法尊 , 1902-1980), Zhi Feng (芝峰 , 1901-1971), Ta Hsing, Tzu Hang, Wei Fang (葦舫), Mo Ru (默如 , 1905-1991), Yin Shun, and Ju Zan (巨贊 , 1908-1984), all eloquent speakers and prolific writers. Likewise, the lineups of teachers at these Buddhist colleges were also exceptional: Liang Qichao, Liang Shuming (梁漱溟 , 1893-1988), Tang Dayuan (唐大圓 , 1885-1941), Zhang Husheng (張化聲 , 1933-2013), Tang Yongtong (湯用彤 , 1893-1964), Xiong Shili (熊十力 , 1885-1968), Jiang Weiqiao, and Huang Canhua (黃懺華 , 1890-1977). Each and every one exerted remarkable influence on the revival of Buddhism.

To promote the globalization of Buddhism, Master Taixu founded the World Buddhist Studies Center in Wuchang, offering Buddhist studies courses in Sanskrit, Chinese, Pali, and Tibetan. He also dispatched monastics study abroad in Japan, Tibet, India, and Sri Lanka. Among them were Venerables Fa Fang, Fa Zun (法尊 , 1902-1980), Zhi Feng, Ta Hsing, and Ta Yong (大勇 , 1893-1929). By promoting Buddhist education to revive Humanistic Buddhism, we have thus met one of Buddha's original intents.

1. Rise of Buddhist-Affiliated Educational Undertakings in Post-Republic of China

In those times, Buddhism was subject to secessionist warlord regimes, typified by pious Christian Feng Yuxiang's (馮玉祥 ,

1882-1948) persecution of Buddhism across China. Fortunately, Master Taixu was good friends with Chiang Kai-shek (蔣介石 , 1887-1975), and was once invited to speak of the *Heart Sutra* to the KMT government.

As Buddhism experienced the annexation of temple properties for conversion into schools, Chiang Kai-shek issued the following orders:

1. Righteously practicing monastics Buddhists are to be protected.
2. Educated intellectual monastics are to be spared.
3. Temple grounds are to remain solemn and pure, illegitimate monastics or Buddhists are not to be permitted from posts such as abbots or managers of the temple. In addition, any Buddhist undertaking that is of benefit to social welfare is to be safeguarded.

As stated by Master Daoan: "The endeavors of Dharma cannot prevail without sovereign benefaction." Some of the KMT's senior statesmen such as Dai Jitao (戴季陶 , 1891-1949), Zhang Ji (張繼), Zhou Lu (鄒 魯 , 1885-1994), Ju Zheng (居 正 , 1876-1951), Yu Youren (于右任 , 1879-1964), and Qu Yingguang (屈映光 , 1883-1973) were Buddhists and proffered at least some protection for Buddhism in times of turmoil.

Sadly, even heroes such as Chiang Kai-shek fall for beauty. After marrying Soong May-ling (宋美齡 , 1897-2003), he converted to Christianity, and Buddhism's connection with him was no more. At such a chaotic time, Buddhism was fortunately able to survive under the Christian philosophy of freedom of belief, which is surely a common ground for all religious followers in the world.

The year the Japanese declared unconditional surrender, I was studying at Jiaoshan Buddhist College. Buddhists in the Jiangsu and Jinghu region were ecstatic at hearing the news. Gradually, lay Buddhists with a passion for Buddhism, and Triple Gem refuge takers grew in numbers, bringing forth prosperity for Humanistic Buddhism.

Venerable Abbot Xue Fang (雪煩 , 1909-1994) from Dinghui Temple undertook the restoration of Jiaoshan Buddhist College. Teachers were busy teaching and publishing the *Middle Stream Monthly*. Each month, we students were asked to assist in packaging and posting the magazine. Once done, our teachers would give each of us each a copy of the magazine, which was extremely rewarding for the day's work.

During that time, Buddhist-affiliated primary and junior high schools prospered. In order to commemorate Master Zong Yang, my master—Venerable Master Zhi Kai (志開 , 1911-1979) founded Zong Yang Junior High School at Qixishan Monastery, and also Da Xiong Junior High School at Nanjing Wofo Temple. Likewise, Venerable Jue Ming (覺 民) founded Pu De Junior High School at Pude Temple in Yuhuatai. There were also Chaofeng Temple Primary School and Fu Shan Tang Primary School in Zhenjiang. Jiaoshan alone founded three gratis primary schools.

I was very fortunate to be brought back to my ancestral temple—Yixing Dajue Temple by my master upon leaving Jiaoshan, and given the position of principal at the Paita Primary School. Although bereft of formal training as a teacher, the experience gained there was invaluable. In those days, hundreds of primary and secondary schools were under the charitable care of Buddhist organizations. I was yet hopeful that we could go on to establish universities, but that dream was cut short by the ongoing wars.

As I traveled to different places, often I came across primary school students who bowed and addressed me as "Venerable." When asked why they did so, their reply was, "Our teachers opened schools for us to learn. They never ask for any money. Our teacher is a good person; he is a Buddhist monk. So we know that all Buddhist monks in this world are good people, just like our teacher." From this, the prosperity of Buddhist education during the Republic of China period can clearly be felt.

It was a pity that the peace long yearned for by the people was fleeting. In no time, the Civil War and Cultural Revolution broke out. Added with the passing away of Master Taixu in 1947, Buddhists were suddenly without a leader. The Humanistic Buddhist movement in Mainland China thus came to a halt.

On the topic of Buddhist monastic education in Taiwan, it all began in 1948 with Venerable Master Miao Guo (妙果 , 1884-1963) from the Chungli Yuan Guang Temple. He was the one who invited Venerable Tzu Hang to Taiwan from Southeast Asia to establish the Taiwan Buddhist College. This was followed by the Taiwan Buddhist Seminar founded by Venerable Ta Hsing at Ling Ying Temple near Chingtsao Lake, Hsinchu. Both Venerable Yen Pei and I served as Deans at the Seminar.

Subsequently, Venerable Pai Sheng (白聖 , 1904-1989) founded the Chinese Buddhist Tripitaka College in Taipei, Venerable Sheng Yin (聖印 , 1930-1996) founded the Tzu Ming Buddhist College in Taichung, Venerable Miao Ran (妙然 , 1915-1997) founded Fa Yun Buddhist College in Miaoli, Venerable Yin Shun founded the Fu Yan Buddhist Institute, and Venerable Nan Ting founded the Hua-yen Buddhist College in Taipei. During those days, *Collection of Works by Master Taixu* was the indispensable textbook for students.

Sadly, many of these Buddhist colleges closed due to lack of students, teachers, funds, or combination thereof. Moreover, since graduates were unable to pursue a career out of their studies, these colleges were thus short-lived.

2. Settling in Yilan, a Place for Buddhist Youths

Having vowed never to be a Buddhist monk dependent on Buddhism, besides writing and lecturing, I began actively recruiting youths in Yilan starting from 1953. Subsequently, the Dharma propagation team, Buddhist Youth Choir, youth group, children's class and Sunday classes were established. Venerables Hsin Ping, Tzu Hui, Tzu Jung, Tzu Chia (慈嘉), Hsiao Pi-hsia (蕭碧霞), Lin Ching-zhi (林清志), Chen Hsiu-ping (陳修平), Chang Zhao (張肇), and Lin Wen-hsiung (林文雄) were amongst those youths.

At the same time, I also established the Guang Hua Tuition Center, the first government sanctioned Buddhist-affiliated education institute. Among the students was Professor Cheng Shyr-yen (鄭 石 岩), former standing member of the Ministry of Education's Student Affairs Committee. Venerables Tzu Hui and Tzu Jung both served as principal of Tzu Ai Kindergarten, the first Buddhist-founded kindergarten. Current Executive Deputy Abbot of Fo Guang Shan Monastery—Venerable Hui Chuan (慧傳) was one of the children attending. If deprived of education, how could we have fostered talents to propagate Humanistic Buddhism?

Youths are fundamental to the development of Humanistic Buddhism. Being aware of this, many have come together to promote Buddhist education. Particularly, classes at Fo Guang Shan Tsung-Lin University have continued for over fifty years, nurturing over

Tzu Ai Kindergarten

five thousand graduates, which I believe is a record in the history of Buddhism. Thus far, Venerables Tao Kuan (道觀) in Chiayi, Pu Hui (普暉), Hui Che (慧哲), and Chen Fang (真芳) in Taichung, Chen Wu (真悟) in Toufen, Hsing Ying (性瀅) and Wu Cheng (悟證) in Hsinchu, and Ta Ying (達瑩) in Hualien were all students at Tsung-Lin.

3. Talents are Essential to the Journey of Revitalization

Other than the Buddhist College, Fo Guang Shan has also organized Summer Camps for College Students. Many former participants are now paragons exerting tremendous influence in the society of their respective countries. For instance, Dr. Chen

Chao-long (陳肇隆), Honorary President of Kaohsiung Chang Gung Memorial Hospital, acknowledged as the father of liver transplant in Asia; Dr. Lin Fang-yu (林芳郁 , 1950-), president of Taipei Veterans General Hospital; practicing doctors in America such as Dr. Shen Jen-yee (沈仁義), Dr. Cheng Chao-yang (鄭朝洋), and Dr. Lee Steve J.H. (李錦興); and also practicing physicians in Japan such as Dr. Fukuhara Shingen (福原信玄) and Dr. Lin Ning-feng (林寧峰), formerly president of BLIA, Tokyo Chapter.

Other youths include: Chao Tsui-hui (趙翠慧), currently President of BLIA Chunghwa Northern Region Association; Hsueh Cheng-zhi (薛正直), Chairperson of KMT Yunlin Region Party; Honorary Professor Lu Wei-ming (呂維明) of National Taiwan University Department of Chemical Engineering; Chu Chao-chi (朱朝基), the young man who donated the Maitreya Buddha statue since enshrined at the Mountain Gate of FGS; Chen Ming-ji (陳明吉), the young artist who sculpted the Triple Gem Buddhas inside the FGS Main Shrine, later becaming a Kaohsiung City councilor. Furthermore, Venerable Chao-hwei (昭慧) from the Hongshi Buddhist College, and even Venerable Yi Kong (依空), Executive Board member of University of the West were both participants at the summer camps. In view of the talents discovered across the world, how can we not be hopeful for the revival of Humanistic Buddhism?

Besides monastic education in the Buddhist College, social education promoted by Buddhists began as early as the period of Japanese occupation. For example, Tainan Kuang Hua High School, Taibei High School in Taipei, Tzu Hang High School founded by the Inner Court of Maitreya Bodhisattva, and also Chih-Kwang Senior High School founded by Venerables Wu Yi (悟一 , 1922-2003), Nan Ting and myself.

Toshodaiji Temple: Master Jianzhen's Journey to Japan - Scroll 1 (section 1)
JAPAN, Nara; Kamakura period (1185–1333), dated 1298; By Rengyo;
Ink and color on paper; H: 37.3 cm

The propagation of Humanistic Buddhism requires us to proactively reach out to serve people and value education. That is why Fo Guang Shan founded Pu-Men Senior High School in 1977, and subsequently founded Jun Tou Primary and Secondary School in Nantou, as well as Jun Yi Primary and Secondary School in Taitung. In light of the need for tertiary education, in 1990, Fo Guang Shan founded University of the West (formerly Hsi Lai University), the first Chinese Buddhist-affiliated tertiary institute in the West. This was followed by Nanhua University in Chiayi, Fo Guang University in Yilan, Nan Tien Institute in Australia, and Guang Ming College in Philippines, a total of five universities.

Presently, Buddhist-founded education institutes in Taiwan also include Huafan University founded by Venerable Hsiao Yun (曉雲 , 1912-2004), Hsuan Chuang University founded by the Buddhist

Association of the Republic of China, Dharma Drum Institute of Liberal Arts founded by Venerable Sheng Yen (聖嚴 , 1931-2009), and also Tzu Chi University in Hualien. Moreover, there are also Buddhist-founded primary and secondary schools, as well as Chu Hai College in Hong Kong, and Singapore. These are tangible deeds by Humanistic Buddhists embodying the Buddha's original intents.

Nevertheless, it is insufficient to merely rely on these institutions in Hong Kong, Singapore, and Taiwan. If the Mainland could embrace Buddhism for the establishment of universities, it would greatly enhance the growth of country and society. It is hoped the vast population of Mainland China could also benefit from Buddhist-founded schools, contributing to the nation's duty of fostering talents and patriotic missionaries. Ultimately, the entire world will benefit.

In order to commemorate Master Jian Zhen's (鑑真 , 688-763) Dharma propagation works in Japan, Zhao Puchu, former president of the Buddhist Association of China collaborated with the Bureau of Religious Affairs, under the State Council, in the hopes of establishing Jian Zhen University at Yangzhou Daming Temple. In support, Fo Guang Shan even donated Jian Zhen Library. Unfortunately, when Zhao passed away, the project was not pursued any further, a true pity.

For the revival of Chinese Buddhism to be possible, Buddhists must actively interact with both society and people. They must do so while holding true to the Buddha's original intents by contributing to the wellbeing of the people, broadly developing good affinities, and establishing education institutes at all levels of schooling. This is the only way to revive Buddhism.

Yuan Tung Temple: Great Hero Hall; TAIWAN, New Taipei City

3) Dharma Propagation Activities and Organizations

In 1912, after the founding of the Republic of China, although works for New Buddhism appeared promising under the leadership of Masters Jichan (寄禪 , 1852-1912) and Taixu, opposition was nonetheless persistent. Internally, there was the obstinate dominance of Zhejiang monastic conservatives and authoritative lay monarchs, whilst externally featured the separatist military regime, temple seizures by the army, domestic conflicts, and obligatory conversion of temple properties into schools.

To ensure organizational Buddhist reform as well as effective resistance to external oppressions, Master Taixu and Venerable Ren Shan founded, in 1912, the Buddhist Progress Society at the Jetevana Vihara in Nanjing. They held a preparatory meeting at Jinshan Temple. However, due to overly hostile remarks made by

Venerable Ren Shan, the Jinshan Confrontation Incident occurred. As a result, the conception of the Buddhist Progress Society came to no avail.

That same year, Venerable Jingan (敬安 , 1851-1912) (also known as Jichan the Eight Fingered Ascetic) united monastic elders in the Jiangsu and Zhejiang area, along with Venerable Daojie (道 階 , 1870-1934) from Beijing Fayuan Temple, to establish the Chunghua Buddhist Association at Shanghai Jingan Temple. In 1912, the inauguration ceremony took place at Shanghai Liuyun Temple, which was attended by over one hundred monastic representatives from all seventeen provinces including Venerables Yuan Ying, Di Xian, and Taixu. Unanimously, Venerable Jingan was elected President of the first national Buddhist association in history. The association was later renamed the Buddhist Association of China, today the most authoritative Buddhist organization in Mainland China. Subsequently, Buddhist societies, centers of study, and medical societies were established with vocations of publication, education, and charity to propagate Buddhism back into society.

As the Buddhist Association of China carried on, confrontations between Venerable Taixu and Venerable Yuan Ying, once friends, return to mind. With Master Taixu on the side of Sangha reform opposing Venerable Yuan Ying vying for the Jiangsu and Zhejiang region monastic conservatives, as well as the dissension and discord amongst their respective disciples; these two monastics once like brothers sharing similar values went their separate ways.

At that time, Master Taixu and Chiang Kai-shek shared a close friendship. Whenever Buddhism faced persecution, such as the compulsory conversion of Buddhist property into schools instigated twice by Tai Shuangqiu (邰 爽 秋 , 1897-1976) from Central University, the conservatives sought Master Taixu to consider contingency plans. Ostensibly united, once these persecutions alleviated, they would alienate Master Taixu anew in order to protect their power and wealth. They opposed Master Taixu's proposals for: 1) reform of Buddhist asset management, 2) reform of Buddhist systems, and 3) reform of Buddhist teachings, resorting to any means in hindering the development of Humanistic Buddhism. Not only were Master Taixu and his "New Buddhism" advocates despondent, even the Nationalist government found their behavior unacceptable.

Consequently, in 1945, following victory against the Japanese, Chiang Kai-shek issued an order for Master Taixu to reinstate the Buddhist Association of China by establishing a Chinese Buddhist Reform Committee, whose members included: Taixu, Master Changkya (章嘉 , 1890-1957), Xuyun, Yuan Ying, Chang Yuan (昌圓 , 1879-1943), Quan Lang (全朗) and Li Zikuan (李子寬 , 1882-1973). Among them, Taixu, Changkya, and Li Zikuan were appointed committee executives. Subsequently, in 1946, the committee organized a Buddhist Association of China Committee Training Seminar at Jiaoshan Buddhist College. The program was the charge of our teacher, Venerable Zhifeng, and thus I was fortunate to be involved in the program.

1. Lifetime Dedication to the Propagation of Buddhism

As Master Taixu spoke quietly in a heavy Zhejiang accent, I honestly did not understand much of his speeches in the training seminar. The only part that still echoes in my mind is: "We must do it for Buddhism! We must do it for Buddhism!"

One day, I unwittingly crossed paths with Master Taixu, I stepped aside and joined my palms respectfully. Likewise he stopped, looked at me, and then said, "Good, good, good." Though the meeting was brief, his simple words of 'good' and "for Buddhism" left a tremendous influence on my endeavors in propagating Humanistic Buddhism.

Sadly, Master Taixu's health deteriorated due to overwork and he passed away, in 1947, aged fifty-eight. That same year, the Buddhist Association of China held its first national General Conference in Nanjing, attended by the directors of each province as well as the Mongolian and Tibet regions. At the Conference, Master Changkya was elected Director-General of the Association. However, as the Civil War broke out, the Association was relocated to Taiwan with the Republic of China government, and thus embarked on a different journey.

Venerable Tung Chu also brought the Association's sign to Taiwan. Madam Sun Chang Ching-yang's offer of ten million old Taiwan dollars, along with Li Zi-kuan's five million old Taiwan dollars, were used to buy Taipei Shandao Temple and its conversion into the headquarters for *Ocean Waves Magazine* and the Buddhist Association of China—Taipei Office.

At the election of the second Board, Master Changkya continued as Director-General, along with nine executive directors: Changkya, Pai Sheng, Sun Hsin-yuan (孫心源), Hsing Yun (星雲 , 1927-), Chang Ching-yang, Chao Heng-ti, Wu Chung-hsing (吳仲行 , 1898-1973), and Lobsang Yeshi (羅桑益西 , 1912-1981). In protest of elders such as Nan Ting, Tzu Hang and Tung Chu not being selected, added to my youth and difference of opinion with the leader; I wrote a letter to the Association declining the position. For this I was criticized as ignorant and ungrateful.

In a later re-election, Venerable Pai Sheng gained more votes than Li Zi-kuan and was elected Director-General. He later held onto the position for forty years, managing the Association through autocracy and turning it into a one-man Buddhist Association, excluding a majority of Buddhists. This restricted the potential of the Buddhist Association of the Republic of China, and hindered the revitalization of Humanistic Buddhism, which was truly a pity.

As a result, Buddhist leaders in Taiwan had no choice but to depend on their own power and faith to continue propagating Humanistic Buddhism. For example, Lee Bing-nan's lay Buddhists, Venerable Pai Sheng's precept conferral, Venerable Yin Shun's scholarship, Venerable Nan Ting's Dharma lectures, and Venerable Tzu Hang's young monastics began promoting young Buddhist movements, Dharma propagation on radio and television, precept conferral, and Buddhist chanting associations in Taiwan. Gradually, Humanistic Buddhism retraced its roots back to Buddha's original intents.

i. Buddhist Youth Movement

Buddhist youth movements began with Chou Husan-te, who established Buddhist societies in universities. Being aware of Buddhism's need for youth, and youth's need for Buddhism, between 1953 and 1954, I already considered initiating a Buddhist youth movement. When the opportunity arose, I invited a dozen youths such as Wang Shang-yi, Wu Yi, and Chang Shang-te from National Taiwan University and other schools to Shandao Temple.

At the meeting, these youths decided to gather a group of, at most, eighty young adults at Yuan Tong Temple in the Chunghe Township of Taipei County for an excursion, a temple visit and activities. However, Venerable Wu Yi promptly cautioned me, "Next time please don't bring this many young adults to Shandao Temple again, because we cannot afford the expenses." I became quite anxious, for without a base in Taipei, I would only be able to meet these youths on the street.

Just then, I came across Chou Husan-te, and asked him: "Mr. Chou, these young adults will meet at Yuan Tong Temple in Chunghe this Sunday, and as I already have prior commitments, would you be able to guide them?" Mr. Chou happily obliged, and so took the matter of university student activities into his own hands.

Other than the University Student Buddhist Foundation from the early days, Venerable Nan Ting also contributed to the Buddhist youth movement. He convinced Chan Le-wu (詹勵吾 , 1904-1982) from Canada to sell his four-story house on Chongqing South Road and contribute the money towards University Student Scholarships, which later became the Torch of Wisdom Association—Presently the *Torch of Wisdom Monthly.*

With Chan Le-wu's sponsorship, Chou Husan-te established the Torch of Wisdom Association and inspired youths to write, as well as gave away free books on Buddhism. For example, he printed a few hundred thousand copies of Lee Heng-yue's *Introduction to Modern Day Intellectuals* and gave them to youths for free, emboldening them to write reflections on the book for rewards of scholarships. Starting in 1957, he established Buddhist societies in various universities such as National Taiwan University's Sunrise Buddhist Studies, Normal University's Jhong-Dao Club, Chengchi University's Oriental Culture Society, and Chung Hsing University's Wisdom Ocean Society. These would have been impossible without the support of lay elders assuming teaching positions within the universities such as Zhou Bang-dao, Lee Bing-nan, Chou Hsuan-te, and Chan Le-wu.

As martial law was not yet rescinded, the China Youth Corps was the only organization with permission to organize youth events. I was fortunate to befriend Sung Shih-hsuan (宋時選 , 1922-2010), Executive Officer of the China Youth Corps, and also one of Chiang Ching-kuo's (蔣經國 , 1910-1988) most trusted men. Upon hearing my proposal for a Chan Summer Camp, he happily agreed, "That's a very good idea!" As a result, in 1969, I began organizing Buddhist Youth Summer Camps at Fo Guang Shan.

To ensure smooth management of the summer camp, I borrowed a few China Youth Corp flags with the help of Zhang Pei-geng (張培耕), then committee member at the Kaohsiung China Youth Corps, and erected them outside Fo Guang Shan. This exempted us from government interference, and the camp was thus problem free. As the Corps was under Chiang Ching-kuo's leadership, the flags meant his patronage, guaranteeing our freedom to do anything. Consequently, through the camps, outstanding Buddhist youths such as Venerable Yi Kung, Venerable Chao Hwei, Hsueh Cheng-chih, Ku Ching-mei (古清美)and You Huey-jen (尤惠貞) were nurtured.

In the summer that followed, though we only offered one hundred vacancies for college students for the two-week Buddhist education experience, we were astounded to receive over six hundred applications from over forty colleges and universities. Other than extending into one extra batch, we had to purchase extra necessities. As this was during the time of Fo Guang Shan's founding, we had limited budget and resources; therefore Zhang Pei-geng liaised with the army to borrow over a thousand blankets, and also thirty army trucks to help transport these youths to excursion sites, saving me a large sum of expenses. At the end of these camps, one hundred and eight youths bade to take refuge to become formal Buddhists.

It can be said that other than Chou Hsuan-te's Torch of Wisdom Society, Fo Guang Shan's Buddhist Youth Summer Camp, Lee Bing-nan's Minlun Society, and Venerable Chan Yun's (懺 雲 , 1915-2009) Fast and Precept Association were also among the Buddhist youth movements that successfully attracted young people to Buddhism. Though most were not financially moneyed, all were passionately and actively propagating Humanistic Buddhism to the youth.

ii. Radio and Television Broadcasts

In the 1950's, radio was the public's main source of information and knowledge, therefore Venerable Nan Ting from the Huayan Lotus Association and lay Buddhist Chao Mao-lin (趙茂林) dedicated their efforts to propagating the Dharma on the radio for decades uninterrupted.

Wishing to do likewise, I began writing *The Biography of Sakyamuni Buddha*, often pulling all-nighters solely to produce enough scripts for all four participating radio stations—BCC, Ming Pen, Ming Sheng, Minelectro Radio, and Yunlin CBC. Subsequently, Venerable Tzu Hui, Tzu Jung and others also began hosting these radio programs. The power of the media began to rise, allowing Humanistic Buddhism that holds true to the original intents of Buddha to be heard throughout Taiwan.

There is a very touching story about Lee Yu (李玉), host of the "Buddhist Voice" Program on the *Biography of Sakyamuni Buddha* at Yunlin CBC radio station. One of my disciples was an

Tongdosa Temple Great Hero Hall
SOUTH KOREA, South Gyeongsang, Yangsan

elderly bhiksuni diagnosed with terminal cancer. When she sought advice for ways to face death, I said to her, "As a monastic, all you need is to focus on what you can do for Buddhism, and pay no attention to matters of life and death." Thus, she began raising funds for the radio program, encouraging people to contribute five dollars. As a result, she managed to raise a thousand dollars for the radio station, enabling Lee Yu's station to sustain for many more years. Miraculously, this bhiksuni's cancer disappeared without any treatment.

There is a saying, "Imagine if classrooms were movie theatres." This makes ample sense to me, for when children come by inept teachers in the classroom, their time in class would be as unbearable as prison, but the situation can be swiftly improved by the use of movies.

Hence Fo Guang Shan, following the use of radio, began to propagate the Dharma via movie and television. It began with *The Biography of Sakyamuni Buddha* in the Jin Guo Theatre, with a director by the name of Liang who scripted overly sensual scenes between Siddhartha and Yasodhara. As consultant to the movie, I objected the idea, but was deemed by the director as overly backward. Therefore I withdrew from the project. After the movie was shown, some Buddhists saw my name listed as consultant to the movie, and came to stir up trouble at our Sanchong Buddhist Cultural Service Center out of protest.

In 1962, Taiwan's first television station—Taiwan Television Enterprise (TTV) was born. The daily broadcasts consisted mostly of programs produced by Christian organizations or the Catholic Kuangchi Program Service. Buddhism was excluded from these opportunities till 1979, when a television producer named Pai Hou-yuan (白厚元), a Muslim, proposed a daily half-hour Buddhist program on TTV priced at one hundred and twenty thousand dollars per episode. This truly was an impossible price for me.

Yet, for the propagation of Buddhism, I was willing to exhaust all resources to produce the first television program "Nectar" which aired for twenty-four minutes each time. This event was advertised on Central Daily News with the following announcement,

As of September 4th, 1949, the Buddhist program—"Nectar" will air on TTV every Wednesday evening from 7:00 to 7:30pm.

However, upon seeing this advertisement, Madame Chiang Kai-shek (Soong Mei-ling) (宋美齡 , 1897-2003) immediately forbade the program from airing. Not even Hau Pei-tsun (郝柏村) or

Chiang Wei-kuo (蔣緯國 , 1916-1997) could dissuade her. Apoplectic, I remonstrated to TTV General Manager Liang Hsiao-huang (梁孝煌 , 1914-2014), who explained that it was my three-minute appearance on the show that resulted in the ban.

"I am not preaching Buddhism. It is merely the promotion of a proper understanding of the Ullambana Festival," I protested.

"Monastics are not permitted to appear on television," said Liang.

"Aren't there characters of Buddhist monks on your drama shows?" I asked.

"Those are not real monks, so it's acceptable," replied Liang.

Without a choice, I was forced to remove those three minutes, leaving twenty-one minutes remaining in the show.

On another occasion, a journalist from Central Daily News informed me that news about Venerable Tzu Hang's postmortem body relic would be banned if Madam Chiang were in Taiwan, but since she left for the United States, they were able to publish a full page report. Madam Chiang's Christian faith essentially restricted any Buddhist program from airing on television, but I remained valiant for the sake of the Dharma, and continued to contest for Buddhist rights.

It was no simple task to have programs airing on all three prevailing television stations, each lasting the usual three months of a given season. Artists or programs were exclusive to specific stations at that time, meaning that they could not appear on other stations. Thus it was quite the feat being able to appear on all three.

Some time later, in 1980, renowned television producer Chou Chih-min (周志敏) assisted in making the second Buddhist program—"Gate of Faith," which aired on CTV, a popular program watched by nearly two million viewers each time. This was possible ensuing the passing of Chiang Kai-shek in 1975, after which Chiang Soong Mei-ling departed Taiwan for the United States.

Fo Guang Shan's subsequent television broadcasts included "Hsing Yun's Chan Talk," "Daily Verse," and "Hsing Yun's Stories"on TTV, "Hsing Yun's Talk" on CTV, and "Hsing Yun's Dharma Words" on CTS. For each recorded episode I was paid six thousand dollars. Circumstances have indeed changed over these last thirty-years. At one time, I had to pay the station one hundred and twenty thousand dollars per episode, and now it is the station paying me six thousand dollars. This undoubtedly denotes the public's acceptance and recognition of Buddhism.

Other than the abovementioned, my novel *National Master Yu Lin*, being quite popular, was adapted into scripts, radio shows, a movie, and theater. Of note, the television show—"Continued Fate of Love", produced by Gou Feng twenty years ago, became a huge hit both in and out of Taiwan.

Beforehand, one-hour afternoon shows in the Peking Opera were the norm. However, two words drawn out through long theatrical singing really did not entice the interest of the audience, let alone fathom what they were singing about. I have always felt the need to re-adapt the Peking Opera in order to attract a bigger audience.

Likewise, Buddhism shares a similar fate to theatre. If steadfastly conservative and unchanging, devoid of popularization and generalization in its means of propagation, no one will be teaching, learning or even believing in Buddhism any longer.

iii. Conferral of Precepts

Zenrinji Temple Amitabha Hall: Amitabha Buddha
JAPAN, Kyoto; Kamakura period (1185–1333); Wood; H: 77.6 cm

All through the Japanese occupation, monastic precepts were not practiced in Taiwan. As the saying goes, "With precepts the Sangha therefore prevails, with Sangha the Dharma therefore prevails." Continuance of the Sangha by conferring precepts thus became critical. An initial attempt to hold a Triple Platform Full Ordination Ceremony was made, in 1952, by the Ta Hsien Temple in Tainan Guanziling. Venerable Pai Sheng took the opportunity to negotiate with the government and put the Buddhist Association of the Republic of China in charge.

For that particular ceremony, Venerable Kai Tsan (開參) was appointed the Sila Archarya, Venerable Chih Kuang (智光) the Instructing Archarya, Venerable Tai Tsang the Karma Archarya, Venerable Tao Yuan as the Teaching Archrya along with Venerables Cheng Lien, Nan Ting, Hui Feng (慧峰), and Zhu Yun as the witnessing Masters, as well as Venerables Pai Sheng as Kaitang, and Chieh Te (戒德 , 1909-2011) as Peitang. Owing to unexpected obligations, Venerable Nan Ting became unavailable, and I replaced him. As a result, I became one of the ten witnessing masters in the first Triple Platform Full Ordination Ceremony held in Taiwan.

Statutes of the Buddhist Association of the Republic of China allowed a temple to host only one comprehensive ordination ceremony per year. Hence Yuan Kuang Temple on Lion Head Mountain, Taipei Shi Pu Temple, Keelung Ling Quan Temple on Yue Mei Mountain, Taipei Ling Yun Temple in Kuan Yin Mountain, and Taichung Pao Chueh Temple all took turns hosting the ceremony.

In those days, the Buddhist Association of the Republic of China held dominion, and no temples were allowed to organize precept ceremonies or issue ordination certificates without their permission. In 1967, I tried registering as host for the event, but was refused permission till 1977, whilst other temples hosted at least two to three times.

As Fo Guang Shan Monastery was not yet an officially registered temple in Kaohsiung County, I envisaged holding the ceremony at Yilan Lei Ying Temple or Keelung Chi Lo Temple. Auspiciously, with the aid of Chen Po-fen, I was able to successfully obtain permission, and thus brought the event to Fo Guang Shan Monastery.

To maintain equilibrium, I invited Venerable Ching Hsin (淨心 , 1929-2001) to act as Chief Coordinator (Kaitang). However, for the issuances of ordination certificates, the Association charged five hundred dollars per certificate for both monastic and lay precepts. Despite payment, Venerable Ching Liang (淨良) still refused to issue the certificates. So, I paid it no mind. Full ordination ceremonies are meant as a benefit for social order and enhanced moral ethics. If I adhered to this principle, no one could impede me in holding ordination or precept ceremonies.

In 1997, Fo Guang Shan hosted its first Triple Platform Full Ordination Ceremony, lasting three months. All procedures followed those set by traditional monasteries in Mainland China. An Instructing Archarya was invited to teach, rehearse, and formally confer the precepts, as well as tutor the preceptees, akin to a short-term Buddhist College program. Other than Venerables Chen Hua (真華 , 1922-2012) and Zhu Yun, and myself as the Three Archaryas, domestic and overseas monastics such as Venerables Yue Chi (月基), Wu Yi, Long Tao (隆道), Kai Cheng (開證 , 1925-2001), Zhu Mo, Pu Jing (普淨 , 1902-1986), Jin An (鏡盦 , 1900-2000), and Thien An (天恩) were also invited to be witnessing Masters and teaching Masters. The solemn ambience of the ceremonies, as well as the meticulous enactment of the procedures rewarded Fo Guang Shan with the "Exemplary Ordination Ceremony" accolade.

i) Conveying Triple Platform Full Ordination Procedures Back to Mainland China

Unique to the ceremony at Fo Guang Shan was the restoration of the Two-Division Ordination Ceremony, which in time past was omitted. I instructed Venerable Tzu Hui, the executive director of the ceremony, to abide by the rituals of the two divisions of bhiksus and bhiksunis each being conferred by witnessing masters of their respective genders. In this way the Triple Platform Full Ordination Ceremony was thus complete, starting from the Sramanera Precepts Platform to the Bhiksu/Bhiksuni Precepts Platform, ending in the Bodhisattva Precepts Platform. Afterward, Venerable Ching Hsin, then Director-General of the Buddhist Association of the Republic of China, assimilated this procedure in his subsequent ordination ceremonies. As a result, this procedure is also applied in Mainland China today.

In the early period of Mainland China, only bhiksus were allowed to act as guiding Venerables in a Triple Platform Full Ordination Ceremony, while bhiksunis solely performed the functions of assistants and support. Yet all monastics were given the role of "guiding venerables" at Fo Guang Shan's ordination ceremonies, for the Dharma values aspiration and will. Regardless that one may be man or woman, lay or monastic, only by attaining the spirit of equality can our minds truly connect with that of the Buddha.

The full ordination ceremony was later held at Fo Guang Shan Hsi Lai Temple in the United States. Construction of Hsi Lai Temple, the biggest Buddhist temple in North America, began in 1978, and was finally completed a decade later on November 26th, 1988, with Venerable Tzu Chuang as the founding Abbess. In tandem, a Ten-Thousand-Buddha Triple Platform Full Ordination Ceremony was held and attended by three hundred monastics from sixteen countries.

In 1991, the Ten-Thousand-Buddha Triple Platform Full Ordination Ceremony was hosted anew at Fo Guang Shan for three months. In excess of five hundred monastics from America, Korea, Thailand, Nepal, Malaysia, Indonesia, Hong Kong, Singapore and Vietnam convened for the longest and most comprehensive ordination ceremony in the history of Chinese Buddhism. Abiding fully by traditional monastic rules in addition to the experience of an alms procession, the preceptees were able to experience the routine of the Buddha's time.

At one time, Bodhisattva Precepts were not observed in the Theravada tradition, thus the followers were unable to aspire for the Bodhi Mind and reach out to people to propagate the Dharma, which is truly regretful. So, at the 1997 International Buddhist Seminar held at Fo Guang Shan, both monastic and lay delegates from the Southern, Northern, and Tibetan traditions co-signed a petition for Fo Guang Shan to travel to India and confer the bhiksuni precepts.

In February 1998, the entreaty became reality under the cohesive efforts of Fo Guang Shan along with Theravada, Tibetan, and Chinese Buddhist organizations. Over one hundred and fifty preceptees from Indonesia, Thailand, Nepal, Africa, Japan, Korea, Europe, America, and other countries realized full ordination, while fifteen hundred lay Buddhists participated in a Triple Gem Refuge Taking and Five Precepts Ceremony. This event enabled the renaissance of the bhiksuni order in India and Theravadan countries that had long

Ajanta Cave 26: Life of the Buddha - Defeat of Mara
INDIA, Maharashtra, Aurangabad; circa mid-to-late 5th century; Stone

been discontinued since the 11th century, marking a very important page in the history of Buddhism.

With regards to lay Buddhist precepts, time was that the Five Precepts and Bodhisattva Precepts observances lasted for seven days. To adapt to the needs of modern times, whilst still emphasizing the spirit of eternally abiding the precepts above momentary pledges, these ceremonies are now two-day overnight events offering greater convenience to people. Moreover, adapting sports stadiums and community centers into Buddha shrines for these ceremonies under the witness of the Three Masters is also a form of pragmatism.

ii) Establishing pure regulations that hold true to the spirit of the precepts

For householders holding a deep appreciation for monastic life but unable to relinquish their family commitments, with the exception of the one-day Eight Precepts retreat introduced by the Buddha; Fo Guang Shan held, in 1998, its first Short-Term Monastic Retreat. We received eight thousand applications with only one thousand admitted for the three separate retreats. This was an unprecedented event in the history of Buddhism.

Throughout the Short-Term Monastic Retreat, participants are required to take the Ten Sramanera or Ten Sramanerika Precepts and lead a secluded monastic life. Concurrently, they are obliged to refrain from watching entertainment such as dancing or singing, sitting or lying on high and comfortable beds, or wearing of fragrances and floral decorations. Thus, one is wholly transcended from secular life, and able to experience the spiritual wealth of emptiness.

It is likewise for precepts. Contents of precepts established by Buddha according to differing conditions need to be attuned to respective eras, locations, and cultures. Be it monastic or lay precepts, as long as one can abide by the four core principles: no killing, no stealing, no sexual misconduct, and no lying, as well as be willing to practice the Four Demeanors, Four Immeasurable States of Mind, and the Four Universal Vows, one already qualifies to be an outstanding Buddhist.

In such a way, Chinese Buddhist masters were quite astute by stipulating pure regulations as an alternative for precepts. Whilst the conventions of monasteries such as Tianning Temple and Jin-shan Temple may each differ, all remain close to the spirit of precepts. The Fo Guang Shan Order also has the Fo Guang Shan Pure Regulations Handbook for members to adhere to. The purported "three thousand demeanors and eighty thousand subtle actions" lies within our ability to deal with people and matters in real life. The conscientious practice of precepts, concentration, and wisdom

Vaishali: Asoka Pillar

to suppress our greed, anger, and ignorance, is also a means for us to quell our afflictions and habits through benefiting all sentient beings. Hence, we can also gain acceptance by others. As once stated, "Buddhahood is attained the instant our human characters are perfected." This was, and is Buddha's original intent in establishing the precepts for this world.

iv. Buddhist Chanting Association

In the early days of Taiwan, chanting Buddha's name was the most popular custom amongst Buddhists. For instance, the Taichung Buddhist Lotus Society founded by Lee Bin-nang, Fengshan Buddhist Lotus Association by Venerable Zhu Yun in Kaohsiung, and the Yilan Buddhist Chanting Association by me. Moreover, the Ling Yen Mountain Temple founded by Venerable Miao Lien (妙蓮 , 1922-2008) in Puli focused mainly on chanting Buddha's name. Among the aforesaid, Lee Bingnan's Buddhist Lotus Society is regarded as the forerunner.

Lee Bing-nan, courtesy name Hsueh Lu, took refuge under Master Yin Guang when young, and dedicated his life to propagating Pure Land Buddhism. In 1950, he founded the Taichung Buddhist Lotus Society with Tung Cheng-chi, Chu Huang-yan, Hsu Tsao-sheng (徐灶生), and Chang Sung-po (張松柏). Numerous chanting classes were held weekly. Lee's work was a major cause for the prosperity of Pure Land Buddhism within Post-Recovery Taiwan.

Lee was well-learned in worldly knowledge and Buddhist studies. Though he was said to have engaged in the dual propagation of Confucianism and Buddhism, he in fact applied the essence of

Confucian thoughts in the form of Buddhist practices. He also founded Bodhi Hospital, Tzu Kuang Library, music bands, and harmonica bands, as well as arts and literary classes to integrate old and new generations as one. In appealing to youths, he steered clear of monastic communities and taking in students, creating new opportunities for Buddhism.

The Taichung Buddhist Lotus Society was as prosperous as Master Hui Yuan's (慧遠 , 334-416) Donglin Temple from bygone days. They held collective chanting services and promoted Pure Land practices. Stories of supernatural responses experienced by lay Buddhists Lee Ching-yuan (李清源) and Lin Ching-jiang (林清江 , 1940-1999) were recorded in *Experiences of Passing Away Under Buddha's Blessings*. Lin Kan-chi (林看治 , 1907-1992), author of the book, was also one who aspired to be reborn in the Western Pure Land. After his body was cremated, hundreds of relics remained. Also, Lee Chi-hwa (李濟華 , 1882-1962), Director of Taipei Buddhist Chanting Association committed to the practice of chanting Buddha's name, was also able to presage the time of his passing. For all these lay Buddhists to be so well attained in their cultivation, Lee Bing-nan surely was an important mentor for Pure Land practices. It can be said there was "Huiyuan of the past, Hsueh Lu of today" when it comes to Pure Land Buddhism.

Lee's faith in Pure Land was unshakable. When Venerable Yin Shun introduced his work *New Pure Land Concepts*, criticizing the Western Pure Land, Lee's students initiated a movement in Taichung to burn the book. Unwilling to make enemies with Lee's enormous organization of lay Buddhists, when Venerable Yin Shun was in the Philippines; he tried to make amends by fundraising meant for Lee's Master Taixu Memorial.

Pious followers of Lee regarded his passion and dedication to propagating Pure Land Buddhism as something exceedingly rare and valuable. Others criticized him for his attachment to Pure Land and disregard for other Buddhist Schools that merit as much devotion and value. To date, the only lay Buddhist organization that remains devoted to the Pure Land faith is that of Lee. Regretfully, without someone to carry the baton or a permanent cultivation center, the organization often needs to rent space at Taichung Ling Shan Temple for chanting services. After Lee passed away, the association became leaderless.

i) The Pure Land Cave: An Experience of the Beauty of Buddha Land

Speaking of the Pure Land practice of chanting Buddha's name, I too have some personal experience. It all began in 1953 when I founded Yilan Buddhist Chanting Association at Lei Ying Temple. In the following years, Seven-Day Amitabha Retreats began with traditional monastic routines. At 5am, the morning session began, Bud-

Byodoin Temple Phoenix Hall:
Figures Making Offerings - Bodhisattva; H: 72.1 cm
JAPAN, Kyoto, Uji; Heian period (794–1185), dated 1053; Wood

dhist formal meals were taken at noon, followed by the main session between 7-9pm, the most dedicated and focused session of the day.

Other than the above, I also promoted the Saturday Chan and Pure Land services. As proper meditation halls and chanting halls were rare in those days, we could only unite both inside the Buddha shrine. With a quarter of the time dedicated to reciting the sutra, another quarter chanting the Buddha's name, one quarter circumambulating the Buddha, and the final quarter for meditation, each session lasted around two hours.

As many Buddhists found chanting Buddha's name a most suitable way of practice; I therefore established the Luodong Buddhist Chanting Association, Toucheng Buddhist Chanting Association, Taipei Buddhist Chanting Association, Huwei Buddhist Chanting Association, and Longyan Buddhist Chanting Association. It can be said that, at that time, the dual practice of Chan and Pure Land became mainstream Buddhist cultivation, bringing Buddhism in Taiwan to its peak.

Concurrently, I also constructed the Fo Guang Shan Pure Land Cave, opened to the public in 1981, to share with the world the wondrous beauty of the Western Pure Land of Ultimate Bliss. Some asked why I chose not to build the Eighteen Hells to frighten people from doing evil deeds. Personally, is it not better to promote positive thoughts through experiencing the beauty and virtue of Buddha's Pure Land? I firmly believe that Buddha taught Humanistic Buddhism to bring light, hope, and joy to the world. Faith should never serve the purpose of creating fear in people's minds.

Since the founding of Fo Guang Shan, there are now over two hundred temples around the world. Having established Saturday as the standard time for chanting, envisage over three hundred Buddha shrines, each filled with an average of five hundred participants, conducting services in unison. Within the same extent of time, there would be fifteen hundred thousand people chanting simultaneously. Is this not a manifestation of the Pure Land of Ultimate Bliss?

All told, throughout my seventy years as a monastic, no less than a quarter of my time has been dedicated to Chan and Pure Land practices. Just the Seven-Day Amitabha Chanting Retreat alone occupied nearly twenty thousand hours of my life. My purpose of promoting Pure Land chanting is that, through chanting

Fo Guang Shan Monastery Pure Land Cave: Arhats
TAIWAN, Kaohsiung; Dated 1981; Cement

Buddha's name, people will be able to better and purify themselves, self-reflect, and self-improve. Furthermore, one will eventually better one's family, society and nation. Thus, without expecting people to do single-minded and attentive chanting, this actually turned out easier to accept for many.

v. Buddhist Societies

In the earlier days, most Buddhist organizations were not government-accredited, while the few that were simply monopolized the privilege without assisting the development of Buddhism.

In 1986, after Chiang Ching-kuo declared the end of martial law, Taiwan opened up to assemblies, organizations, opinions, publications, and overseas travels. Numerous Buddhist societies were established to propagate the Dharma. Some of the prevailing Buddhist societies in Taiwan include: Buddhist Association of the Republic of China, BLIA Chunghua Headquarters, Lay Buddhists' Association Republic of China, Chinese Buddhist Temple Association, Chinese Young Buddhist Association, Chinese Bhiksuni Association, Chung-Hwa International Merits Association of Buddha-puja and Sangha-dana, and Tzu Chi Foundation.

Founded in 1991 as the "Chuanghua Buddha's Light Association" in Taipei, the association was then renamed "Buddha's Light International Association World Headquarters" (BLIA for short). It was inaugurated at the Music Center in Los Angeles, in 1992, with in excess of 4,000 members from over forty-five countries worldwide. Elected as President, I was joined by Wu Po-hsiung (吳伯雄), Mizutani Kosho, Yan Foon Gu, Henry Yau (游象卿), and Ven. Bhikkhu Aniruddha as elected Vice Presidents. During the inauguration, I spoke on the theme, "Joy and Harmony" elaborating on how Humanistic Buddhism remains true to the Buddha's original intents in six points:

1. From monastic to lay Buddhists,
2. From temples into society,
3. From self-learning to altruism,
4. From quietude to activity,
5. From students to teachers,
6. From locality to the world.

The founding of BLIA opened a door for lay Buddhists to take part in Dharma propagation, not only fulfilling Buddha's spirit of equality, but also sees the influence of Humanistic Buddhism further enriched.

With the objectives:

1. To advocate humanistic Buddhism
2. To establish a Pure Land in this world
3. To purify the minds of people in this world
4. To be dedicated to world peace

The BLIA now has over one hundred and seventy chapters, around two thousand sub-chapters, and millions of members in more than seventy countries, across the five continents.

In July 2003, BLIA also became the first Buddhist organization to be accorded NGO with special consultative status by the Economic and Social Council of the United Nations (UNESCO). This honor would have been impossible without the joint efforts of both the monastic and lay members of the Association.

Following the founding of BLIA, in 1994, the BLIA Young Adults Division (BLIA-YAD) was founded with Venerable Hui Chuan as President. In just a few years, YAD divisions across the world and Taiwan were established. Of note, the Taiwan YAD Headquarters initiated the "New Life: Five Precepts for Youth" to promote the Five Precepts among youths. Annually, tens of thousands of young adults have responded to the movement by observing the Five Precepts: No killing, no stealing, no sexual misconduct, no lying, and no intoxicants.

Furthermore, the annual Charity Trips to India, Mainland China, Malaysia, Philippines and Brazil offer young adults opportunities to provide sanitation, teaching, and medical consultation services. Over one hundred Sumagadhi and Sudhana Lecturers have been trained to deliver talks in schools to promote the Three Acts of Goodness Movement. In 2015, the Marvelous Malaysia Young Buddhists Concert attracted eight thousand youths to sing their passion and mission for Buddhism. These new champions of Dharma propagation provide boundless hopes for the future. To date, there are nearly two hundred existing YADs actively reaching out to schools and communities, highlighting the influence of Humanistic Buddhism in purifying human minds.

My idea was to enable not just monastic and lay Buddhists to learn and practice the Dharma but also allow people from all walks of life, young and old, man and woman to grow as one. Thus the concept of BLIA certainly had a place for children's education. In 2000, Buddha's Light Scouts was formed at Fo Guang Shan, and subsequently chapters all over the world. Being the first international Buddhist scouts group, Buddha's Light Scouts now includes Pre Cub Scouts, Cub Scouts, Boy Scouts, and Rover Scouts. Not only do they pay regular visits to the elderly dwelling alone, they even participated in the recovery works for the Morakot Typhoon Disasters. These scouts wholly, and fittingly demonstrate a spirit of wisdom, kindness, and courage.

i) Different Faiths, Same Purpose: Purifying Human Minds

For a long time, Buddhists solely focused on repetitive chanting of Buddhist sutras without reading or reflecting on the contents, which truly concerned me. As the Buddhist procedure of learning involves "entering the state of Samadhi through hearing, reflecting, and practicing the Dharma," I created the Humanistic Buddhist Reading Association in January 2002 to promote reading. For over a decade, Venerable Chueh Pei (覺培) formed over two thousand reading groups, and actively promoted various reading techniques, reading seminars, and even reading expositions. The development of the Reading Association has further enhanced interest and spiritual growth in Buddhists.

In February and May 2015, Chunghua Federation of Traditional Religious Associations and United Association of Humanistic Buddhism were subsequently established. Both associations symbolize the realization of Humanistic Buddhism's spirits of "Respect and Tolerance," as well as "Peace and Equality." It is hoped that through the Chunghua Federation of Traditional Religious Associations, different religious organizations are able to embrace similarities and celebrate differences through continued interactions and exchanges. While differing in our faith, we all nevertheless share a common goal: to work together in purifying society and human minds.

This is why every December 25th, since its founding, the

Buddha Museum has been hosting the World Reunion of Religious Associations by inviting all deities to celebrate a day of holy reunion. Yearly, more than two thousand religious organizations and fifty thousand participants from around the world attend. In seeing deities and devotees filing into the Museum in orderly fashion, regardless of region or age, I cannot help but be reminded of Buddha's Dharma gatherings on Vulture Peak, where heavenly and human beings alike joined before the Buddha. We are truly reliving the Buddha's time!

Furthermore, under the collaboration of Tzu Jung, Hui Chuan, Yi Jung (依融), Man Yi (滿益), Chueh Pei, and Miao Le (妙樂), the newly established United Association of Humanistic Buddhism now comprises over two hundred temples or Buddhist organizations, as well as over four hundred individual members such as: Da Hsiung Vihara, Cifa Chan Monastery, Fo Guang Shan, Luminary International Buddhist Society, Chunghua Bhiksunis Association, Ling Jiou Mountain Buddhist Society, Bliss & Wisdom Society, and so on. Individual members include: Wu Po-hsiung, Yeh Ching-fong (葉金鳳), Cora Wang (王力行), Chien Feng-wen (簡豐文), Chang Yia-chung (張亞中), Huang Giin-tarng (黃錦堂), Ting Shou-chung (丁守中), Pan Wei-kang (潘維剛), Wu John Chih-yang (吳志揚), Hou Shi-chyuan (侯西泉), and Hong Yuh-chin (洪玉欽).

Last year, to broaden the inspiration of Humanistic Buddhism, we founded the Buddha's Light Missionary Association, Chunghua, to promote books and publications. Within the first year alone, we gave away a few million copies of *365 Days for Travelers: Wisdom from Chinese Literary and Buddhist Classics*, *Hear Me Out: Messages from a Humble Monk*, and *Hear Me Out: Reflections* to thousands of hotels, hostels, airline companies, schools, libraries, hospitals, and

Western Pure Land; CHINA; Qing dynasty (1644–1911);
By Ding Guanpeng; Ink and color on paper; 295.8 x 148.8 cm

National Palace Museum, Taipei, Taiwan

correctional centers. Unprecedented, the book launch was held at the Great Hall of the People in Beijing. I believe that this collection of Buddhist and literary classics will allow Buddha's Humanistic Buddhism to shine in every human mind, and every corner of the world.

Just as Buddha avowed on the vajra seat, "How amazing! How amazing! All living beings possess the wisdom and virtue of the Buddha. It was merely concealed by their delusions and attachments." Every human being has the buddha-nature, and can attain buddhahood. The monastic and lay assemblies, who both propagate and protect the Dharma, certainly mutually maintain Humanistic Buddhism. The dissemination of Humanistic Buddhism rests on the shoulders of all Buddhists. Since this is an ineluctable responsibility, why discriminate between you and I as opposed to simply striving as one?

4) Charitable Undertakings to Serve Society

In order to benefit humanity, Buddhism advocates the bodhisattva practices of the Six Paramitas that lead to concurrent liberation of oneself and others. The practice of these Six Paramitas begins with generosity, starting with financial charity, which is limited to momentary relief. But it also involves higher levels of giving, such as the teachings of the Dharma and fearlessness. The latter two forms of generosity are hardest to apprehend, since most people are aware of philanthropy only in the form of money. This is why charity is a favored option among Buddhists, whilst culture and education, though equally as important, are considered more difficult and less preferred.

Buddhist charity works began as early as Buddha's time. Buddha's disciples built public bathrooms, called on the sick, and provided free medicine. Sudatta the Elder, King Bimbisara, and Visakha donated housing and viharas. King Asoka held open banquets to feed the famished, built pharmacies, and welfare houses to provide supplies such as medicine and food to travelers, the sick, and the destitute. They were all forerunners in Buddhist charity and social welfare.

After Buddhism came to China, many Buddhist masters abided by the Buddha's teachings and conducted charitable activities to serve society. Furthermore, they established free schooling, planted trees and forests, dug wells besides offering water, paved roads and built bridges, gave away free porridge and caskets, founded loan centers, "inexhaustible storehouses", and infirmaries. Any work that benefits and assists living beings is an instrument of the Bodhisattva path through which Humanistic Buddhism is connected with society.

The list of charitable deeds by eminent masters from the past is endless. Yet one should not dismiss contemporary charitable acts by Humanistic Buddhists. Especially after the Xinhai Revolution, Buddhist reform movements began, and Buddhists thus actively played their role in relieving living beings from distress. Although temples were damaged by floods and droughts, once restored, they also set up charity groups and established retirement homes and orphanages. In times of chaos and distress, they provided relief to victims of disasters, rescuing wounded soldiers, providing emergency relief aids. They also established Buddhist hospitals and monastic rescue teams to save soldiers on battlefields, bury the deceased, as well as conduct prayer services for the victims and the affected. Undoubtedly, Humanistic Buddhism has conducted charitable activities and social works at all levels of society.

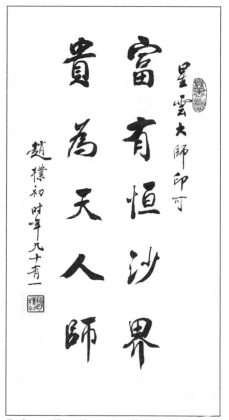

Fo Guang Shan Monastery: Calligraphy Dedicated
to Master Hsing Yun; TAIWAN, Kaohsiung;
Dated 1996; By Zhao Puchu; Running script;
Hanging Scroll; Ink on paper; 93 x 49 cm

Since the early Republic of China period, many lay Buddhist associations already existed such as the Association of Righteous Buddhist Faith in Hankou, Shanghai Pure Karma Society, Buddhist societies in Chengdu, Chongqing, and Henan, and Lay Buddhist Societies in Shanghai, Beijing, Tianjin, and Changsha. In times of calamity and conflict, many bodhisattvas such as Xiong Xiling

(熊希齡 , 1870-1937), Di Baoxia, Wang Yiting (王一亭 , 1867-1938), Li Chenbai (李塵白), Gao Henian (高鶴年 , 1872-1962), Jiang Weinong (江味農 , 1872-1938), Wu Bihua (吳璧華), Kang Jiyao, Zhu Qinglan (朱慶瀾 , 1874-1941), Xi Zhongxun (習仲勛 , 1913-2002) (father of President Xi Jinping), and Zhao Puchu have stepped up to help Buddhism through hard times by offering their time and money. Some temples even offered camp space for troops and shelters for the displaced. Are these not great acts of generosity?

Looking back to my days at Qixia Vinaya College, perhaps the greatest feat that Qixiashan Monastery ever realized was taking in over two hundred thousand refugees during the Sino-Japanese War in 1937. General Liao Yaoxiang (廖耀湘 , 1906-1968), a high-ranking commander who fought against the Japanese, was hiding among the refugees. The monastics at Qixiashan helped conceal his identity, helping him reach the frontlines to continue his duty in defending the country. Have Buddhists not contributed to their country and society? Throughout this occurrence, my master, Venerable Master Zhi Kai made tremendous contributions, surely the cause of his promotion to superintendent, and then Abbot of Qixiashan.

1. Sincere Acts of Generosity through the Four Givings

I once divided generosity into four stages:

Stage one: the giving of money.
Stage two: the giving of labor.
Stage three: the giving of language.

Stage four: the giving of heart.

In stage one, sometimes giving too much money does not truly help. Even when willing to volunteer one's labor, at times there is not much to be done. In contrast, there can never be too kind a word spoken, especially to offer one's kind intention and blessing. In passing on the Truth and Dharma. To always be ready to give others faith, give others joy, give others hope, and give others convenience. Such kind acts as performing a handful of good deeds, or showing a face full of smile are all forms of giving.

To a more profound degree, though I have neither given money nor my labor, but simply felt joyful and praised those who did give; the merit attained is same as the benefactor. In fact, the merit of rejoicing in others' act of giving is even greater. This is the bearing of a practitioner of Humanistic Buddhism.

The essence of generosity is attainment of "Emptiness of all three aspects of giving," namely, formless giving. The act of generosity in Buddhism is empty of desire for profit and fame or quid pro quo. Above all, the act of generosity must not be used as a disguise for investments. It is against the law of cause and effect to use people's charitable donations for any other purposes.

Venerable Ta Hsing told me that when someone makes a donation to him for the purchase of fruits, he would mark the red packet accordingly and use it for no other purpose. If the donation was for tea, he would mark "tea" on the packet. This ensured that the cause and effect of his actions were clear. Thus, if someone donates money for charity and relief aid, but you spend it on purchasing real estate or any other endeavor, you are behaving contrary to cause and effect. This is wrong. Donations made for construction of temples should be used only on construction, not on real estate or opening department stores. Donations made to carve Buddha sculptures should be expended only on Buddha sculptures, not establishment of schools. Black and white cannot be confounded. Charitable endeavors must be carried out righteously and ethically be in accordance with the law of cause and effect.

Acts of kindness, as advocated by Humanistic Buddhism, serve the purpose of reviving the bodhisattva deeds of Buddha from his previous lives into the present. Specifically, they impart the largesse of fearlessness and formlessness. Just as Venerable Tzu Hang said, the life of Buddhism rests upon three types of endeavors: culture, education, and charity. Moreover, other than these three, true Buddhist endeavors must be done based on the spirits of the Four Ways of Embracing, Six Paramitas, and Thirty-Seven Factors of Enlightenment.

The charitable endeavors of Humanistic Buddhism place emergency relief as priority over poverty, because its essence is Dharma propagation. The greatest form of charity lies in the salvation of human minds rather than aid provided in material or monetary forms. Thus the true import and substance of charity is extremely profound. While material and monetary support will eventually end, the gift of Dharma will offer a lifetime, and even lifetimes of benefits.

Charity and relief works can also comprise admonishment against killing and the promotion of the sanctity of human life. For example, Lu Bicheng (呂碧城 , 1883-1943) traveled to Europe and America to promote the sanctity of life. Master Hongyi and Fen Zikai's collective work on *Illustrations of Life Protection* offered solace and peace to those living in chaotic times. During my early days in Taiwan, this book was widely circulated. Later, when I built the Buddha Museum, I embodied the one hundred and fifty-four illustrations into murals along the covered walkways as means to promote the protection of life. Humanistic Buddhism exemplifies the mission of benefiting society and liberating all living beings. Beginning from a time bereft of nature and environmental protection awareness, Buddhists were already advocating the right to life in times of monarchical rule and civil rights.

Speaking of the right to life, instead of liberating lives, one should be protecting lives since such acts carry the purpose of nurturing compassion and love for animals, as well as raising awareness of environmental protection. The notion that one can accumulate merit by releasing lives on celebratory occasions such as one's seventieth or eightieth birthday is mistaken. To procure and release animals is actually an act of killing, not of merit.

It is unfeasible to purchase all animals requiring freedom. The only way to save lives is through compassionate hearts. It is hoped that all means of life liberation can be achieved by holding true to the spirit of "ceasing all evil and practicing all good." This is the best form of safeguarding life. Rather than spending three or five thousand dollars to purchase then release a tortoise, one may as well spend that money on educating people with the right attitude of not taking life and the sanctity of living beings.

2. Prison Programs to Nurture Compassion and Self-Awareness

With regard to correctional center visits, the work began with the "Correctional Center Dharma Propagation Team" initiated by Venerable Nan Ting, Chao Mao-lin, many others and myself. Venerable Kuang Tzu, Ma Hsing-hui (馬 性 慧), Li Zi-kuan, Liu

Chong-yi (劉中一), Chen Hui-fu (陳慧復), and I were among the many who took turns to visit. I have visited nearly every prison in Taiwan. For instance, the prisons in Taipei's Tucheng, Hsinchu, Taichung, Yunlin, Pintung, Kaohsiung, Hualien, Lanyu (Orchid Island), and Ludao. I even visited Stanley Prison in Hong Kong and several in America. Furthermore, I was the first Counselor of Rehabilitation and Education appointed by the Department of Justice.

I led a dialogue on life and death, as well as rehabilitation, with death row prisoners in Tucheng, likewise with over two thousand convicted of major crimes, nearly all still in their prime. I said to them, "If all two thousand of you became monastics just like me, imagine how much your compassion and contribution could help Buddhism and society."

I conducted a Triple Gem Refuge Ceremony for inmates of Kaohsiung Women's Prison. A majority of them were imprisoned for violation of the Act of Negotiable Instruments. Specifically, these women were used as shills, facades that shielded illicit activity such as drug trafficking, and in fiduciary fraud by being used in illegal activities such as check kiting as well as money laundering. This resulted in their conviction as perpetrators of crimes they had not committed. It was woeful to see women making such sacrifices for their husbands. In truth, it is the women who made the most contributions to this world by their sacrifices.

When Ma Ying-jeou (馬英九) was Minister of Justice, he frequently invited Fo Guang Shan monastics to Tainan Ming De Drug Rehabilitation Center to aid as missionaries, living on the premises as well as spending twenty-four hours of every day with inmates. This was unheard of. I also advocated, to former Minister of Justice Liao Cheng-hao (廖正豪), for the establishment of Halfway Houses to serve as rehabilitation zones for inmates for four months upon completing their sentence and provide them counseling.

In prison, security guards impose all manners of restrictions, but in a halfway house a moderate level of freedom is offered. For example, the right to receive visitors, opt for their preferred diet, smoking cigarettes, and even outdoor excursions. When felons are subjected to a greater sense of human kindness and love, the chances of recurring hatred and anger will be minimized, and their ability to adapt to normal life improved.

That is why the Law needs to be enforced with a positive outlook to life, to achieve the purpose of rehabilitation. Fo Guang Shan held activities such as the Eight Precepts Retreat, Triple Gem Refuge Taking Ceremony, and even Short-Term Monastic Retreats insides prisons to assist the process of rehabilitation and purification, as well as aid inmates in developing their compassion and self-awareness. Any repudiation of their worth within and to society will only drive them back to acts of crime.

In recent years, the lanterns displayed at Fo Guang Shan's New Year Festival of Light and Peace have all been works of correctional center inmates. In the process of creating these lanterns, not only did their characters change, they were able to regain their self-esteem and sense of honor. In 2012, the Changhua Prison Guwu Percussion Troupe even performed at the Buddha Museum, which was well received by the public.

In recent years, industrial development has fuelled the speed of global warming, causing endless natural disasters and man-made calamites. In response to disasters such as the 1951 Hualien Earthquake, 921 Earthquake, Typhoon Nari, the SARS outbreak, Southeast Asia Earthquake Tsunami, Sichuan Earthquake, and Typhoon Morakot, Fo Guang Shan has actively participated in works of disaster relief along with other organizations.

In July, 2014, the TransAsia air crash in Penghu and Kaohsiung gas explosions shook Taiwan. Buddhist, Catholic, Muslim, Taoist, Christian, and I-Kuan-Tao organizations united inside Kaohsiung Arena and jointly held the "National Interfaith Prayer Service for the 731 Kaohsiung Gas Explosions and 723 Air Crash in Penghu." The service was attended by tens of thousands alongside President Ma Ying-jeou and presidents of all five government branches to pray for the victims.

3. Giving a Sense of Dignity in the Process of Acceptance

The duty of disaster relief must be done with respect for the personal identity of the affected. We cannot use this as an opportunity to advocate Buddhism or ask for contributions or recognitions of our works. When Typhoon Morakot struck, Fo Guang Shan offered shelter to victims who were Christians, and even arranged for pastors to come and lead them in prayers. Upon completion of their mission, a pastor prayed to a Buddha statue and said, "Thank you Buddha, for assisting us in carrying out God's will."

In truth, the work of relief is not carried out to save anyone but our own homes and ourselves. When the Sichuan Earthquake occurred, I reached out to the affected areas and declared, "I am here to repay you all." The giver and receiver are equal in merits. The act of receiving what is given also has its merits. Relief work must be done with a sense of dignity, and charity must be given under the circumstances that people feel at ease in receiving it.

Furthermore, we offered assistance to the Churches. A Christian Sister, having served in Taiwan for decades, wished to return home to retire, and we were more than happy to sponsor her travel

Vaishali: Vishwa Shanti Stupa

expenses. When Cardinal Paul Shan SJ (單國璽, 1923-2012) fundraised for Mount Beatitude, Fo Guang Shan likewise made contributions to the project. The charitable works in Humanistic Buddhism span beyond faiths, beyond regions, with no expectations, and without gains.

4. Dharma's Purifying Effect on the Mind's Greed, Anger and Ignorance

The charitable endeavors of Humanistic Buddhism carry the mission of spreading Buddha's loving-kindness and compassion to the world and enhancing people's faith in the Dharma. For this reason, Fo Guang Shan's Cloud and Water Mobile Clinic extend to remote areas to provide medical care. The Fo Guang Senior Citizen's Home provides the solace of faith for the elderly in their latter years. Da Ci Children's Home, for the past forty years, has assisted over eight hundred children in starting their own families. In addition, events such as the Compassion and Loving-Kindness Campaign, Retrieve Our Hearts, and also the establishment of the Public Education Trust Fund give out awards such as Truthful, Virtuous and Beautiful Media Award as well as the Three Acts of Goodness School Awards. Fo Guang Shan has also constructed over fifty Water and Cloud Mobile Library Trucks to bring books and knowledge to children in remote areas. These are all means through which the meaning of charity is further enriched and elevated.

Without the guidance of a truly wise mind, generosity is far from the ultimate Buddhist teaching of compassion, and merely an act of kindness. Buddha's original intent in teaching is to eliminate the root of suffering by purifying human minds of the Three Poisons: greed, anger and ignorance. This is the only way to truly free humanity from the tribulations of natural disasters and manmade calamities.

Throughout the long span of Buddhist history, the spread of Buddhism would have been impossible without the great act that is generosity. Yet, in Humanistic Buddhism, the practice of giving in the form of wealth, Dharma, and fearlessness are more transcending and precious. In our contemporary society permeated by fear and insecurity, irrespective of the extent of law enforcement or availability of security systems, countless still feel vulnerable. Therefore, for people to be free of fear, the gift of Dharma to elevate moral standards and enhance righteousness is fundamental.

The aforementioned endeavors of the Bodhisattva path are all in accord with the spirit exhibited by the Buddha, from ancient Indian times to modern Chinese society. To transform humanitarian charities into the selfless bodhisattva aspiration, that expects nothing in return, is a practice in accord with the buddha mind as well as the needs of humanity. By keeping true to the Buddha's original intents, we stay true to the ultimate principles of charity.

5) International Propagation for the Globalization of the Dharma

The spread of Humanistic Buddhism does not only take place in this world. Indeed, the Dharma spreads across the boundless dharma realms and the three thousand great chiliocosms. As told in the *Amitabha Sutra*, "Each morning, all beings in His land each wraps a rich variety of lush flowers in their garments and offers them to the billions of buddhas in lands of all directions." To follow this tradition in the Buddha lands, our international Buddhist events today are but trivial matters.

During the Republic of China era, International Buddhist conferences, delegations, and interfaith dialogues already existed. For example, in 1924, the World Buddhist Federation initiated by Master Taixu took place in Lushan, Jiangxi. The following year, Master Taixu led a delegation from the Buddhist Association of

China to Japan for the East Asia Buddhist Conference. This was the first official meeting between contemporary Chinese and Japanese Buddhists.

In 1928, Master Taixu went to Europe and America to give Dharma lectures. There, he founded the World Buddhist Studies Center in Paris. He was the first Chinese Buddhist monk to bring the Dharma to Europe and America, where Cai Yuanpei introduced him to renowned philosopher Bertrand Russell. In order to promote the internationalization of Buddhism, Master Taixu subsequently sent students to Japan, Tibet, India, Sri Lanka and other countries to pursue their studies.

When the Sino-Japanese War broke out, Master Taixu founded the Buddhist International Delegations in 1939 and travelled to Burma, India, Sri Lanka, Singapore, Malaysia and other countries to foster a resistance movement against Japan. Upon arrival in India, he received a grand welcome by cheering crowds teeming the streets. On this event, he wrote a poem:

> *Gandhi, Taixu, and Nehru;*
> *always greeted by thunderous cheers from the crowd.*
> *From Varanasi to Kushinagar;*
> *the streets are always filled with people.*

In 1943, the Chinese Religious Fellowship was founded, uniting religious organizations and their followers in resistance against Japan. I distinctly remember Master Taixu being the Buddhist representative, General Pai Chung-hsi (白崇禧 , 1893-1966) as the Muslim representative, and Cardinal Bishop Paul Yu (于斌 , 1901-1978) as the Catholic representative. In the face of national crisis, religious groups inherently united and nurtured fellowships.

Some time later, the Civil War drove numerous monastics from the Mainland to Hong Kong, Taiwan, Singapore, and Malaysia, bringing Humanistic Buddhism to other nations. For my part, although war brings nothing but misfortune, it is not an utter loss if, in the process, philosophical and cultural dissemination is kindled.

In 1963, the international spread of Humanistic Buddhism began in Taiwan through the Buddhist Delegation of the Republic of China initiated by the Buddhist Association of the Republic of China. The delegation visited Thailand, India, Malaysia, Singapore, Philippines, Japan, Hong Kong and other countries. As the spokesperson, I have chronicled all the particulars in my books *Traces Over the Sky and Ocean* and will not expound on them further here.

As Buddhist studies and sectarian development in Japan were quite prosperous, coupled with the short distance from Taiwan, exchanges occurred frequently. In 1974, the China-Japan Buddhist Progress Society was founded with Venerable Master Niwa Renbo, Director of Japan's Soto School, and myself as Presidents from both sides. Throughout the past decades, we had the honor of making acquaintances with outstanding leaders from Japan. For example, Furukawa Taiko—abbot of Myoshin-ji of the Rinzai Sect, and prominent professors such as Tsukamoto Zenryu, Mizuno Kogen, Nakamura Hajime, Hirakawa Akira, Kamata Sihgeo, Makida Tairyo, Ando Toshio, Maeda Egaku, Mizutani Kosho. Regularly, they visited Taiwan and Fo Guang Shan to present papers or teach at Tsung-Lin University. When Venerables Tzu Chuang, Tzu Hui, Tzu Jung, and Tzu Yi (慈怡) studied abroad in Japan, they too had a chance to confer with these eminent professors.

Japanese Buddhism followed a different path from Chinese

Buddhism. Their faith shifted from Buddha to patriarchs, from public temples to family heritage, and from observing precepts to simply acting as priests, solely preaching without having to lead a strictly disciplined monastic life like that of bhiksus. As Buddhist priests, having a family is acceptable.

In terms of Korean Buddhism, after I initiated the China-Korea Buddhist Progress Society in 1974, Fo Guang Shan has remained in close contact with the Jyoge Order's Three Triple Gem Temples—Tongdosa Temple (representing the Buddha gem), Haeinsa Temple (representing the Dharma gem), and Songgwangsa Temple (representing the Sangha gem), alongside renowned schools such as Dongguk University, and Geumgang University. Annually, Fo Guang Shan welcomes, on average, a dozen groups from Korea. Korea enjoys a long history of Buddhism, yet it is a pity that nearly all renowned monasteries are found in remote and isolated mountain forests. In contrast, Christian Churches built at crossroads have thrived tremendously. In fact, if we wish for the pervasiveness of Buddhism in this world, then we must first consider the locations of the temples to provide better access for the public.

1. Passions for the Dharma that Led to Worldwide Dissemination

In 1978, Venerables Tzu Chuang and Yi Hang (依航) settled in a small church within Los Angeles in the United States with the mission of constructing Hsi Lai Temple. One day, Venerable Thien-An from the University of California visited with a group of eighteen Theravadan bhiksus, cramming the spaces of the temple. To welcome my fellow Dharma propagators in a strange land, I cooked a vegetarian feast. In scholarly exchanges, then Harvard Ph.D. student Pruden also dwelt at Fo Guang Shan for a year, as a fellow.

With Hsi Lai Temple in America as a starting point, Humanistic Buddhism thus began to spread to the West and to the rest of the Five Continents. Considerable gratitude goes to Chinese immigrants and local governments in various parts of the world. For example, our endeavor in Brazil was made possible with Chang Sheng-kai's (張勝凱) generous donation of his house, which subsequently was rebuilt as Templo Zu Lai. In the Netherlands, Luo Fu-wen (羅輔聞) petitioned for the government to donate a piece of land for construction of He Hua Temple. In Switzerland, He Zenwei (何振威) convened four thousand Buddhists and helped establish the local BLIA Chapter. In Australia, construction of Nan Tien Temple was made possible with the support of the CEO of BHP and Wollongong Mayor Frank Arkell. In Malaysia, Dong Zen Temple is visited on average by one million people each New Year, which would have been impossible without the blessings of Venerables Zhu Mo, Jin Ming (金明), and Guang Yu (廣餘), as well as Tan Sri Dr. Koh Tsu Koon (許子根), then Chief Minister of Penang and also Mr. Khoo Poh Kong (邱寶光). With their enthusiasm and passion for the Dharma, the global spread of Humanistic Buddhism thus found its root.

The key to international propagation lies in the nurturing of multilingual talents. Throughout the past decades, there are Venerable Tzu Hui (慈惠) who is fluent in both Japanese and Taiwanese, as well as Venerable Miao Guang (妙光) who speaks English and continues the works of international academic exchanges under the FGS Institute of Humanistic Buddhism. In Japan, there are Venerables Man Jun（滿潤）and Tzu Yi who have supervised the construction of Housuiji Temple in Gunma. In Hong Kong, Venerables Man Lian（滿蓮）and Yung Fu（永富）continue to organize the annual large-scale Dharma events in Hong Kong Coliseum and Victoria Park. In Brazil, Venerables Chueh Cheng（覺誠）, Miao Yuan（妙遠）, and Chueh Hsuan（覺軒）provide education to impoverished children. In the Philippines, Venerables Yung Guang（永光）and Miao Jing（妙淨）are leading the cast of "Siddhartha: The Musical" on a world tour around America, Malaysia, Singapore, Hong Kong, and Mainland China. In Europe, there is Venerable Man Chien（滿謙）, and also Venerables Ru Hai（如海）and Chueh Hsin（覺心）in Spain, Chueh Rong（覺容）and Miao Da（妙達）in France. In Chile, there is Miao Guan（妙觀）. In America, Venerables Hui Dong（慧東）, Ru Yang（如揚）, and Chueh Chuan（覺泉）engage in interfaith dialogues locally and at the United Nations. In Berlin, Venerable Miao Yi（妙益）now leads German nationals in the daily maintenance works of the temple such as morning and evening chanting, table services, cooking, and shrine attendance works. Similarly in Chung Tian Temple, Brisbane, the daily routine is managed by a group of Australian nationals. After a few decades, localization of Humanistic Buddhism is gradually happening.

2. Acculturating to Local Customs, and Development of Unique Characteristics around the World

What does localization mean? Localization is about contribution and fellowship. Localization means to follow each culture, each place, and each custom to develop a unique feature in different ways.

Localization does not imply the 'removal' of any elements but the action of 'giving.' It is hoped that through Buddhism, the people in each local area are given a more enriching spiritual life. This is exactly how Humanistic Buddhism holds true to Buddha's original intent—To be accepted by people.

The spread of Humanistic Buddhism around the world not only faces differences in policy and culture, interfaith dialogue with the Christian, Catholic and Muslim communities is also crucial. For this reason, I always encourage local Catholics and Christians to follow two faiths. This is akin to showing interest in both literature and philosophy at school.

Abiding by the principle of respect and tolerance in my travels around the globe, I have been received by world leaders such as Indian Prime Minister Jawaharlal Nehru, His Majesty King Bhumibol Adulyadej of Thailand, President Diosdado Pangan Macapagal of the Philippines, Vice President Al Gore of the United States, Malaysia Prime Minister Mahathir Mohamad, Singapore Prime Ministers Lee Kuan Yew (李光耀 , 1923-2015) and son Lee Hsien Loong (李顯龍), Australian Prime Minister Tony Abbott, and various leaders from Indochina countries. I also met with religious leaders such as Pope John Paul II, Pope Benedict XVI, and Cardinal Paul Shan Kuo-hsi SJ from Taiwan.

Worth mentioning is the World Fellowship of Buddhists (WFB), which was co-founded in 1950 by Master Taixu, Dr. Gunapala Piyasena Malalasekera from Sri Lanka and others in Colombo. In 1988, I had the pleasure of creating the cause for the WFB to step outside of Asia for the first time to hold the WFB 16th General Conference at Hsi Lai Temple in the United States. It was the first time in over decades for Buddhists from both sides of the Taiwan Strait to sit in the same conference in a Western country. This is said to bear similar significance with the 2015 meeting between Chinese President Xi Jinping and Taiwan President Ma Ying-jeou in Singapore. Other WFB General Conferences were subsequently organized at Nan Tien Temple in Australia, and Fo Guang Shan in Taiwan.

The WFB event in 1988 led to an invitation by Zhao Puchu, President of the Buddhist Association of China to the International Buddhist Progress Society to organize a five hundred member "International Buddhist Dharma Propagation China Tour Group" from America to visit Buddhist temples in various Chinese provinces. The group was received by Yang Shang-kun (楊尚昆 , 1907-1998), then President of the People's Republic of China for a one-hour meeting. We were then joined by Li Xiannian (李先念 , 1909-1992), then Chairman of the Chinese People's Political Consultative Conference in the Beijing Great Hall of the People for another meeting, followed by a banquet. It was unprecedented for monastics to be received inside the most supreme hall of the Communist Party, and also the highest form of reception to be given since the reform and opening of the Party.

In 2002, the Buddha's finger relic was escorted to Taiwan, yet another significant event. Under the signed authority by Jiang Zemin (江 澤 民), then General Secretary of the Communist Party of China that said, "Hsing Yun as the lead, united efforts in welcoming, enshrinement as one, and security as the top priority," the Buddhist circle of Taiwan was thus authorized to unite, regardless of sects or traditions, in escorting Xi'an Famen Temple's most treasured Buddha's finger relic to Taiwan. Then Chairperson of the Mainland Affairs Council of the Republic of China, and also 2016 President-elect, Tsai Ing-wen (蔡英文) assisted in arranging two Dragon Airlines charter flights to fly from Taipei via Hong Kong to Xi'an, creating a record in Cross-Strait direct flights. The entire process was recorded and broadcasted by Phoenix TV. Before direct flights opened up between the two Sides, Buddhism had already linked them together.

In 2003, under the support of Professor Tian Qing (田青) from the Chinese National Academy of Arts and Ye Xiaowen (葉 小文), then Director of the Bureau of Religious Affairs under the State Council, Fo Guang Shan Buddhist Monastic Choir was invited to perform inside the Beijing Forbidden City Concert Hall and Shanghai Grand Theatre. In hearing my closing remarks on stage at the Grand Theatre, many of the Elder monastics at the concert broke into tears, because they had never seen any monastic permitted to publicly give an address. To them, it was truly comforting to see monastics given such opportunities after so many years of suppression.

Subsequently, Director Ye and Professor Tian proposed the establishment of the Chinese Buddhist Music Performance Group in 2004 with Venerable Sheng Hui (聖輝), Vice President of the Buddhist Association of China as Chief, and Venerable Abbot Hsin Ting (心定) of Fo Guang Shan and Venerable Xuecheng, Secretary-General of the Buddhist Association of China as Vice Presidents. Under the collaborative works of Venerables Tzu Hui, Tzu Jung, and Yung Fu, over one hundred monastics from the Four Major Buddhist Schools as well as the Theravada, Chinese, and Tibetan traditions were assembled to perform at national halls in Hong Kong, Macau, and Taiwan as well as top-class theatres such as the Kodak Theatre in the United States and Queen Elizabeth Theatre in Canada. If such collaborative works continue, how can a friendly, peaceful, and united Cross-Strait relation not be possible in the future?

After the Cultural Revolution, the "Three Nos" policy was established by the Republic of China government, insisting on "no contact, no compromise and no negotiation" with the Communist Party. As a result, any religious conferences were held as internal affairs. When the First World Buddhist Forum was under preparation, the Bureau of Religious Affairs actually sent a charter flight to take me to Hainan to hold a consultation. Subsequently the Forum listed Venerable Kok Kwong from Hong Kong, Venerable Yi Cheng (一誠) from the Buddhist Association of China, and Panchen (班禪) Lama from Tibet amongst the eight conveners. The First Buddhist Forum was held in Hangzhou, the Second in Wuxi and closed in Taipei, marking yet another page in Cross-Strait Buddhist exchanges.

In February, 2013 I received an invitation to join the Taiwan Delegation lead by Lien Chan (連戰), Honorary Chairperson of the Nationalist Party to visit Xi Jinping, General Secretary of the Communist Party of China, and Hu Jintao (胡錦濤), President of the People's Republic of China. When I shook hands with Xi Jinping inside the Beijing Great Hall of the People, he said to me, "I have read your books." In reply, I said, "I have written a piece of calligraphy that says 'ascending high to see far.'"

From as early as 2006, when I was in Zhejiang to attend the First Buddhist Forum, I already had the opportunity to meet with Mr. Xi when he served as the Governor of Zhejiang. When he initiated construction of the Maitreya Big Buddha at Xuedou Temple, I wrote a piece of calligraphy that said, "Humanistic Maitreya," now engraved on the seat of the Maitreya Big Buddha. Some time later, I had another opportunity to meet with him again in Beijing. In 2015, when I attended the Boao Forum in Hainan, Mr. Xi was present at the group photo with our delegation. He reminded me of his father, Mr. Xi Zhongxun, a pious Buddhist who helped preserve Master Huineng's body relic when he served as Secretary of Guandong Provincial Party. I am truly grateful to them for their protection and support for Buddhism.

After that meeting with Mr. Xi, I was then received by Yu Zhengsheng (俞正聲), Chairman of the Chinese People's Political Consultative Conference. During the meeting, I proposed permission from the Party for the World Fellowship of Buddhists and the Buddha's Light International Association to hold their meetings in Mainland China to enhance fellowship and social harmony. With much gratitude, he agreed and enabled the WFB to hold their general conference in Xi'an in October 2014. The following October, BLIA held its Board of Directors Meeting at FGS Ancestral Temple—Yixing Dajue Temple. This extraordinary event would not have been possible without the assistance of Yu Zhengsheng, Wang Zuoan (王作安), Director of the State Administration for Religious Affairs, Wang Zhongsu (王中蘇), Secretary of Yixing City, and Yixing City Mayor.

As I look back to instances of international exchanges, the list goes on and on. For example, the World Tantric and Sutric Buddhist Conference, International Buddhist Academic Conference, World Fellowship of Buddhist Youth Academic Conference, Catholic and Buddhist International Dialogue and Conference, and various other inter-tradition, interfaith, and academic events. This gave me the opportunity to make acquaintances with eminent leaders such as Venerable Bhikkhu Sanghasena, Bhante Pannila Ananda, and Venerable K. Sri Dhammananda. In addition, Fo Guang Shan has also become Brother Temples with Wat Phra Dhammakaya in Thailand. For the past twenty years, the International Buddhist Monastic Seminar has been held annually. These are all important events in international Buddhist exchanges.

Other than the above, Professor David Chappell from University of Hawaii, Professor John McRae from Cornell University, Professor Stanley Weinstein from Yale, Professor Lewis R Lancaster from University of California, Berkeley, and also Professors from the Mainland such as Fang Litian (方立天), Lou Yulie (樓宇烈), Yang Zengwen (楊曾文), and Lai Yonghai (賴永海) are good friends of Humanistic Buddhism.

3. Friendly Exchanges Leading to the Actualization of the Humanistic Buddha Land

A world Buddhist movement requires the participation of all Buddhist leaders from the Mainland and Taiwan to make globalization of Buddhism possible. What we have achieved so far is the establishment of University of the West in America, Nan Tien Institute in Australia, and Guang Ming College as well as the Academy of Art in Philippines who are propagating the Dharma in the form of musicals. There is also the Nan Hua Performing Arts School from Nan Hua Temple in South Africa. In Brazil, the Soccer Team made up of the Sons of Zulai is actively propagating Humanistic Buddhism through the means of soccer games. The Vienna Youth Philharmonic Orchestra plays the sounds of the Dharma not only through their performances but also by composing their own music and lyrics. In India, Venerable Hui Xian (慧顯) continues the education program for some one hundred novices in hopes of revitalizing Buddhism there. It is hoped that these children will one day play a role in India's Humanistic Buddhism. In recent years, Fo Guang Shan has also become an annual gathering place for over a thousand students from some four hundred universities as a place for self-discovery and learning.

In the past, international travel was exclusive, not to mention costly for international Buddhist activities. Today, monastic and lay Buddhists are found on all five continents of the world, working hand-in-hand to propagate Humanistic Buddhism. In particular, the Buddha Musuem has been receiving guests from all over the world since its opening in 2011. We are in an era of fellowship that has transcended all backgrounds such as religion, and nationality. Is this continued exchange and fellowship under the spirit of oneness, coexistence, and mutual respect not already a manifestation of the Buddha Land?

We hereby dedicate the abovementioned merits to all living beings within the Dharma realm. May happiness and peace be with all. Last but not least, may we dedicate all merits to the Buddha and show our gratitude to him by propagating Humanistic Buddhism, which holds true to Buddha's original intents.

Chapter Six

Conclusion

Summary of Chapter Six

Humanistic Buddhism denotes the Dharma, the Buddha's teachings for humanity. Its sacredness is indubitable. It adheres to the truths of all the Buddha's fundamental teachings and holds the Three Jewels as its core. However, it also emphasizes the humanistic, relevant, altruistic, joyful, universal, and timely characteristics of Buddhism, as well as the global spread of the Dharma.

Only one side of Buddhism was shown, bereft of a comprehensive interpretation of the doctrine, resulting in a divergence from the Buddha's original intents. Unsurprisingly, the spread of Buddhism was thus limited.

In the future, Humanistic Buddhism shall evolve from the passive attitude of "suffering, emptiness, and impermanence" into one that is positive, beneficial, and essential. Its shall expand from a monastic focus to one that encompasses both lay and monastics, men and women alike. It shall advance from being reclused in distant mountains and forests to connecting with society and adapting to urban life. It shall emerge from being confined to temple grounds and individual practices, towards integrating with family life, as well as with service and contribution as ways of cultivation.

Humanistic Buddhism shall transform temples and families into places of practice. Bridging the gap between seclusion and society, it will ensure greater interaction between Buddhists. Similarly, Humanistic Buddhism shall strive to be socially relevant in whatever ways conditions require. All Buddhists shall unite and advocate the spirit of Buddhism. Peace and stability shall be achieved through a Humanistic Pure Land of the Five Harmonies. This is why we propose Humanistic Buddhism: holding true to Buddha's original intents.

Conclusion

Ever since I found my faith in Buddhism, I gradually realized that this religion is also found in various countries and regions of the world. Thai people follow Thai Buddhism. Burmese people follow Burmese Buddhism. Vietnamese people follow Vietnamese Buddhism. Mongolian, Qinghai and Tibetan people follow Tibetan Buddhism. Korean people follow Korean Buddhism. Japanese people follow Japanese Buddhism. Indeed, Chinese people follow Chinese Buddhism.

Amongst the many Chinese faiths, my earliest belief in Buddhism began with Guanyin Bodhisattva, and later incorporated within that of Amitabha Buddha, Ksitigarbha Bodhisattva, and Samantabhadra Bodhisattva. Consequently, as I realized that Sakyamuni Buddha, Lord of the Saha World, founded Buddhism I finally discerned how intricate my faith was.

As my faith developed, I eventually gathered the many foci of belief back into one, that is, the Buddha. My faith was thus in Sakyamuni Buddha, the founder of Buddhism.

The Buddha manifests in billions of forms, many of which comprise the aforementioned buddhas and bodhisattvas. In such regard, the candor of my faith is further affirmed. Thus, when in the presence of a Guanyin Bodhisattva statue, I would be prostrating to Sakyamuni Buddha. Before an Amitabha Buddha effigy, I would be prostrating myself to Sakyamuni Buddha as well. In the same manner, when facing a Sakyamuni Buddha statue, I could also be prostrating to Amitabha Buddha and the Medicine Buddha.

Subsequent to the Buddhist saying, "All buddhas are on the same path, and all lights interpenetrate one another," I am certain that my actions are correct. Each buddha embodies all other buddhas, while all buddhas symbolize the one buddha. All the buddhas and bodhisattvas are represented by the supreme one—Sakyamuni Buddha.

My faith in the Buddha inspired me to write *The Biography of Sakyamuni Buddha* at the young age of 25. In those days, some referred to Sakyamuni Buddha as 'Buddha,' others called him 'Tathagata,' some regarded him as "the world honored one," and others addressed him as 'the Noble Sakya.' Likewise, Tathagata also has the Ten Epithets. Despite these many names, I still believe all are redundant save one—'Buddha.'

Ever since my decision to simply refer to the Buddha as 'Buddha' in *The Biography of Sakyamuni Buddh*a, this is the only title found in my writings.

Humanistic Buddhism is Buddhism founded by Buddha. Buddhism split into Early Buddhism, Sectarian Buddhism, Northern Buddhism, and Theravada Buddhism. In China, there is Huayan Buddhism, Tiantai Buddhism, Consciousness-Only Buddhism, and Pure Land Buddhism. It is simply impossible to follow all these numerous and varied types of faith. For example, Chan Buddhism alone is comprised of Five Schools and Seven Sects. Exactly which school or sect do I, as a Buddhist, belong to?

This edifies me about the so-called faith. In this world, people will insist on their own chosen faiths. Some contend in their faith in Pure Land Buddhism, some in Consciousness-only Buddhism, others Chan Buddhism, and some on Three Treatises Buddhism. Deeming all else as inferior or mistaken, people will each have their specific faith, believing theirs paramount. Truthfully, all are Buddhism. The only people who are impairing the Dharma are Buddhists themselves.

There was a gongan about a Chan Master who suffered of

Wat Chin: Life of the Buddha - Miracle at Sravasti
THAILAND, Ayutthaya; 7th–8th century; Sandstone;
H: 129 cm; Bangkok National Museum, Thailand

rheumatism in his legs. His two disciples took on the duties of massaging each of his legs. When the senior disciple massaged his right leg, the Master complimented the junior disciple for doing a wonderful job with his left leg, making the senior very unhappy. When the junior massaged his left leg, the Master spoke about how his senior disciple did a great job with his right leg, causing un-happiness in the junior. As they became jealous of each other, they decided to break their Master's other leg so that the other disciple would be without a leg to massage. This is a flaw of human nature to show no forbearance to those who are better than them.

In order to impart their own hatred, they sacrificed both legs of their master. Is this not a phenomenon among all Buddhists? They defame each other merely to legitimize their own faith without perceiving they are actually extinguishing the future of Buddhism. If we continue to demean and condemn one another for being wrong or inferior, how can Buddhism ever prosper? The future of Buddhism is only possible with the power of all Buddhists united.

Life of the Buddha - Return to Kapilavastu; THAILAND; circa 1750–1780; Ink and color on paper; L: 66.5 cm; Bodleian Library, University of Oxford, UK

There are many who developed arrogance and selfishness after becoming Buddhists. Some, as missionaries, took the contributions of devotees for granted. Others, as scholars, criticized and divided Buddhist faith by means of rivalry and depreciation. In the end, what crumbles is Buddhism, leaving everyone with ruins. All that has been done is nothing but defamation and sabotage. Have you ever come across any scholar or expert criticize and compare the Bible?

Among Buddhists, Chan practitioners would belittle Pure Land followers, deeming them as ignorant. Pure Land practitioners on the other hand would accuse Chan followers of being delusional. Some believe in self-reliance, while some favored being dependent, all belittling each other, oblivious that their futile bickering has only one consequential outcome: the ruin of Buddhism. They may as well simplify their faith and integrate all into a single teaching. Let each other believe in their own chosen faith without defamation. Such is the true way of a decent believer. This is comparable to the organs encompassing your face. Let the eyes, ears, and nose each do their job. Any act of comparison is meaningless. Only with collaborative effort can we be made whole.

With a single Sakyamuni Buddha featuring billions of manifestations in Buddhism, we should all be allowed to follow our own chosen faith and abide each other. Shall this magnanimous bearing be demonstrated, then my faith in the supreme one—Sakyamuni Buddha will be further affirmed.

Having grown up in Qixiashan Monastery and Jiaoshan Monastery for over a decade, I seldom saw any lay devotees visit the monastery. Living within were only a few dozen or hundred monastics passing their days and nights chanting and eating. I pondered if this was all Buddhism could ever be?

Some time later, when I returned to my ancestral temple—Dajue Temple in Yixing, I never saw visiting devotees during my two year stay. The only people were my senior Dharma brother, farmers, some workers and myself. Was Buddhism not supposed to be "Amitabha found in every home, and Guanyin in every family"? If the Chinese believed in Buddhism, why had Sakyamuni Buddha never existed in their faith?

From when my faith in Buddhism began, I always believed in that Buddha. Yet why is Sakyamuni Buddha only found inside monasteries or mountain forests instead of families and society? The only path to a righteous faith is for all Buddhists to establish their faith in the founder—the Great Buddha.

Stemming from such thoughts, I vowed to bring Buddhism out of the mountains and into society, to ensure that monastics interact with lay Buddhists, and to take Buddhism from temples into homes. I also pledged to shift a faith that focused on meaningless metaphysical discussions to one devoted to serving society. It was also vital to alter Buddhism's focus on monastic cultivations of chanting, meditation, and reciting Buddha's name to being open to all Buddhists for collective cultivation, fellowship and interchange.

During my days at Jiaoshan Buddhist College, I attended the Buddhist Association of China's Committee Training Seminar organized by Master Taixu (太虛 , 1890-1947). I held my own philosophy about the establishment of a "new Buddhism," and was aware that Buddhists must be cautious about internal disputes and external threats. Generally, what Buddhism needs is reform. Despite my passion to engage in Buddhist reform movements, the little weight I carried gave me no leverage. Consequently, the only thing that I achieved was the publication of the monthly *Raging Waves* magazine. When my master—Venerable Master Zhi Kai

(志開 , 1911-1979) heard of this, he donated fifty reams of paper as encouragement. The support of my Master for my first endeavor meant a lot to me, because it inferred that I had not done it out of my own selfish purpose.

Later, when I assumed the posts of Superintendent and then Abbot at Huazang Monastery in Nanjing, though the tenures were short, I was already nurturing a blueprint for "new Buddhism." The vision involved endeavors in education, culture, philanthropy, organization of devotees, and an enlarged Buddhist community. In those days, Huazang Monastery already owned a textile mill, a primary school, and a hot water vendor. All these services held direct links to people's daily living. For this reason, I believed the future of a new Buddhism must involve social services and connection to the people in order for it to endure.

Regrettably, the conservatives within the Monastery hindered such vision and passion. Some twenty monastics residing in the monastery depended on chanting services as a way to survive and to cover daily expenses. However, if a monastery were to do nothing but chanting, unable to teach or propagate the Dharma, or offer service to society; I wondered if they were still in accord with the Buddhist objectives of altruism and propagation. The task of Buddhist reform was a difficult one.

By chance, I arrived in Taiwan with the Monastic Rescue Team and was fortunate enough to find residence at Yuan Guang Temple in Chungli, doing chores and services for two years. Later, I assumed a position as Dean at the Taiwan Buddhist Seminar in Tsingtsao Lake in Hsinchu for a year and a half. Subsequently, I found lodgings in Yilan. Conscious that I was still young, and determined, surely I would be able to accomplish great things for Buddhism.

Lei Yin Temple in Yilan started off as a small branch of the

Longhua Sect. Inside lived a seventy-year-old bhiksuni, an old laywoman, and three households of military dependents. The only space they could offer to a Dharma speaker like myself was a small room behind the Buddha statue in the Main Shrine. Given the poor living conditions, coupled with my ten years of monastic training, I was able to nurture my traits of patience and endurance.

I began to think of the needs of youths, children, and care for the disadvantaged minority, as well as women in Buddhism. I wondered what conditions were needed in order to convey them from where they were to the face of the Buddha.

The process was not uneventful, but I finally felt that I was settled down in Yilan. Why? Many youths were willingly attending my Dharma talks, while veterans and teachers from Yilan Secondary School, Yilan Agricultural School, Yilan Ladies Secondary School, and the Signal Communication Corps School joined me as friends and devotees. They contributed to the founding of the Buddhist Choir, Dharma Propagation Team, and even the Humanities and Sciences Tuition School.

With my faith in the Buddha as my core, I felt it was essential for monastics and lay devotees to coexist in harmony. So, I opened the temple door to devotees for chanting and cultivation activities. I also organized events such as the Chanting Association, Meditation Association, Women's Association, Youth Association, Student Association, Children's Class, and others. These served as practical means for people from all walks of life to come in front of the Buddha to discover physical and mental well-being, through his blessings and teachings. Thus I also advocated: "Discover your practices in Chan, Pure Land, and collective cultivation, as well as your understanding in all forms of Dharma."

Buddhism in Yilan became lively and dynamic. Lei Ying Temple was so small that it offered no space for a conversation lounge, and people had to stand in the corridors to chat, but no one complained. Also, there existed a large community of I-Kuan Tao followers in Yilan, yet they were all willing to join me in propagation works. The development of Buddhism in Yilan would not have been possible without the support of these people. Due to this, I was free from the subjections of conservative Buddhists throughout the decades of my stay in Yilan.

At first, I was uncertain why Buddhism had to be further divided into many names such as "Humanistic Buddhism," "Life Buddhism," or "World Buddhism," but I nevertheless decided to

Amaravati: Paying Respect to the Buddha's Footprints; INDIA, Andhra Pradesh, Amaravati; Satavahana period (circa 200 BCE–250 CE), circa mid-1st century; Limestone; H: 40.6 cm; Government Museum, Chennai, Tamil Nadu, India

keep it simple by propagating a Buddhism suitable for all.

As time went by, I came to discover that Buddhism truly evolved along with history, culture, diverse backgrounds, as well as the changing needs of time. No matter the needs, Buddhism must be centered on humans and help them discover happiness, safety, and transcendence, in addition to perfection of their character. Therefore, I came to focus on something that regarded human nature the same as buddha-nature, a principle based on "a buddha comes from a perfected human," and "humans are buddhas-to-be," namely, the unity of humans and buddha—Humanistic Buddhism.

I truly believe that Humanistic Buddhism can encompass all types of Buddhism together with the complex system of faiths and names that have existed throughout the past two thousand years. Humanistic Buddhism shall redirect Buddhism once divided by geography, time, and individual bias back to Buddhism that is rooted in self as a human being and the Buddha. Steadily, I found myself on the path of Humanistic Buddhism for it truly befits the needs of humanity and, in my belief, is the only path that shall guide the world towards the light of hope.

Humanistic Buddhism is centered on the Three Jewels and the fundamental teachings of impermanence, suffering, emptiness, selflessness, Three Dharma Seals, Four Noble Truths, Noble Eightfold Path, Threefold Learnings, Four Ways of Embracing, and Six Paramitas. The word 'Humanistic' is emphasized in the hope that all Buddhists shall value the spread of Dharma within this world in need of it. The neglect of this world, and of the daily needs of humanity will result in the marginalization of Buddhism. Humanistic Buddhism offers Dharma that purifies and elevates human character in a world filled with temptations of the Five Desires and Six Sense Fields.

Back in those days, my mind was focused solely on propagating Humanistic Buddhism. Many times I declined the invitation to be Director General of the Buddhist Association of Yilan County. In my mind, if I was unable to join the Buddhist Association of China in the Mainland, then what meaning was there in being the Director General of a Buddhist Association in Yilan? Hence, throughout the decades of my stay in Yilan, I was referred to by no particular title but simply "the Venerable from Yilan," or "the Venerable from the Northern Gate." Most people were even unaware that my Dharma name was Hsing Yun.

Amidst all these endeavors, I never forsook publication works. On a weekly, sometimes monthly basis, I traveled to Taipei to edit articles for *Awakening the World Periodical, Life Magazine,* as well as *Awakening Sentient Beings* or *Bodhedrum.*

In the 1950s, a few youths from Yilan finally established the Buddhist Cultural Service Center in Sanchongpu, near Taipei, for the publication of Monthly Buddhist Texts in vernacular language, as well as distribution of some Buddhist instruments and objects.

The cause for the Center was a question raised by the youths, "Master, other than believing in Buddhism, what else can we do?" The query struck me like a thunderbolt. Indeed! Other than believing in Buddhism, what else can devotees do? I therefore encouraged them to establish a kindergarten and the Buddhist Cultural Service Center as ways to offer their service to the world. Among these youths were those who later would become Venerables Hsin Ping (心平), Tzu Chuang (慈莊), Tzu Hui (慈惠), and Tzu Jung (慈容).

Nevertheless, these accomplishments drew envy and jealousy from the Buddhist Association of the Republic of China. In fear that I would supplant them, they began to hinder and impair my movements in different ways. For example, declining to pass on the

Children Paying Respect to the Buddha
CHINA; Ming dynasty (1368–1644);
By Chen Hongshou; Ink and color on silk;
149.5 x 67.5 cm; Palace Museum, Beijing, China

applications of our youths to study abroad in Japan, or rejecting our applications for leading pilgrimages to India and other nations. Fortunately, some government officials offered alternatives to these youths.

This prompted me of the need to join the Buddhist Association of China to remove such obstacles. In those days, merely a few young monastics were actively propagating the Dharma. Consequently I was fortunate enough to receive the support and guidance of some elders. Several even nominated me for membership to the standing committee.

However, my mind was set only on the role of Secretary-General, a position that could have truly allowed me to plan and promote activities for Buddhism. Moreover, I felt undeserving of the committee position since I owed neither assets nor resources, which would disgrace the Association by having someone so insignificant assume such a role in it. For this reason, I wrote an article, "My reasons for declining the position of standing committee of the Buddhist Association of the Republic of China."

Certainly, difficulties were also due to my young age and inexperience. Particularly, the articles I published in *Life Magazine* and *Raging Waves*, with my opinions on reform, clearly offended the elders and conservatives. Our names were like the "Four Bandits," (Sun Yat-sen (孫中山 , 1866-1925), Yang Heling (楊鶴齡 , 1868-1934), Chen Shaobai (陳少白 , 1869-1934), and Yu Lie (尤列 , 1866-1936) of the Kuomintang Party, and also of the founders of the Communist Party such as Mao Zedong (毛澤東 , 1893-1976). People shirked any connection with us. Furthermore, being a native of Jiangsu, I was mindful of the fact that many townsmen also coveted a position in the Association. This made it more difficult to accomplish anything.

This ambience persisted till 1963, when the Buddhist Association of the Republic of China organized a delegation to Southeast Asia and America. I was nominated by some of the more opened-minded central committee members of the Nationalist Party who had read my articles in *Life Magazine,* as well as *Awakening the World Periodical.* Comprehending that the leaders of the Buddhist Association opposed my nomination, they held a vegetarian banquet for these Elders in an attempt to persuade them, and remind them of the Nationalist Party's influence. Consequently, the Elders reluctantly agreed to add my name to the list of delegates and appointed me as spokesperson for the delegation.

The deputation visited Hong Kong, Philippines, Japan, Malaysia, Singapore, Thailand, and even Buddha's homeland— India, thereby fulfilling my greatest wish. Moreover, it was also an eye-opening experience for a young and philomath Buddhist like me.

During our visit to India, Indian Prime Minister Jawaharlal Nehru received the delegation. Rather regrettably, my speech during the meeting was published on the front page of the *Central Daily News* instead of that of the delegation Chief, prompting his intense disapproval. Consequently, my relationship with them became especially strenuous. Not only was I prohibited from leaving the country for future representations of the Buddhist circle, my attempts in any new Buddhist endeavors were rigorously suppressed. I was not even permitted to respond to the summons of President Chiang Kai-shek (蔣介石 , 1887-1975).

As averse as I am to mention the merits and demerits of the Buddhist Association, as all are merely mundane affairs and have little to do with the propagation of Buddhism; I nevertheless suffered an endless array of criticisms and accusations. Several from the Buddhist circles held me as "Hsing Yun the destroyer of Buddhism," "Hsing Yun the Mara of Buddhism," or "Hsing Yun who is pushing Buddhism towards destruction with his choir." Notwithstanding, my faith and passion for Humanistic Buddhism remained firm and unyielding. Everything was purely for the sake of Buddhism.

Whenever eminent monks from the Mainland gathered in Taipei, a mere phone call would bring me out of Yilan to accompany these guests, or respond to an edict to attend a meeting. The endless salutations and farewells left me with no time to tend to my propagation works. Starting from the 1960's, I continuously travelled back and forth between Kaohsiung and Yilan to cultivate affinities with devotees. Occasionally the devotees from Kaohsiung were so eager and passionate that I became hesitant to live in Kaohsiung, as that passion could sometimes be as scorching as the weather down South.

Reluctant to wane such passion, and recognizing the difficulty to initiate anything in the North; coupled with the fact that no monks from the Mainland were agreeable to settling in the South, I journeyed southward on my own. I consequently erected Kaohsiung Buddhist Hall, Shou Shan Temple, and Fo Guang Shan Monastery. Contentedly free from the convoluted concerns of the Buddhist circle in Taipei, I became "the Mainland monk in Southern Taiwan" and relished the indulgence of fully focusing on Dharma propagation and education works as well as the rapports with the native Buddhist elders there.

Based in Taipei, the Buddhist Association of the Republic of China was elated to learn of my departure, and several vowed to ensure that I would never return. Not once did I take this statement to heart. Years later, I managed to construct Pu Men Temple,

Yonghe Temple, Sanchong Cultural Square, Taipei Vihara in Song-shan, and Jin Guang Ming Temple in Sanxia.

Thus far, that I was able to establish branch temples across Taiwan and worldwide comes from my strong motivation resultant from such duress. Sometimes loss may turn out to be gain. Providing we have faith and never fear adversities, we may be driven to become stronger and braver in undertaking yet greater things in the future.

Later, when I founded Tsung-Lin University at Fo Guang Shan, the Buddhist Association even held a meeting in Taipei to entertain means to subvert it. Gratefully, then Secretary-General of the Association Feng Yung-chen (馮永楨), spoke up, "If we cannot even topple the Catholic seminaries or Christian Bible colleges, why attempt to bring down a Buddhist college?" His daring speech and

Fo Guang Shan Jin Guang Ming Temple: Main Temple Gate
TAIWAN, New Taipei City

fortitude spared me yet again from another woeful occurrence.

Regardless, I remained disposed and supportive to the Buddhist Association of the Republic of China. For example, having already been excluded from the World Fellowship of Buddhists Conference, I continued to contest for the Association's right to participate. In view of my struggles, I was merited to be elected Director-General, my youth notwithstanding. However, Venerable Pai Sheng (白聖 , 1904-1989) had held the position for over forty years. No matter what we had to say, these Elders insisted on knocking us with the baton instead of passing it on.

That is why I saw the Buddhist Association of the Republic of China as key to Buddhist reform. Yet grasping the ineffectuality of that affiliation, I thus resolved to become self-dependent and founded Fo Guang Shan, starting with educational endeavors. At this time, the government accepted our proposal to establish the Young Buddhist Association of the Republic of China. This was of course vehemently opposed by the Association who went to extremes to ensure that this did not happen.

Respectfully, Tung Shu-pan (董樹藩 , 1932-1986), Chairperson of the Mongolian and Tibetan Affairs Committee mediated with them, and advocated for the establishment of the Chinese Han-Tibet Culture Association, with me as President. However, given the circumstances amongst the Han and Tibetan cultures, the proposal went unfulfilled.

In light of the way Venerable Pai Sheng seized control of the Buddha Association of the Republic of China without ever valuing the need to foster talent, thereby severely impeding the development of Buddhism; I deemed it a lesson. At age fifty-eight, having served for eighteen years, I voluntarily retired as the Head Abbot of Fo Guang Shan. This was to ensure that Fo Guang Shan had an established constitution, and to entrust the responsibility of managing the order in the hands of my disciples. I then journeyed overseas alone to pursue my works in Dharma propagation.

Successively, Hsi Lai Temple in Los Angeles, I.B.P.S., New York, He Hua Temple in the Netherlands, Nan Tien Temple and Chung Tian Temple in Australia, Templo Zu Lai in Brazil, Nan Hua Temple in South Africa, and Fo Guang Shan France were founded, empowering my work of Dharma propagation to embrace all five continents. In addition, in 1992, we instituted the Buddha's Light International Association World Headquarters in Los Angeles, under whose umbrella are now several million members across a few thousand chapters and sub-chapters across the world.

The Buddha's teaching of "reverse contributory factor" serves as a reminder for all prevailing monastics to respect, encourage, and support each other. Even should we encounter enemies, instead of getting agitated, we might as well be motivated. There will eventually be opportunities for us to realize our vows. For this I

Fo Guang Shan Hsi Lai Temple
USA, California, Hacienda Heights

remain hopeful and determined in the propagation of Humanistic Buddhism.

Consequently, I firmly believe that only by being good to others will good causes and conditions occur. Any desire to defeat or demean others is futile, for we will only bring ourselves down. The aforesaid chronicle was merely a brief one in which I open my heart to the Buddha. We shall strive to learn from the Buddha's arduous cultivation of doing the impossible, and enduring the unbearable.

Speaking of Humanistic Buddhism, in the spring of 2000, whilst having breakfast at Fo Guang Shan with Dr. Charles HC Kao (高希均), Professor Emeritus of Wisconsin University, he asked me, "What is Humanistic Buddhism?"

Never having thought of this question, I nevertheless provided an answer. "Humanistic Buddhism is, 'What was taught by the Buddha, needed by human beings, that which purifies, and that which is virtuous and beautiful.'"

"Wonderful! I now know what Humanistic Buddhism is." Replied Dr. Kao joyously.

For an honorable professor, who was not a Buddhist, to grasp the meaning of Humanistic Buddhism from just a few simple words, an enlightened mind is clearly needed. From this it can be seen that only with prajna wisdom as well as a mind that is clear and aware can the profound meaning of Humanistic Buddhism be thoroughly perceived.

As I reminisce on my life as a monastic, any endeavor I have been involved in has been for the sole purpose of propagating Humanistic Buddhism. Such efforts comprised: erecting monasteries for monastic cultivation, founding Tsung-Lin University, and advocating the dual practice of Chan and Pure Land Buddhism as well as daily spiritual cultivation. I vowed to liberate people

Budai; CHINA; Ming dynasty (1368–1644), dated 1503; Ink and color on silk; 169.8 x 97.8 cm; Museum of Fine Arts, Boston, Massachusetts, USA

from suffering and adversity, as well as value family happiness and peace. Therefore, I proposed the Four Givings: Give others faith, give others joy, give others hope, and give others convenience, in addition to the Three Acts of Goodness, Five Harmonies, Seven Admonitions, and Noble Eightfold Path. Subsequently, the teachings of Humanistic Buddhism began to spread.

Upon hearing that the elderly faced a communication gap with the younger generations, I vowed to establish retirement homes. Upon hearing that children from broken families were left uncared for, I built a children's home. Upon hearing that children from impoverished families may be on the verge of forsaking their education, I founded kindergartens, primary schools, and secondary schools. Upon hearing the need for mass media communication, I established radio stations, a television station, and a newspaper company. Anything needed by humanity is my responsibility, and I shall endeavor to give, in the form of Dharma, in every way possible.

As the devotee community grew larger and more resourceful, I recalled that while there were already many religion-founded universities across the world, and dozens of Buddhist-affiliated universities in Japan, Chinese Buddhists had yet to establish any universities. In fact, at one time, the word "*tsung-lin*" meant university. It was a place of learning for students from all derivations. Regretfully, the monastery's abbot held no grand vows or visions. His sole focus for the monastery was a place for monastics to inhabit instead of expanding it as a public school or place for spiritual cultivation. It was now time to amend its meaning, instead of simply establishing monasteries, we may as well found universities.

I thus initiated the "Million-Member Fundraising Campaign"

and established five universities in and out of Taiwan. However, having never received a formal education, and thus unqualified to even teach in a secondary school; how was I to establish a university? Auspiciously, the law still allows me to serve as founder and board chairman, and there are, at present, more than a thousand teachers instructing at universities, secondary schools, and primary schools founded in my name.

I am grateful for all the opportunities that have made the establishment of FGS's universities possible. Also for the affinities shared by many who have invited me to give lectures on campus as well as bestowed upon me doctoral degrees and the title of emeritus professor. For instance, I have taught Buddhist Studies for six years at the Christian-affiliated Tunghai University, and also served as Dean of the Institute of Indian Cultural Studies at Chinese Culture University for many years. In my mind, justice will be served as long as we make solid accomplishments.

At this point, I cannot help but ponder. In the long course of history, how can people of all nations, races, social strata, gender and age accept Buddhism? If Buddha was able to convert some ninety-six 'heretics,' why is it that we are not able to do so with humanity today?

Thinking further, why is it that bodhisattvas and deities have larger followings than the Buddha? Is it because Buddha has not offered them the wealth, safety, and longevity that deities have supposedly bestowed on them, or the deliverance and salvation which bodhisattvas have offered? Hence, these believers feel a deeper connection with deities and bodhisattvas, yet are unable to take in the universal and eternal truth of Dependent Origination taught by the great Buddha. It is truly regretful to see this!

As I recall, how is it that Mazu (媽祖), Lu Dongbin (呂洞賓),

Guan Yu (關雲長) and the City Lord (王爺), once followers of Buddhism, are now deities with independent followings that have outgrown the Buddhist community?

Buddha entrusted the Dharma to his disciples in the hope that they would further propagate and exalt their faith. The future of Buddhism lies not solely on the Buddha but all Buddhists. For our own faith, for the Buddha, for the future of humanity, and for ourselves, we shall ensure that the Buddha's light shines universally. Once the light of the Buddha illuminates our own minds, we shall also be free from all affliction, ignorance, sorrow, sadness, suffering, and hardship.

For this reason, I have proposed the following Buddhist principles:

1. Glory goes to the Buddha
2. Success goes to the multitude
3. Benefit goes to society
4. Merit goes to devotees

Our faith in Humanistic Buddhism lies not within the blessings of the Buddha but in our aspirations to contribute to his endeavors and all living beings. This is the only way for Buddhism to have a future.

The Dharma incorporates all teachings and forsakes nothing. With such inspiration, Buddhists never neglect anyone in need. We are willing to do anything, and everything. With the concerted effort of monastics and lay Buddhists, men and women, Humanistic Buddhism shall be widely propagated and touch all corners of the world.

In our endeavor to reconnect Buddhism with real life, practitioners of Humanistic Buddhism, comparable to Buddha's countless manifestations and Avalokitesvara's thirty-two forms of responsive manifestations, have reached out to society through expedient means to serve, contribute, and cultivate affinities. With unceasing diligence, the following achievements and innovations in Dharma propagation have been accomplished over the past decades:

1. **Education:** Primary, secondary, and tertiary schools, Buddhist colleges, institutes of Buddhist studies, Chinese schools, devotees seminars, urban Buddhist College programs, and public education trust funds.
2. **Media:** Magazines, newspaper, radio station, television station, and online courses.
3. **Art:** Exhibition centers, art galleries, publication of the *Encyclopedia of World Buddhist Arts*, and museums such as the Buddha Museum.
4. **Food:** Vegetarian restaurants and Water Drop Teahouses to provide vegetarian meals.
5. **Charity:** Cloud and Water Mobile Clinic, children's homes, retirement homes, sickbays, hospice rooms, Community Service Team, and Mentality Protection Center Vehicles.
6. **Activities:** Summer camps, Young Adults Divisions, children's classes, BLIA Scouts, Devotees' Dharma Gathering, alms processions, social movements, Buddhist weddings, Dharma lectures, pilgrimages to India, pilgrimage groups, Cloud and Water Mobile Library Trucks, Forums, Million-Member Fundraising Campaign, correctional center Dharma programs, Dharma visits to Armed Forces and remote islands.
7. **Sports:** Basketball teams, baseball teams, gymnastic teams, soccer teams, and cheer squads, augmenting Buddhist faith

Seokguram Grotto: Sakyamuni Buddha
SOUTH KOREA, North Gyeongsang, Gyeongju;
Unified Silla dynasty (668–935); Stone; H: 3.26 m

among athletes.

8. **Conferences:** International conferences such as the Symposium on Humanistic Buddhism, International Sangha Conference, World Buddhist Forum, various Cross-Strait Buddhist and cultural forums, World Fellowship of Buddhists general conferences taken beyond Asia into FGS branch temples in America and Australia.

9. **Academic publications:** Publishing houses, collections of papers from various international academic conferences, *A*

*Collection of Contemporary Buddhist Works: Chinese Buddhist
Academic Series, Universal Gate Buddhist Journal, Humanistic
Buddhism: Journal, Arts and Culture,* and hundreds of other
magazine and journal publications.

10. **Spiritual cultivation:** Holiday retreats, Humanistic Buddhist
Reading Association, Short-Term Monastic Retreats, and Triple
Platform Full Ordination Ceremonies.

11. **Music and dance:** Music groups, Buddhist choirs, and Buddhist
music concerts.

12. **Constitution:** Establishment of organizations, advocating
equality between monastic and lay Buddhists, the BLIA Lay
Dharma Lecturer, Sudana and Sumagadhi Lecturer's systems,
advocating gender equality, and petitioning for Buddha's
Birthday to be listed as a national holiday.

These Buddhist undertakings have subsequently been taken in
hand by numerous youths who continue to provide further opportunities for people to be of service and play a role in the development
of Buddhism. Many of these young Buddhists established Buddhist
Monastic Choirs, performing in different parts of the world, each
time well received by the locals. Evidently, we are living in the
golden era of Humanistic Buddhism.

Besides the aforesaid endeavors, we are grateful for the good
causes created by the Mainland leaders to develop Cross-Strait
Chinese cultural exchanges. For instance, five million people
attended the welcoming of the Buddha's finger relic to Taiwan.
The concerts of the Chinese Buddhist Music Performance Group in
different parts of the world were also quite successful. Later, I was
given permission to restore my ancestral temple—Yixing Dajue
Temple that now houses the Yunhu Program, Yangzhou Program,

and Humanistic Program. In the prosperous time of Humanistic Buddhism it is hoped that we Buddhists will place greater resolve on what we can do for the Buddha and Buddhism instead of what they can offer us.

"Humanistic Buddhism" is simply Buddhism itself, and not some contrived attempt at distinctiveness. Since Buddha was born in the human world, if his teachings were not Humanistic Buddhism, would it be better to call them Rebirth Buddhism? Animal Buddhism? or Hell Buddhism, Asura Buddhism, or even Hungry Ghost Buddhism? This is illogical.

Humanistic Buddhism inspires us to establish a Buddha's Pure Land in this world. Just as Master Taixu said, "The attainment of Buddhahood is concurrent with the perfection of our human characters." The Dharma should help each Buddhist find spiritual peace and eradicate one's greed, anger, and afflictions to find a home in life, maintain harmony within family, love self as well as others, and enjoy life.

Especially, contemporary Buddhists are gradually discovering that just a single phrase in Humanistic Buddhism or a single teaching by the Buddha suffices to truly change their lives, their families, their attitude, and their ways of dealing with the world. Having benefited from the teachings and practices of Humanistic Buddhism, one will come to realize that Buddha Land and Pure Land can be found right here, in this world. Providing our human characters are refined and improved, we are not distant from the Buddha.

This is exactly what Humanistic Buddhism proposes. It is hoped that the Buddha's spirit of sacrifice and benevolence can be fulfilled forthwith, so that the history and Dharma of Humanistic Buddhism can prevail. It is also hoped that outstanding Buddhist organizations and leaders will step forward to guide the world in the continued heritage of Buddhism. May those who share similar aspirations come together to "Let the Buddha's light shine universally, and the Dharma stream flow eternally." As the saying goes, "The duty of Dharma propagation lies in the hands of monastics."

In summary,

- Humanistic Buddhism holds true to Buddha's original intents.
- Humanistic Buddhism is Buddhism in its truest form.
- Humanistic Buddhism is for humanity.
- Humanistic Buddhism is universal Buddhism.
- Humanistic Buddhism is a ray of hope for the future of humanity.
- Humanistic Buddhism is a compass for life.
- Humanistic Buddhism is a spiritual provision for life.
- Humanistic Buddhism offers a mental and spiritual home.
- Humanistic Buddhism serves as a remedy to political, social and economic inadequacy.
- Humanistic Buddhism shall enrich human minds.
- Humanistic Buddhism shall enhance social norms.
- Humanistic Buddhism is a cause for social stability.
- Humanistic Buddhism shall enrich individual harmony through well-being, interpersonal harmony through respect, family harmony through deference, social harmony through cooperation, and world harmony through peace.

None of the above arise from my individual intent. Instead, these are what the Buddha intended to teach the world. Thus we hereby dedicate everything to Buddha and hold true to his original intents. It is hoped that present-day monastics and lay Buddhists may offer their utmost sincerity to the Buddha. That anyone who does not bear faith in Buddhism is willing to understand Buddha's teachings, specially Buddhism's influence on spiritual well- being, as well as Buddhism's contribution to the Chinese People and Chinese culture.

It is okay if you do not believe in Buddhism, because Buddha does not need you to believe in him. What matters is that you believe in your own compassion and kindness that enables you to think for others, refrain from unwholesome deeds, and inspire all good deeds. Should you have the slightest faith in Buddha, how can you not share an affinity with him?

Consequently, regardless of the different levels of faith amongst the millions of Buddhists, faith remains unified, and faith remains our only way of life. If we were able to hold true to Buddha's original intent in rediscovering the joy and freedom offered by our faith, then life would be truly carefree.

Based upon this principle, I persist in my service for Humanistic Buddhism as well as my endeavors for the New Buddhism Movement. Whether this is a merit or demerit matters not to me. As I explained in an article in the *Merit Times*, "I am not a Buddhist monk who 'feeds on' Buddhism." Rather than depending on Buddhism, I strive to ensure that the future of Buddhism lies in me. This has been my lifetime motto.

As I reminisce on my lifetime's endeavor to propagate the Dharma, I am reminded of the arduous path undergone by Master Taixu. He too experienced disagreements with the Buddhist Association of China, thereby powerless to realize his vision. It seems like I have followed after him, and I cannot help but lament on the circumstances given to Buddhism. I speculate either time, luck, or destiny were on my side.

In the recent Taiwan election, Professor Chai Sung-lin (柴松林, 1934-) demurred about how the people only voted for their favorite candidates instead of those who could truly make a difference. How could there be hope for the Chinese people? It was likewise with the Buddhist Association. People voted only according to factions, discounting people of talent or influence. How could Buddhism progress this way? As stated earlier, "It is the people who glorify the Way, not the Way that glorifies the people." This is perhaps another reason why the revitalization of Buddhism was not possible.

Possibilities for revitalization did arise during the late Qing and Ming periods. For example, when Master Taixu proposed *Rensheng Fojiao* (Life Buddhism), those jealous of him tried to suppress and sabotage him, thwarting his vision. Fortunately, many of his peers each played to their strengths and sustained the propagation of Buddhism. For instance, Buddhist masters Xuyun (虛 雲 , 1840-1959) and Lai Guo (來 果 , 1881-1953), Pure Land master Yin Guang (印光, 1862-1940), Master Zong Yang (宗仰, 1861-1921) who was affiliated with the Cai Yuanpei Education Association in Shanghai, Venerable Yue Xia (月霞, 1858-1917) who focused on Huayan Buddhism, Venerable Dixian (諦閑, 1858-1932) from the Tiantai School, and also Venerable Yuan Ying (圓瑛, 1878-1953) the eloquent Dharma teacher.

Circumstances were undeniably difficult for Master Taixu. Owing to traditionalist obstructions, Master Taixu only ever served, for a short period, as Abbot of Hangzhou Jingci Temple. He was precluded from any other position. Nevertheless, he established Buddhist colleges such as Minnan Buddhist College and Wuchang

Master Taixu   Master Xuyun   Venerable Yuan Ying

Buddhist College to foster talents, many of whom later emerged as elites of Buddhism.

For example, Venerables Daxing (大醒 , 1900-1952), Fa Fang (法舫 , 1904-1951), Le Guan (樂觀 , 1902-1987), Wei Fang (葦舫), Zhi Feng (芝峰 , 1901-1971), Yin Shun (印順 , 1906-2005), Chen Kong (塵空), Mo Ru (默如 , 1905-1991), Fa Zun (法尊), Fa Hui (法慧), and Liao Can (了參). Furthermore, there were many young monastic from across the Mainland: Master Hui Jue (會覺) from Zhejiang Wuling Buddhist College, Master Wei Xian (惟賢 , 1920-2013) from Sichuan Huayan Temple, Master Ming Zhe (明哲 , 1925-2012) from Qingdao Zhanshan Temple in Shandong, Master Xue Fan (雪煩 , 1909-1994) from Jiaoshan in Jiangsu, Master Dong Chu (東初 , 1908-1977), Master Ming Shan (茗山 , 1914-2011), and also Venerable Zheng Guo (正果 , 1913-1987) who served as President of the Buddhist Association of China after the Cultural Revolution, Venerable Zhu Mo (竺摩 , 1913-2002), and Venerable Ju Zan (巨贊 , 1903-1984). They were all pupils and successors of Master Taixu.

In addition, there were laymen such as Yang Renshan (楊仁山 ,

1837-1911), Ouyang Jian (歐陽漸 , 1871-1943), Tang Dayuan (唐大圓 , 1885-1941), Ding Fubao (丁福保 , 1874-1952), Chen Hailiang (陳海量 , 1909-1982), Liang Qichao (梁啟超 , 1873-1929), Dai Jitao (戴季陶 , 1891-1949), Qu Yingguang (屈映光 , 1883-1973), and Zhao Hengti (趙恆惕 , 1880-1971) who actively contributed to the revitalization of Buddhism. All are truly great bodhisattvas and protectors of the Dharma.

As hope for new Buddhist endeavors was kindled, the separatist regime, the Anti-Japanese Resistance War, and the civil war erupted end to end, bringing the revitalization of Buddhist to a halt by force of arms.

Auspiciously, the torch of the Dharma was relayed to Taiwan with the advent of monastics from the Mainland. In light of the chaotic times, many of them remained passive and conservative

Fo Guang Shan Buddha Museum
TAIWAN, Kaohsiung

368

towards the development of Buddhism. Several even tried to encourage relinquishing the idea of founding Fo Guang Shan as the ongoing turmoil meant that Taiwan was nigh on being removed from the United Nations. They told me that there was no hope in attempting whatsoever in Taiwan and might as well stop wasting my time. Regardless, holding true to my principle of "continuing to strike the bell for each day that I remained a monk," I strove on with my works of propagation.

As we recall the possible causes for Master Taixu's unsuccessful New Buddhist Reform Movement, several points stand out; one being that he passed away before the age of sixty-two, that the conservative forces of the Sangha remained too powerful, and finally, he lacked a foundation for his mission. Nevertheless, his students and disciples have all been stupendous in continuing his efforts. For

this, I hold Master Taixu in great esteem.

Still, though some of his disciples categorized me under the "Taixu Sect" based on what I had accomplished, I never considered myself his successor. All I have done is carry out my duty as a disciple of the Buddha. What I cannot refute is my spiritual compatibility with his aspirations and compassion. No matter the suppression and ostracism I was subjected to, and irrespective of any public opinion or criticism against me and Buddhism; I am fortunate to be blessed with something that Master Taixu was not: the support of a large following of disciples and devotees. Their efforts have made possible the establishment of temples worldwide.

To date, Fo Guang Shan has stood for over sixty years, thirty of which I have been a retired abbot. There is presently a following of over one thousand monastic disciples, two hundred of which hold a Master's or Doctorate degree. Some two hundred of these disciples are also in their prime, waiting to elevate and propagate Humanistic Buddhism.

Concurrently, many outstanding leaders of the Fo Guang Shan Order are currently carrying out their duties across the five continents. I am confident that they will continue their endeavors in propagating the Dharma and allow the era of Humanistic Buddhism to shine. Providing the heritage of Buddhism endures, what need is there to fear for the future of Humanistic Buddhism?

Having propagated the Dharma in Taiwan for over sixty years, I clearly remember the countless eminent masters who have contributed to the spread of Buddhism in Taiwan. For example, Master Miao Guo (妙果 , 1884-1963), Venerable Bin Tsung (斌宗 , 1911-1958), Venerable Cheng Kuang (證光 , 1896-1955), Venerable Chi Hsing (智性 , 1884-1964), Venerable Chi Yu (智諭 , 1924-2000), Venerable Hsiu Ho (修和), Venerable Sheng Yin (聖印 ,

1930-1996), Venerable Pu Miao (菩妙 , 1921-2009), Venerable Kai Cheng (開證 , 1925-2001), and Venerable Long Tao (隆道 , 1906-1987).

Buddhism in Taiwan is not the sole representative. Other than the United Association of Humanistic Buddhism, there are also many outstanding organizations. For example, Huayen Lotus Association, Huafan University, Dharma Drum Mountain, Thousand Buddha Mountain, Museum of World Religions founded by the Lin Jiou Mountain Buddhist Society, Ling Yen Mountain, Chung Tai Chan Monastery, Ching Chueh Buddhist Sangha University at Kuang Teh Temple, Xiang Guang Temple, Fu Zhi Feng Shan Si, Tzu Chi Foundation, Hai Ming Temple, Ci Fa Si, Cih Ming Temple, and many others. Their roles in the history of Humanistic Buddhism shall be contingent on their vows and aspirations.

Hope abounds that the Buddhist colleges founded by Taiwan's historic monasteries such as Ling Quan Temple, Guanyin Mountain, Shitou Mountain, Fa Yun Monastery, Yuan Kuang Ch'an Monastery, Da-Sian Temple, Dagan Mountain, Kai Yuan Temple, Nanputuo Temple, Tung-shan Ssu, and Fu Yan Vihara can continue to nurture talents for Buddhism. To all aspiring young bhiksus and bhiksunis whose names I am unable to hereby list, may you continue to strive in letting the light of Humanistic Buddhism shine.

Moreover, it is hoped that scholars, professors, laymen, and eminent leaders who are pious Buddhists or friends of Buddhism will follow the examples of Buddhists such Wu Po-hsiung (吳 伯 雄) and his seniors: Tai Chi-tao, Lee Ben-nan (李 炳 南 , 1891-1986), Lee Tzu-kuan (李子寬 , 1882-1973), Chou Hsuan-te (周 宣德 , 1924-1988), Nan Huai-chin (南懷瑾 , 1918-2012), and Yang Baiyi (楊白衣 , 1924-1986) in recognizing the value of Buddhism

and empower it to radiate. It is in the hands of both monastic and lay Buddhists to ensure the light of Humanistic Buddhism shines forever.

Following the Cultural Revolution in Mainland China, Zhao Puchu (趙樸初, 1907-2000) began to carry the name "Humanistic Buddhism," which in my opinion was the right thing to do. If anyone should object, it means a failure to understand what Buddhism truly is. Since Humanistic Buddhism is originally Buddhism itself, any rejection of it means the rejection of Buddhism. Try stating any fact that makes Humanistic Buddhism not what it is? Since the Dharma never forsakes any teaching, why forsake the word 'Humanistic'?

Some people are concerned with Humanistic Buddhism being overly mundane and even profane. Actually, the spirit of Humanistic Buddhism involves "this-worldly" undertakings with an "other-worldly" mind. Namely, it is a combination of both tradition and modernity. By tradition is not meant whichever tradition has existed for hundreds or even thousands of years. Instead tradition in this instance denotes advocating Buddha's fundamental, genuine wisdom and cultivation. This is why I say that Humanistic Buddhism holds true to Buddha's original intents.

Fortuitously, there are many rising talents in Mainland China, such as Venerable Xuecheng (學誠) currently President of the Buddhist Association of China, who are disposed to propagating Humanistic Buddhism. Given my limited knowledge of the numerous talents out there in Mainland China, I hereby apologize for being able to name but a few at my old age.

Nonetheless, it is fervently wished that mutual support is tangible and existent. As the saying goes, "The light of the Dharma cannot shine without the mutual praise of monastics." I sincerely hope that not only will monastics aspire to develop the Bodhi Mind and undertake the endeavors of Humanistic Buddhism, may they also find the heart to tolerate each other. It is the only way for Chinese Buddhism to flourish. The bigger your heart, the greater your success. May you countenance unceasing exchange and unity, willingly be in the company of virtuous ones, support your juniors, foster young talents, and allow the light of Humanistic Buddhism to shine as one. As affirmed in the lyrics of "Rhythm of the Buddhist Youth,"

> *The devotion of his children is swelling*
> *the mighty ocean of his following,*
> *As the age of enlightenment now is drawing near.*

May all children of the Buddha reward his grace by empowering the torch of Humanistic Buddhism to blaze bright, the turning of the Dharma wheel to continue, and the Buddha's days be exalted for eternity.

Appendix One:

Chronology of the Buddha's Life

Birth

(563B.C.E.)

- Born as Siddhartha Gautama in Lumbini on April 8th of the Lunar calendar in the kingdom of Kapilavastu in Northern India. To date, Lumbini, along with the asoka tree under which the prince was born remain a protected site by the Nepalese government.

- His father, King Suddhodana, and mother, Queen Maya were the rulers of Kapilavastu. The prince belonged to the Sakya clan and the Ksatriya caste.

- Queen Maya, died seven days after the prince was born, leaving him in the care of his aunt, Mahapajapati Gotami.

- Asita, a seer, predicted that Siddhartha will either become a monarch who will unite all lands, or renounce the worldly life and become a Buddha to liberate all sentient beings.

Age 8

- Siddhartha was educated in the subjects of the Four Vedas and the Five Sciences. King Suddhodana also summoned 500 children of the Sakya clan to study as his classmates to prepare them for aiding the prince in his future reign.

Age 12-18

- Siddhartha received military and martial arts training, excelling his Sakyan peers. Not only was he able to lead and command an army, he has also mastered weaponry and wrestling. Using a bow that could only be drawn by the strength of a thousand men, the prince's arrow pierced through seven iron drums and shot into the ground. A well also appeared around the arrow, and was thereby named the Arrow Well. The prince's reputation was widespread.

Age 12-18	• Unlike his peers, Siddhartha grew up differently. He often pondered about even the smallest things in life such as, "Why do the weak fall prey to the strong?" or "What is the cause of life's sufferings? How can we be free from such sufferings?"

Age 19-24	• Six years after being married to Princess Yasodhara, the eldest daughter of King Suprabuddha of Devadaha, their son Rahula was born.

Age 25-30	• One day, Siddhartha ventured outside the palace walls and encountered the Four Sights of old age, sickness, and death, leaving him in serious grief. His final encounter with a dignified renunciant inspired him to renounce.
	• Upon hearing Siddhartha's wish to renounce, King Suddhodana was so afraid that Asita's prophecy would come true that he built three splendid palaces, each for spring, summer, and winter. He even arranged beautiful and seductive entertainers to serve the prince, wishing that this would cause Siddhartha to indulge in pleasure. Although Siddhartha had a luxurious and comfortable living, his questions and queries prevailed in his mind.
	• One night, when everyone was asleep, Siddhartha woke up Chandaka, his servant, and left the palace on his horse Kanthaka. He then cut off his hair and renounced his princely life.

Age 25-30

- The prince crossed the Ganges River and practiced in a forest near Rajagrha, some 500 kilometers from home. King Suddhodana therefore dispatched five officials including Ajnata Kaundinya to accompany Siddhartha in his practices.

- Upon seeing Siddhartha begging for alms in Rajagrha, King Bimbisara was deeply moved by his demeanor and offered half of his kingdom in attempt to persuade Siddhartha to abandon his practices. Remaining adamant, Siddhartha promised to return and deliver the king once he attained enlightenment.

- In Rajagrha, Siddhartha first sought advice in Arada and Udraka, the two most renowned ascetics of the Samkhya School in India. They had already achieved the dhyanas of nothingness and of neither thought nor non-thought. Nevertheless, they were still not liberated from defilements, and no better teacher could be found.

- For six long years, Siddhartha and his five companions practiced extreme asceticism in the forest in Uruvela alongside other Brahmins and hermits.

Age 31-35

- In the six years of ascetic practice, Siddhartha ate no more than a sesame seed or a grain of wheat per day. Emaciated and on the verge of death, he realized that asceticism was not the perfect practice and decided to abandon it. His five companions scorned him for his degeneration. Siddhartha went alone to bathe in the Nairanjana River, near Mount Gaya. After accepting a shepherd girl's offering of milk, he regained his strength.

- According to the Vinaya, after the Buddha attained enlightenment, he moved to seven different places around the bodhi tree and continued to contemplate the profound truth of Dependent Origination. He then taught about the state of self-enlightenment in his 21-day discourse of the *Avatamsaka Sutra*. However, the teachings on the levels of being a bodhisattva and the Buddha's way of realization were too profound and incomprehensible for ordinary beings.

- At Deer Park in Varanasi, the Buddha took the Five Bhiksus as his first disciples, marking the beginning of the Sangha. He gave three lectures on the splendid meaning of the Four Noble Truths, the first turning of the Dharma Wheel. As a result, the Triple Gem: Buddha, Dharma, and Sangha were complete.

Age 31-35

- Afterwards, the Buddha ordained Yasa, son of a rich elder in Varanasi, and his relatives and friends, numbering 55 in total. At the time, there were 61 arhats in the Sangha.

- After listening to the Buddha's teachings, Yasa's parents happily took refuge in the Buddha and became the first upasaka and upasika, the foundation for an organization comprising both monastics and laity.

- In the following twelve years, the Buddha travelled across India, teaching the Agamas. He mainly taught the Four Noble Truths, Noble Eightfold Path, Twelve Links of Dependent Origination, the Thirty-Seven Conditions Leading to Bodhi, and non-self.

Age 36-41

- At the side of Nairanjana River of Mount Gaya, the Buddha liberated the three Kasyapa brothers who worshipped fire—Uruvila Kasyapa, Kaya Kasyapa and Nadi Kasyapa—as well as their 1,000 followers, solidifying the foundation of the Sangha.

- The Buddha returned to Magadha and taught the Dharma to King Bimbisara as promised more than a decade ago. The king built the first Buddhist monastery, Venuvana Vihara in the capital Rajagrha. It was divided into sixteen buildings, each containing sixty rooms for the Buddha and the Sangha's living quarters. There were also 500 towered-pavilions and 72 lecture halls.

- Sariputra and Maudgalyayana became the Buddha's ordained disciples and helped propagate the Dharma, a significant event in the Buddha's Sangha. Afterwards, Mahakasyapa, the foremost among brahmans, also ordained and joined the Sangha. With kings and scholars taking refuge in the Buddha one after another, the Buddha's teachings became even more wide-spread. 1,250 disciples followed the Buddha in his travels, and became permanent followers in the Sangha.

Age 36-41

- Elder Sudatta and Prince Jeta from Sravasti, a city in the northern kingdom of Kosala, donated a grove and trees. Under Sariputra's planning and supervision, Jetavana Monastery was constructed as a new dwelling for the Buddha and his disciples. King Prasenajit of Kosala also took refuge in the Buddha, becoming a significant and loyal Dharma protector.

- The Buddha often traveled north and south, between Bamboo Grove Monastery and Jetavana Monastery. With Magadha, Kosala, and Matsya as centers of his propagation, the Buddha traveled all over India and taught many disciples.

- Due to Sudinna's breaking of his vows, the Buddha established the precepts, and the rule that a Upavasatha ceremony must be held every fortnight to recite the precepts.

Age 42

- For the next eight years, the Buddha taught the *Vimalakirti Sutra, Sutra Asked by Visesacinta Brahma Deva, Sandhinirmocana Sutra, Golden Light Sutra,* and *Mahasamnipata Sutra.* These lectures expanded both partial and all-embracing teachings, and teachings delivered through both skillful means and essence. This period of teaching is thus called *vaipulya.*

Age 43-49

- As the Sangha gradually expanded along with their propagation, King Suddhodana sent his minister Udayin to Sravasti to invite the Buddha to return to Kapilavastu to teach the Dharma. Princes of the Sakya clan, such as Purna, Ananda, Devadatta, Nanda, Aniruddha, Bhadra and other royal youths, were all inspired by the Buddha's benevolence and joined the Sangha community.

- Upali, who belonged to the lowest caste and was a barber for royalty, renounced with the Buddha's consent. Since then, the Buddha's Sangha had broken the segregation of castes and instead advocated equality. This was against brahmanical social order and shocked many in India.

- Rahula, the Buddha's son, was ordained. The Buddha thus established the ten precepts for srameneras, marking the beginning of novice monks in the Sangha.

- King Suddhodana, the Buddha's father, died at the age of 93. The Buddha carried the casket himself. Mahamana, Aniruddha's older brother, ascended the throne and ruled Kapilavastu.

- The Buddha's aunt, Mahapajapati, led 500 court ladies to Vaisali and became his ordained disciples, marking beginning of the bhiksuni community.

Age 50-71

- For 22 years starting from this period, the Buddha taught teachings on Prajna and the Middle Path to eliminate attachment and to direct his disciples to the essence of the Dharma. These were the origin of the Buddha's teachings in the *Lotus Sutra*.

- Liberated Hariti.

- The Buddha chose Ananda as his full-time attendant.

- Jiva, a great physician, served the Buddha.

- Liberated serial-killer Angulimala.

- Under the influence of Devadatta, Prince Ajatasatru rebelled and imprisoned his father, King Bimbisara, declaring himself the new king.

Age 70-78

- The Buddha taught *Amitayurdhyana Sutra* (*Sutra of the Meditation on the Buddha of Immeasurable Life*) to King Bimbisara and Queen Vaidehi. King Bimbisara died in prison.

- Devadatta schemed to split the Sangha, but was stopped by the Buddha.

- King Ajatasatru repented and took refuge in Buddha.

- Kosala's Prince Virudhaka usurped the throne. King Prasenajit fled. King Virudhaka attacked and occupied Kapilavastu, despite the Buddha's three failed attempts to stop him. The Sakya clan was thus eliminated. King Virudhaka also killed Crown Prince Jeta.

- King Ajatashatru annexed Kosala and Kapilavastu into Magadha.

- In the next seven years, seeing the maturation of his disciples' understanding of the Dharma, the Buddha expounded the *Lotus Sutra*. He revealed the true essence of the Dharma, as well as the Tathagata's original intention of being born into this world.

- The Buddha crossed the Ganges River to teach the Dharma in the kingdoms of Vrji and Vaisali.

Age 79

- Preparing to attack Vrji, King Ajatasatru sent his minister Varsakara to seek the Buddha for advice. The Buddha taught him "The Seven Non-Regressing Dharmas" and successfully dissuaded the king from starting a war.

- Mahapajapati, Sariputra, and Maudgalyayana, entered nirvana.

- The Buddha said to his disciples before he entered nirvana:

  "Do not grieve. Everything with life in this universe is impermanent. If you wish that I permanently stay in the world, yet do not act in accordance with the Dharma I have taught, what would be the use of living for millions of years anyway? If you all act in accordance with the Dharma I have taught, I will live forever in your hearts. My Dharma-body will pervade the universe, and I will be together with all of you and with all sentient beings in the future."

Age 80

- Ananda asked the Buddha four questions:

  "1. How shall we start the beginning of the sutras?
  2. After you enter nirvana, who shall be our teacher?
  3. Where should we abide?
  4. How should we deal with vicious bhiksus?"

  The Buddha said to the congregation,

  "You should begin each sutra with 'Thus have I heard.' You should rely upon the precepts as your teacher. You should abide in the Four Bases of Mindfulness. You should quietly disregard vicious bhiksus."

Age 80

(483B.C.E.)

- The Buddha chose to enter nirvana peacefully in meditation on the Eight Bases of Overcoming and Eight Kinds of Liberation between two sala trees in Kusinagara. Mahakasyapa was the last to venerate at the Buddha's feet after he entered nirvana. After cremation, the Buddha's relics were divided between eight kingdoms, where stupas were built for these relics. People regarded the stupas as if they were the Buddha; it allowed them to recollect the Buddha's merits of teaching in the human world.

Sacred Sites

- Site of birth: **Lumbini.**

- Site of ascetic practices and attainment of Buddhahood: **Bodhi Gaya.**

- Site of teaching the *Avatamsaka Sutra* and the *Agamas* as well as the first turning of the Dharma Wheel: **Deer Park.**

- Site of establishing the Bhiksuni Sangha: **Vaisali.**

- Site of teaching the *Lotus Sutra*: **Vulture Peak**

- Site of teaching the *Diamond Sutra*: **Jetavana**

- Site of teaching the *Mahaparinirvana Sutra* and of parinirvana: **Kusinagara**

Appendix Two
List of Titles

365 Days For Travelers: Wisdom from Chinese Literary and Buddhist Classics 獻給旅行者 365 日—中華文化佛教寶典

A Collection of Contemporary Buddhist Works: Chinese Buddhist Academic Series (Fazang Wenku) 法藏文庫

A Collection of Parables (Zhongjing Zhuan Za Piyu) 眾經撰雜譬喻

A Collection of Records on the Emanation of the Chinese Tripitaka (Chu Sanzang Ji Ji) 出三藏記集

A Commentary on Avalokitesvara Bodhisattva's Universal Gate Chapter (Guanshiyin Pusa Pumenpin Jianghua) 觀世音菩薩普門品講話

A Complete Collection of Stories on Buddhism (Fojiao Gushi Daquan) 佛教故事大全

A Critique of Poetry (Shi Pin) 詩品

A Record of Buddhist Practices Sent Home from the Southern Sea (Nanhai Jigui Neifa Zhuan) 南海寄歸內法傳

Abhiniskramana Sutra (Fo Benxing Jing) 佛本行經

Abhiniskramana Sutra (Fo benxingji Jing) 佛本行集經

Agamas (Ahan Jing) 阿含經

Along the River During the Qingming Festival (Qingming Shanghe Tu) 清明上河圖

Amitabha Sutra (Mituo Jing) 彌陀經

Attadanta Sutta (Zhizhang Jing) 執杖經

Auxiliary Teachings (Fu Jiao Bian) 輔教編

Avatamsaka Sutra (Huayan Jing) 華嚴經

Awaken the Masses Weekly (Juequn) 覺群

Awakening Living Beings Magazine (Juesheng) 覺生

Awakening the World News (Jueshi Bao) 覺世報

Awakening the World Periodical (Jueshi) 覺世

Bible (Shengjing) 聖經

Bilingual Buddhist Series: Sutras & Scriptures Doctrines of Buddhism (Zhong Ying Duizhao Foxue Congshu) 中英對照佛學叢書

Bodhedrum Magazine (Putishu) 菩提樹

Book of Liang (*Liang Shu*) 梁書

Buddhacarita (*Fo Suo Xing Zan*) 佛所行讚

Buddhism Taiwan (*Taiwan Fojiao*) 台灣佛教

Buddhism Today (*Jinri Fojiao*) 今日佛教

Buddhist Affinities Across 100 Years (*Bainian Fo Yuan*) 百年佛緣

Buddhist Novels (*Fojiao Xiaoshuo Ji*) 佛教小說集

Buddhist Paper (*Fohua Bao*) 佛化報

Buddhist Pilgrim Monks of Tang Dynasty (*Datang Xiyu Gaoseng Qiufa Zhuan*) 大唐西域求法高僧傳

Buddhist Stories For Children (*Fojiao Tonghua Ji*) 佛教童話集

Buddhist Studies Journal (*Foxue Congbao*) 佛學叢報

Buddhist Youth (*Fojiao Qingnian*) 佛教青年

Buddhistic Occasional (*Fohua Suikan*) 佛化隨刊

Central Daily News (*Zhongyang Ribao*) 中央日報

Chinese Buddhism (*Zhongguo Fojiao*) 中國佛教

Collection of Works by Master Taixu (*Taixu Dashi Quanshu*) 太虛大師全書

Commentary on the FoShuo Bei Sutra (*Fo Shuo Bei Jing Chao*) 佛說孛經抄

Comparative Studies of Buddhism and Science (*Fofa Yu Kexue Zhi Bijiao Yanjiu*) 佛法與科學之比較研究

Complete Collection of Venerable Yuan Ying (*Yuanying Fahui*) 圓瑛法彙 (圓瑛法師全集)

Comprehensive History of the Buddhas and Patriarchs (*Fozu Lidai Tong Zai*) 佛祖歷代通載

Dharma Voice Magazine (*Fayin*) 法音

Dharma Waves (*Fahai Polan*) 法海波瀾

Dharmacakra Pravartana Sutra (*Fo Shuo San Zhuan Falun Jing*) 佛說三轉法輪經

Diamond Sutra (*Jingang Jing*) 金剛經

Dictionary of Buddhist Studies (*Foxue Da Cidian*) 佛學大辭典

Dirghama Sutra (*Foshuo Chang Ahan*) 佛說長阿含

Discerning the Truth (*Bian Zong Lun*) 辯宗論

Dragon Canon (*Long Zang*) 龍藏

Dream of the Red Chamber (*Honglou Meng*) 紅樓夢

Dwelling in the Fuchun Mountains (*Fuchun Shanju Tu*) 富春山居圖

Eighteen Papers on Buddhist Studies (*Foxue Yanjiu Shiba Pian*) 佛學研究十八篇

Ekottaragama (*Sutra*) (*Zengyi Ahan Jing*) 增一阿含經

Encyclopedia of World Buddhist Arts (*Shijie Fojiao Meishu Tushuo Da Cidian*) 世界佛教美術圖說大辭典

Endless Light (*Wujindeng*) 無盡燈

Experiences of Passing Away Under Buddha's Blessings (*Nianfo Ganying Wangsheng Ji*) 念佛感應往生記

Extensive Records of the Taiping Era (*Taiping Guangji*) 太平廣記

Fo Guang Shan Pure Regulations Handbook (*Fo Guang Shan Qinggui Shouce*) 佛光山清規手冊

Genealogy of the Sakya Clan (*Shijia Pu*) 釋迦譜

God of the Eastern Sea (*Donghai Ruo*) 東海若

Great Hero Monthly (*Daxiong*) 大雄

Great Journey to the West (*Datang Xiyu Ji*) 大唐西域記

Guanyin Bodhisattva (*Guanshiyin Pusa*) 觀世音菩薩

Hear Me Out: Messages from a Humble Monk (*Pinseng Youhua Yao Shuo*) 貧僧有話要說

Hear Me Out: Reflections (*Pinseng Shuohua De Huixiang*) 貧僧說話的回響

Heart Sutra (*Bore Xinjing*) 般若心經

History of Chinese Buddhism (*Zhongguo Fojiao Shi*) 中國佛教史

History of Han, Wei, Eastern and Western Jin, and Northern and Southern Dynasty Buddhism (*Han Wei Liang Jin Nan-Bei Chao Fojiaoshi*) 漢魏兩晉南北朝佛教史

History of the Southern Dynasties (*Nan Shi*) 南史

History of Vernacular Literature (*Baihua Wenxue Shi*) 白話文學史

Hong Kong Buddhism (*Xianggang Fojiao*) 香港佛教

Human Life Magazine (*Rensheng*) 人生

Humanistic Buddhism (*Renjian Fojiao*) 人間佛教

Humanistic Buddhism: Journal, Arts and Culture (*Renjian Fojiao Xuebao Yiwen*) 人間佛教學報 · 藝文

Illustrations of Life Protection (*Husheng Hua Ji*) 護生畫集

In Search of Gods (*Sou Shen Ji*) 搜神記

Introduction to Modern Day Intellectuals (*Xiang Shouguo Jiaoyu De Ren Jie-*

shao Fojiao) 向受過現代教育的人介紹佛教
Jiaxing Canon (*Jiaxing Zang*) 嘉興藏
Qisha Canon (*Qisha Zang*) 磧砂藏
Journey to the West (*Xiyouji*) 西遊記
Kaibao Canon (*Kaibao Zang*) 開寶藏
Khitan Canon (*Qidan Zang*) 契丹藏
Koran (*Kelanjing*) 可蘭經
Koryo Canon (*Gaoli Zang*) 高麗藏
Lamp in the Ocean of People Monthly (*Renhai Deng*) 人海燈
Lankavatara Sutra (*Lengyan Jing*) 楞嚴經
Lion's Roar (*Shizihou*) 獅子吼
Literary Mind and Carved Dragon (*Wenxin Diaolong*) 文心雕龍
Lotus (*Hehua*) 荷花
Lotus Sutra (*Fahua Jing*) 法華經
Madhyama Agama (*Zhong Ahan Jing*) 中阿含經
Mahaparinirvana Sutra (*Daniepan Jing*) 大涅槃經
Mahaprajnaparamita Sutra (*Bore Jing*) 般若經
Maharatnakuta Sutra (*Dabaoji Jing*) 大寶積經
Mahparinirvana Sutra (*Daboniepan Jing*) 大般涅槃經
Manji Daizokyo (*Wanzi Zhengzang*) 卍字正藏
Manji Zokuzokyo (*Wanzi Xuzang*) 卍字續藏
Methodology of Buddhist Studies (*Fojiao Yanjiu Fa*) 佛教研究法
Middle Stream Monthly (*Zhongliu*) 中流
Monthly Buddhist Texts (*Meiyue Yin Jing*) 每月印經
National Master Yu Lin (*Yulin Guoshi*) 玉琳國師
Nectar (*Ganlu*) 甘露
New Pure Land Concepts (*Jingtu Xinlun*) 淨土新論
Nirvana Sutra (*Niepan Jing*) 涅槃經
Ocean Waves Magazine (*Haichao Yin*) 海潮音
Older Sutra of Parables (*Jiu Za Piyu Jing*) 舊雜譬喻經
On Principles (*Ben Lun*) 本論
Outline of the Buddhas and Patriarchs (*Fozu Gangmu*) 佛祖綱目
Pinjia Canon (*Pinjia Zang*) 頻伽藏
Prayer Magazine (*Qidao Tekan*) 祈禱特刊

Preface to the Orchid Pavilion Collection (*Lan Ting Ji Xu*) 蘭亭集序
Prince Sudana Sutra (*Taizi Xudana Jing*) 太子須大拏經
Raging Waves (*Nu Tao*) 怒濤
Record of Lay Buddhists (*Jushi Chuandenglu*) 居士傳燈錄
Records of the Buddha Kingdom (*Foguo Ji*) 佛國記
Reports of Buddhist Studies by a Scientist (*Yi Ge Kexuezhe Yanjiu Fojing De Baogao*) 一個科學者研究佛經的報告
Samyuktagama (*Za Ahan Jing*) 雜阿含經
Selection of Works (*Wenchao Jinghua Lu*) 文鈔菁華錄
Shorter Chinese Samyuktagama (*Bieyi Za Ahan Jing*) 別譯雜阿含經
Strange Tales of Liao Zhai (*Liaozhai Zhiyi*) 聊齋誌異
Sujata Sutra (*Foshuo Yuyenu Jing*) 佛說玉耶女經
Sutra of Bequeathed Teachings (*Yi Jiao Jing*) 遺教經
Sutra of Eight Realizations of Great Beings (*Ba Daren Jue Jing*) 八大人覺經
Sutra of Parables (*Fo Shuo Piyu Jing*) 佛說譬喻經
Sutra of the Collection of the Six Perfections (*Liudu Ji Jing*) 六度集經
Sutra of the Month (*Meiyue Yi Jing*) 每月一經
Sutra of the Nine-Colored Deer (*Fo Shuo Jiuse Lu Jing*) 佛說九色鹿經
Sutra of the Right Mindfulness of Dharma (*Saddharma-smrty-upasthana-sutra*) (*Zhengfa Nianchu Jing*) 正法念處經
Sutra on King Prasenajit Covered in Dust After His Mother Passed Away (*Fo Shuo Posini Wang Taihou Beng Chentu Ben Shen Jing*) 佛說波斯匿王太后崩塵土坌身經
Sutra on Past and Present Causes and Effects (*Guoqu Xianzai Yinguo Jing*) 過去現在因果經
Sutra on the Lion's Roar of Srimala (*Shengman Jing*) 勝鬘經
Sutra on the Parable of the Arrow (*Jianyu Jing*) 箭喻經
Sutra on the Perfection of Great Wisdom (*Dabore Jing*) 大般若經
Sutra on the Wise and Foolish (*Xianyu Jing*) 賢愚經
Taisho Canon (*Dazheng Zang*) 大正藏
Taixu's Dharma Propagation Journal (*Taixu Hongfa Zhuankan*) 太虛弘法專刊
Tegen Canon (*Tieyan Zang*) 鐵眼藏
The Biography of Sakyamuni Buddha (*Shijia Zhuan*) 釋迦傳
The Biography of Sakyamuni Buddha (*Shijiamounifo Zhuan*) 釋迦牟尼佛傳

The Buddhist Daily (*Fojiao Ribao*) 佛教日報
The Buddhist Monthly (*Fojiao Yuebao*) 佛教月報
The Classics of Tea (*Cha Jing*) 茶經
The Life of Su Dongpo (*Su Dongpo Zhuan*) 蘇東坡傳
The Merit Times (*Renjian Fubao*) 人間福報
The Mirror of Origin (*Gui Yuan Jing*) 歸元鏡
The Pinjia Canon (*Pinqie Dazangjing*) 頻伽大藏經
The Scholars (*Rulin Waishi*) 儒林外史
The Science of Buddhism (*Fojiao Kexueguan*) 佛教科學觀
The Travels of Old Decrepit (*Lao Can Youji*) 老殘遊記
The Water Margin (*Shui Hu Zhuan*) 水滸傳
The World Buddhist Lay Association Magazine (*Shijie Fojiao Jushilin Linkan*) 世界佛教居士林林刊
The Xuyun Almanac (*Xuyun Heshang Nianpu*) 虛雲和尚年譜
Thousand-Hand Guanyin (*Qianshou Guanyin*) 〈千手觀音〉
Traces Over the Sky and Ocean (*Hai Tian You Zong*) 海天遊踪
Treatise on the Perfection of Great Wisdom (*Dazhidu Lun*) 大智度論
Understanding the Two Truths (*Jie Erdi Yi*) 解二諦義
Universal Gate Buddhist Journal (*Pumen Xuebao*) 普門學報
Universal Gate Magazine (*Pumen*) 普門
Vaipulya Sutras (*Fangdeng Jing*) 方等經
Vairocana Canon (*Pilu Zang*) 毘盧藏
Varsakara Sutra (*Yushi Jing*) 雨勢經
Vimalakirti (*Weimojie Jing*) 維摩詰經
Vimalakirti-Nirdesa Sutra (*Weimojie Jing*) 維摩詰經
Vinaya in Five Divisions (*Wu Fen Lu*) 五分律
Vinaya in Four Divisions (*Si Fen Lu*) 四分律
Wisdom Torch (*Hui Ju*) 慧炬
Xingqixing Jing (*Fo Shuo Xing Qi Xing Jing*) 佛說興起行經
Yogacara Offering Service (*Yuqie Yankou*) 瑜伽焰口
Yogacarabhumi Sastra (*Yuqieshi Di Lun*) 瑜伽師地論